Rhetoric, Politics and Society

Series Editors
Alan Finlayson
University of East Anglia
Norfolk, UK

James Martin
Goldsmiths, University of London
London, UK

Kendall Phillips
Syracuse University
Syracuse, USA

Rhetoric lies at the intersection of a variety of disciplinary approaches and methods, drawing upon the study of language, history, culture and philosophy to understand the persuasive aspects of communication in all its modes: spoken, written, argued, depicted and performed. This series presents the best international research in rhetoric that develops and exemplifies the multifaceted and cross-disciplinary exploration of practices of persuasion and communication. It seeks to publish texts that openly explore and expand rhetorical knowledge and enquiry, be it in the form of historical scholarship, theoretical analysis or contemporary cultural and political critique. The editors welcome proposals for monographs that explore contemporary rhetorical forms, rhetorical theories and thinkers, and rhetorical themes inside and across disciplinary boundaries. For informal enquiries, questions, as well as submitting proposals, please contact the editors: Alan Finlayson: a.finlayson@uea.ac.uk James Martin: j.martin@gold.ac.uk Kendall Phillips: kphillip@syr.edu

More information about this series at
http://www.palgrave.com/gp/series/14497

Jens E. Kjeldsen · Amos Kiewe
Marie Lund · Jette Barnholdt Hansen

Speechwriting in Theory and Practice

Jens E. Kjeldsen
Department of Information Science
and Media Studies
University of Bergen
Bergen, Norway

Amos Kiewe
Department of Communication
and Rhetorical Studies
Syracuse University
Syracuse, NY, USA

Marie Lund
School of Communication and Culture
Aarhus University
Aarhus, Denmark

Jette Barnholdt Hansen (Deceased)

Rhetoric, Politics and Society
ISBN 978-3-030-03684-3   ISBN 978-3-030-03685-0 (eBook)
https://doi.org/10.1007/978-3-030-03685-0

Library of Congress Control Number: 2018963063

© The Editor(s) (if applicable) and The Author(s) 2019
This work is subject to copyright. All rights are solely and exclusively licensed by the Publisher, whether the whole or part of the material is concerned, specifically the rights of translation, reprinting, reuse of illustrations, recitation, broadcasting, reproduction on microfilms or in any other physical way, and transmission or information storage and retrieval, electronic adaptation, computer software, or by similar or dissimilar methodology now known or hereafter developed.
The use of general descriptive names, registered names, trademarks, service marks, etc. in this publication does not imply, even in the absence of a specific statement, that such names are exempt from the relevant protective laws and regulations and therefore free for general use.
The publisher, the authors and the editors are safe to assume that the advice and information in this book are believed to be true and accurate at the date of publication. Neither the publisher nor the authors or the editors give a warranty, express or implied, with respect to the material contained herein or for any errors or omissions that may have been made. The publisher remains neutral with regard to jurisdictional claims in published maps and institutional affiliations.

This Palgrave Macmillan imprint is published by the registered company Springer Nature Switzerland AG
The registered company address is: Gewerbestrasse 11, 6330 Cham, Switzerland

To our colleague and friend, Jette Barnholdt Hansen (1966–2017).
Her passion for the spoken word was a joy of life itself.

Contents

1 Introduction: The Case for Speechwriting 1

2 Speechmaking in the Twenty-First Century 7

3 The Beginning of Speechwriting 27

4 Research and Theory on Speechwriting 39

5 The Rhetorical Canons of Speechwriting 55

6 Genres of Speechwriting 75

7 How Speeches Are Written 93

8 Characterizing the Speaker 119

9 Writing for the Ear 133

10 Writing for the Eye: Pictures, Visions, and PowerPoint 145

11 The Ethics of Speechwriting 165

12	The Functions of Speechwriting in Contemporary Society	177
13	The General Steps in the Speechwriting Process	187
Index		197

CHAPTER 1

Introduction: The Case for Speechwriting

The art and practice of rhetoric and its early emphasis on speaking in public commenced around 500 BCE in Syracuse, Sicily, and at its inception, itinerant teachers known as the sophists, taught others the art of speaking in public, primarily out of local necessity born of a revolt against a local despot and the need to reclaim lost properties. Speechwriting, or the help others provide speakers in designing, drafting, editing, and finalizing speeches, is still the prevalent practice of the speechmaking process. Most speakers, often leaders of politics or industry, entrusted with the production of a given speech, rely on the help of others in securing the most effective speech possible. For some, such help is done informally while others employ professional writers to help them draft and improve the quality of a speech. The assistance involved includes assessing some or all the crucial variables included therein such as figuring out the best arguments to the designated audience, presenting a responsible reasoning process given the issue at hand and seeking to maximize the speech's overall effectiveness by employing attractive phrasing and proper delivery.

Our book presents the case for speechwriting as a practice and a profession that is based on long-standing theoretical grounding. Speechwriting and speechwriters enjoy a long-standing tradition that is quite vibrant in contemporary practices. The political and the businesses worlds, as well as related professions, resort to speechwriters on a continuous basis, seeking efficient, adaptable, and appealing speeches on a host of issues. Beginning with the sophists and through the Greek and

© The Author(s) 2019
J. E. Kjeldsen et al., *Speechwriting in Theory and Practice*,
Rhetoric, Politics and Society,
https://doi.org/10.1007/978-3-030-03685-0_1

Roman periods, treatises on rhetoric through contemporary practices and examples, the art of writing public speeches for clients has stipulated principles and processes that can be taught, practiced, and perfected. Speechwriting is situated in a discipline with a rich history that is based on recognized theories and teachable practices based on well-established rhetorical principles.

Most texts about speaking in public are devoted to the speaking part of the oratorical process and seeking to prepare speakers to develop their own speeches. In the USA and to some extent in Europe too, courses in public speaking are abounded and are often required by some disciplines in academic institutions and across disciplines. The concept of an involved and educated citizenry often grounds this academic need. The prevalence of public speaking courses in the USA, a practice that began early in the nineteenth century, is closely tied to the appreciation of a democratic political system that is founded on the principle of freedom of speech and the subsequent need to educate citizens in the art of speaking ethically and responsibly in public.

Our text takes a different focus, that of instructing the art of writing of speeches with a specific focus on writing such speeches professionally and for clients. We approach this topic with the recognition that the speechwriting process is the habit of many speakers who, to one degree or another, rely on the ideas, their development, input, and feedback of others in the process of crafting, editing, and finalizing effective speeches. Ours is not a handbook. There is plenty of these. Our objective is to offer a well thought through account of the speechwriting process, its theoretical underpinnings, ethical implications, and practices. To accomplish this task, we adhere to the fundamental principles of rhetorical theories and public speaking and adopt them here to the art of writing speeches.

We consider the speechwriter a professional who is an expert in the art of writing and public speaking and who is able to write speeches for clients. We recognize the fact that professionals from different but related fields often lend themselves to the practice of speechwriting. Policy advisors have dabbled in speechwriting as have those with strong writing skills or those from the legal profession. In other settings, professionals in public relations sometime function also as speechwriters. What we seek here is to put the practice of speechwriting under theoretical, conceptual, and ethical lenses in order to ground it in a critical process whereby a thoughtful and critical perspective drives the writing of speeches for clients.

We hope that such a perspective would yield greater understanding as well as improved speechwriting processes.

Despite the growing reliance on technology to enhance and manage multiple and diversified audience able to receive messages, be it the Internet and its voluminous web pages as well as the many social media outlets, human beings still resort to the one activity that has remained constant for some three and half thousand years: speaking in public as the primary mode of communicating with others. From Biblical times to ancient Greece, to the Roman Empire and later, the Holy Roman Empire of the Middle-Ages to the modern world, people still speak in public and they do so most extensively to present ideas, advocate positions, find adherents, and move people in a given direction. The physical and the creative are still the key variables in assessing skills, strength, and potential, often rendered necessary in assessing the credibility and viability of one individual to embody specific ideas. Put differently, our messages are still subsumed in our persona that in turn relies on the creative and performative process of constructing and delivering effective speeches.

Speaking in public then is a practice whereby a person exemplifies key qualities such as wisdom, character, and confidence in front of spectators. Public speaking has not changed much since antiquity in the sense that it is still considered among the most telling characteristic of an individual. On the strength of their rhetorical qualities, leaders have risen to prominence, some pursuing the most altruistic principles while others have resorted to manipulative and unethical practices. At its core, speaking in public is still oral, still an address to others, still a one-shot attempt at achieving a given objective and still the most real of all communication practices even with the aid of the megaphones, public address systems, radio, television, and the teleprompter. The judgments spectators make about speakers are holistic as they account for the selection of topic, organization and structure, style and delivery, and the overall believability as one embodied package. And as an embodied account, speaking in public is a risky task since so much hangs on the success of a performance that cannot be undone or goes through a "do over." For this very reason, those entrusted with the presentation of important topics have sought the help of ghostwriters to ensure that at least some of the more controlled performative aspects of public speaking can be planned and hence secure some measure of success or, at the minimum, to minimize weaknesses or failures. This is where the speechwriter comes in, helping the speaker with a comprehensive understanding of the task ahead and aiding the speaking in narrowing down uncertainties and constructing a viable speaking opportunity.

For better or worse, public speaking has been used by honorable people and those of ill repute. Great leaders such as Abraham Lincoln spoke in public about human virtues to advance the cause of humanity by emancipating slaves while ruthless rulers like Adolf Hitler used the same art to move people in the direction of mass murder. Clearly, the creative art of speechwriting is heavily invested in ethical implications. The ethics of writing speeches for clients, or ghostwriting, are discussed here in order to give the art of speechwriting legitimacy and to allow speechwriter professionals to engage confidently and ethically in this practice of writing speeches for others.

The modern polity as its ancient counterparts relies on public speeches to advance policies or ideas and they will likely remain a staple of most social and political systems. The interaction between leaders and followers often centers on addressing the public, hence, the need for effective speeches. As long as speeches are needed and speakers need speeches, the practice of writing speeches will continue. In principle, speeches are written prior to their delivery and the better speeches are those that have been prepared in advance and that went through an editorial phase. The practice and process of developing speeches have often been in the hands of more than just the speaker alone. Speakers or speechwriters draft speeches, write portions thereof, seek advice from others, and receive solicited and unsolicited drafts or points for inclusion. Some speakers will practice a heavier hand than others over the speechwriting process. Some will have their speeches drafted entirely by others only to be finalized by the speaker prior to delivery. The principle notion advanced here is that speechwriting is usually a collaborative art but that no consistent approach is apparent.

One of the thorniest issues related to speechwriting is the notion that speakers who rely on the work of speechwriters, deliver speeches that they did not write and that such a practice is inherently unethical because the true writers of speeches are not identified nor credited. However, this stance is rather limited and not altogether accurate. There are several reasons that can be cited here as to the legitimacy of writing speeches for others. Most speakers seek input from colleagues, associates, and experts in perfecting their speeches, even when they drafted the speech themselves. When covering a specific topic in a speech, most speakers who are likely leaders of one sort or another, need to rely on the input of others in order to secure effectiveness and avoid making mistakes or errors in judgment or intent. Most speakers seek feedback, advice, and a second opinion in order to avoid a less than favorable impression and to maximize receptiveness, recognizing that no individual can contemplate accurately all the speaking variables involved in a speech situation. The re-drafting and finalizing of speeches then are already the combined efforts of more than just the speaker. Speaking in public requires unique understanding of the public mode of communication and not all speakers possess knowledge and expertise in this field. Hence, the input of those more astute in public presentation can ensure greater effectiveness as well as minimizing weaknesses.

Our aim is to describe and elaborate the process of speechwriting, highlight its theoretical, conceptual, critical, and ethical features in order to present the practice as a teachable art. We divide our book into thirteen chapters. Following the Introduction, we describe in Chapter 2 how speechwriting works in the twenty-first century. In Chapter 3, we describe the classical period in which the concept of speechwriting was first developed. In Chapter 4, we focus on research and theoretical faming of the speechwriting process. In Chapter 5, we delve into the canons of rhetorical theory. In Chapter 6, we develop rhetorical precepts and genres that are essential for speechwriters. In Chapter 7, we discuss the process of writing speeches and the varied types of speechwriters. In Chapter 8, we delve into the relationship between speechwriters and speakers for whom speeches are written. In Chapter 9, we describe features of writing for the ear, and in Chapter 10, we focus on writing for the eye. In Chapter 11, we explore the ethical issues involved in writing speeches for others. In Chapter 12, we describe the functions of speechwriting in contemporary society, and in Chapter 13, we offer practical steps in the speechwriting process.

CHAPTER 2

Speechmaking in the Twenty-First Century

"Fire the Speechwriters"!

In 2009, former speechwriter for President George W. Bush, Matt Latimer, wrote an essay in *Washington Post* urging Barack Obama to eliminate his own profession: "Mr. President," he wrote, "fire the speechwriters; it might be the only way to save the presidency." Latimer argued that "The age of the Internet and cable news has opened the world to an onslaught of ideas, opinions and information," that is "stripping away the grandeur – and power – of the highest office in the land." Speechwriters, he claimed, "have become enablers, manning an assembly line of recycled bullet points so presidents can serve as the nation's pep-talk-givers, instant reactors, [and] TV friends."[1] Presidential candidate Donald Trump has opined during the summer of 2015, that he does not use speechwriters since he does not speak from prepared notes.

Is this the situation for speeches and speechwriters in the twenty-first century? Is speechwriting dying? Are speechwriters really reduced to assembly line workers producing recycled bullet points? We don't think so. On the contrary, we believe that writing and giving speeches is as important as it has ever been, but the dilemma posed by those critical of the role of speechwriters requires that we understand the criticism and address its concerns and explain the misperceptions therein.

[1] http://www.washingtonpost.com/wp-dyn/content/article/2009/09/04/AR2009090402278.html. Accessed January 11, 2016.

Speechmaking is not for every occasion of communication, but in the right circumstances, speechmaking has a rhetorical power that is unequal to any other kind of communication. What we suggest here is that there is a direct correlation between the importance of a given speech and the importance of employing speechwriters to guarantee the success of the specific assignment. At the same time, though, Latimer may have a point: Many leaders, especially political leaders, probably plan and deliver too many speeches. Given this new pressure and the logistics of managing multiple speech events, there are practical reasons why speakers do not and cannot spend time on speechmaking and hence the need for others to help the process.

CEOs sometimes tell us that they do not want "to do" a speech; they just want to get the job done, instead of using valuable time and resources talking to audiences. They do not consider speechmaking a cost-effective activity. It is much easier, they assume, to distribute information online, prepare a short video, send an e-mail, or participate in an interview: Why prepare a formal speech, if engaging in an informal meeting would suffice? Yet, these informal settings, too, are speech acts and they, too, require preparations as the very publicness of a presentation must abide by rhetorical stipulations such as audience analysis and specific appeals to motivate audiences. A speech, then, is not a matter of length or a formal setting as even short statements such as a tweet might benefit from good editing as well as testing it for maximum effect.

Renaissance for Speechwriting

Anyone seeking to write good speeches must start thinking about why people deliver speeches at all—and more importantly: Why other people listen to them. Several key questions guide our quest here: What is in a public speech that requires a special focus? What separates speeches from other forms of communication? What is the unique selling point of a speech? And in the age of Internet, and social media, what role should speechmaking have?

We should start by discarding the notion that the time of speechmaking is over. It is not.

Take the British journalist and member of the European Parliament, Daniel Hannan. When he woke up on March 25, 2009, his phone and e-mail inbox were clogged with texts. The day before, he had delivered a three-minute speech in the European Parliament, calling Gordon Brown, "the devalued Prime Minister of a devalued government." The YouTube clip of his short remarks had attracted over 36,000 hits. It was the most watched video in Britain that day, and some three million people have watched his speech. Hannan is not the only speaker experiencing a speech going viral. Who can forget the eloquent attack that Australia's former Prime Minister, Julia Gillard, launched on her opponent Tony Abbott, accusing him for double standards, sexism, and misogyny? Some 2.5 million people have seen this speech on YouTube.

New media is not a threat to speechmaking but an opportunity. Internet and video are potential vehicles for the speechwriter's words, creating a renaissance of speechwriting. New forms of communication will not displace the good speech. The use of social media, big data, and IT-technology was unequaled during Obama's campaigns of 2008 and 2012 to any other campaign in history. During the 2016 presidential campaign, tweets of Donald Trump proved how much speakers need speechwriters in order to improve content, receptiveness, and overall effect. There is no doubt that new technology helped Senator Obama become president and some would argue that Trump's tweets were successful in his presidential quest. But without the oldest mode of communication—speechmaking—neither would have become president. When faced with growing criticism of less-than-effective speech, a rambling style and incomplete sentences, Trump agreed to deliver few key speeches that were prepared in advance and read from the teleprompter. These few prepared speeches increased in frequency during the last stretch of the campaign and proved that a planned and a well-prepared speech often is superior to one that is not.

Some have dismissed the value of speechmaking relative to the importance of social media. The Arab Spring or Occupy Wall Street could not have happened without social media as a tool for disseminating information and organizing action.[2] It is certainly true that new media are excellent in creating and gathering a crowd. But, what do we do when the crowd has gathered? What did the thousands of people gathered in New York during Occupy Wall Street do? What did the massive crowd in Tahrir Square in Cairo do? They looked for a speaker, a spokesperson, a leader, someone able rhetorically to address the multitude, representing

---

[2] Cf. Clay Shirky, *Here Comes Everybody: The Power of Organizing Without Organization* (London: Penguin Books, 2008).

their aspiration and eloquently generating support and followers so that clear objectives are set.

Every crowd needs a speaker. Because that is how unity is created and purpose and direction are stated. For rhetoric scholar Kenneth Burke, the objective of identifying speaker and audience and making leader and followers consubstantial is key to rhetorical success. This objective is accomplished the way humans have done it for centuries, by giving speeches.

A Speech Is an Event

Speeches have an important place in human history and our time are not different from those preceding us. Several principles are important to contemplate. First and most, a basic thing to remember is that even though speeches are written, and many people read them; speeches are not texts. A speech is an event. It is a physical meeting where one person has undisputed access to many people's attention.

A Speech Is a Situational Event

Common for all speeches is the meeting between a speaker and an audience. A speech is not just a text, but a *physical and situational event unfolding in a specific sphere of time and space*. We distinguish between two main types of public speeches: The *traditional speech* whereby speaker and audience are united in time and space, and the speaker addresses the audience directly without any mediated variable separating them—except, of course for the use of microphones, loudspeakers, and similar technical aids. The *mediated speech* whereby the speaker and audience are separated in time and space. The speaker communicates through the use of mediated variables such as radio, television, or Internet, to address the physically absent audience and whose presence exists but is not visible to the speaker. For example, Ronald Reagan's address after the Challenger disaster in 1986 and Franklin D. Roosevelt's famous Fireside Chats, both transmitted live, were broadcast on radio and on television respectively to mass audiences. Likewise, Barack Obama implemented a weekly video address broadcast on www.whitehouse.gov. These two main types of speeches, of course, come in many different forms: a traditional speech broadcast on television or the Internet, and a mediated speech and an audience present, simultaneously functioning as a traditional speech. Any speaker, and any speech, can now be broadcast and distributed online, enlarging significantly the size of their audience.

The fact that a speech is a physical and situational event is most obvious in the *traditional speech*, which is distinguished from mediated forms of communication by being an actual physical meeting: Speaker and audience share the same space. This allows the speaker not only to influence the audience, it also possible for audience members to influence each other as well as provide the speaker with an immediate feedback. Ironically, mediated technology put an end to mass communication.[3] Listeners and the viewers of broadcasting or online communication are not a mass; they are not part of a group or a crowd. Generally, they sit alone or with few people at home—often rather inattentively. With a *traditional speech*, however, we can make everybody in a crowd react in the same way and at the same time and as such, speeches unite people in a community that in turn is enacted by virtue of the speech that unifies its members.

Even though the traditional speech, like writing or broadcasting, unfolds in time, it is experienced as a continuous and instantaneous situation. An individual can bring the morning paper or an iPad on the bus, but one cannot put a speaker in your pocket. When the speech is done, the words are gone. This experience literally makes the traditional speech unique. The mediated speech can also be experienced as an event, especially when it is transmitted live, as in the case of Reagan's address to the nation after the explosion of the space shuttle *Challenger* in 1986. As other live transmissions in broadcasting, the live broadcasting of a speech has many of the qualities we find in a traditional speech: a sense of simultaneity and a shared experience of the here and now. Even though speaker and audience are separated in space, they are united in time and emotions.

We also note that even speeches broadcasted long after their delivery can create the sense of the speech as an event. When we watch videos of mediated traditional speeches, such as Martin Luther King's "I have a dream," given in Washington 1963, we can imagine the experience and

---

[3] Anders Johansen, "Credibility and Media Development," in *Television and Common Knowledge*, ed. Jostein Gripsrud (London: Routledge, 1999), 159–172; cf. Anders Johansen, *Talerens troverdighet: Tekniske og kulturelle betingelser for politisk retorikk* (The Credibility of the Speaker: Technical and Cultural Conditions for Political Rhetoric) (Oslo: Universitetsforlaget, 2002).

perhaps even contemplate it as though we were there ourselves. In spite of such speeches being mediated, the moving images allow for a "here and now" experience. We know from historical accounts that Lincoln's *Gettysburg Address* entered the annals of great speeches about forty years after its delivery once it was incorporated in high school curriculum. A more recent assessment of this speech is that it continues to speak to different generations and though transformed relative to the circumstances of a given period, it is relived and impacting different generations despite the passage of time.

A Speech Is Oral and Physical

As a form of communication, a speech is first and foremost an embodied oral and physical performance. Even though most speeches are created initially as written text and read from a script, as an embodied performance, it suggests an act that is completely different from its initial textual formation. Indeed, there are fundamental differences between oral and written communication that need to be fleshed out. In contrast to written texts, a speech will always be dependent on the character and use of the speaker's voice. The character of a voice is constituted by its inherent qualities, such as a harsh voice, a tense voice, a modal voice, a breathy voice, a whispery voice, a lax voice, a falsetto, or a creaky voice. Active use of the voice includes features such as intonation, volume, tempo, tempo variations, pausing, tone, and articulation. An audience's physical experience of a speaker's vocal qualities and use of voice contributes to a sense of presence and experience of the speaker's character and an underscoring of the important elements and claims in a speech.

Another important trait of the speech as an oral genre is the instantaneousness and immediacy of the spoken word. The moment the speaker utters a word, it is gone. The aural room is time limited and determined by the moment. We may be cognitively immersed in a written text, but the spoken word literally surrounds us. And though a rebroadcasted speech can give listeners an impression or a sense of the original, older speeches that exist only in text form can be relived but in an imagined and interpretive way. We emphasize this point because some speakers will often cite lines from previous great speeches and as such a different interpretation situated in a different context is introduced to a new audience. Note for example the repetitive use of Franklin D. Roosevelt's line,

"The only thing we have to fear is fear itself." This famous line has been used quoted repeatedly in different times and by different speakers and in different contexts, each seeking the line to strengthen or support a stance and in a context different from the original use.

The fleeting character of the spoken word makes it rhetorically important that a speech is clearly organized, has memorable formulations, makes an impression, and sticks in memory. Speechmaking invites communication that is vivid and graphic. Oral societies have always used stories, examples, contrasts as well as rhetorical tropes and figures to grab attention and make an impression. These oral traits are no longer very prevalent in most contemporary speechmaking given the fact that speeches are first written down and then read aloud. When speakers and speechwriters write speeches, there is always a risk that norms of written communication, such as abstraction, hierarchical structures, and strict logical consistency, can overshadow the qualities of natural orality.

The quality and sound of words provide a physical experience which is characteristic of speechmaking, though conditioned by the size of the audience and on whether the speech is traditional or mediated. A traditional speech with a small audience is normally best delivered without a microphone and the audience physically close to the speaker. Even small variations in the use of the voice are noticeable and can leave a great impression. Before larger audiences, a microphone can help preserve a certain specter of smaller variations and modulations; however, large crowds would still expect a speech that sacrifices the small variations in order to use a higher volume and a more varied specter of voice qualities.

Crowds—especially outdoors—are often restless, inattentive, or involved in mutual conversation, which invites speaker to use body and voice more actively and loud. Television or online videos bring the audience close to the speaker both visually and auditorily, and here again small variations in gestures, facial expressions, and voice become more salient and important. The energetic and intense delivery that may be expedient in a traditional speech will often appear exaggerated and theatrical when viewed on television and mobile screens.

In summary, any speechwriter that seeks to utilize the special qualities of the speech as a physical and situational event needs to be aware of these issues.

A Speech Is a Hierarchical Organization of Speaker and Audience

Compared to other kinds of communication, speechmaking is characterized by a hierarchical structure: The speaker stands alone, facing the audience, often placed on a raised platform. The members of the audience are gathered in a group, united in physical unity, with their joint attention directed toward the speaker. The roles are clearly defined: The speaker has the right to the word; the audience is intended to listen, without the chance of truly getting the word themselves. This is a fundamental difference from everyday conversation (cf. Atkinson), when the interlocutors continuously pay attention to each other, as they operate within social rules of conversational turn-taking, which not only gives an individual the opportunity, but also the obligation to take the word as well as be expected to respond.[4]

This is not the case in speechmaking, which makes it necessary for a speaker to actively use rhetorical devices that grabs and sustains the attention of an audience. Speakers typically use devices such as rhetorical questions, contrasts, three-point-lists, and directly addressing an audience.[5] These rhetorical devices invite audiences to react as a group in unison, responding jointly with applause, laughter, cheering, or physical forms of approval or rejection.

Speakers Create Community

No other form of oral communication can create community and unity the way a speech does. Whereas media audiences are normally at home or at work, scattered in different parts of the company, the city, or even the country, an audience is physically present as a group in front of the speaker. The very gathering in one place for the occasion of a speech constitutes the audience. Leaders can send out a report, an e-mail, or any kind of text. But it does not afford them the opportunity to look the audience in the eyes as when they speak. Of course, they can make a video, look into the camera, and address viewers as "we," but it is very hard to constitute an audience that truly feels as a "we" when a speaker

---

[4] Cf. Max Atkinson, *Our Master's Voices: The Language and Body Language of Politics* (London and New York: Methuen, 1984).

[5] Atkinson, *Our Masters*.

is physically separated from an audience. Good leadership, often an extension of oral communication, for example, assumes bringing people together: emotionally and physically. Only rhetoric can do that.

The traditional speech, then, is in a unique position because the bodily presence of speaker and audience in the same physical space is not reproducible. Only by actually participating and being part of a group with attention directed in unison toward the speaker, can audiences experience the speech. In the physical meeting with an audience, a speaker exposes and offers a *self*, which is not available to audiences reading the speech or listening to it in sound recording, not even to audiences watching it in moving images. The situation of the traditional speech offers a unique meeting, providing the audience with an exclusive access to the speaker. They get what sociologist Erving Goffman has called "preferential access," meaning physical presence, accessibility, and opening up that *only* available to the present "members of a listening audience."[6]

When people as an audience are physically at a public speaking event, even though they are different from each other and from the speaker, it is easy for them to accept the speaker and themselves as "us" and "we" simply because they share the same location and overlaps in values, beliefs, attitudes, and even stance. Being together in the same space is often, in the language of Kenneth Burke, a sign of consubstantiality as they form a group. This very form of physical and mental community is unique for traditional speechmaking, because it unites the speaker, message, and audience into a physical and actual "we." This consubstantiality, however, does not necessarily mean that audience members are in complete agreement with the speaker or with each other. This very consubstantiality affords the speaker the potential for constituting the audience as a unified group.

When individuals present their case in writing, the words become physically separated from the presenter. In a sense, the speech or the arguments therein no longer belong to her, but become an independent rhetorical act on paper, in a newsletter, or on one's homepage. When a speaker is actually present and standing in front of an audience presenting her case, the message therein becomes more than just a position or an argument. It becomes a rhetorical situation whereby a speaker

---

[6] Erving Goffman, *Forms of Talk* (Philadelphia: University of Pennsylvania Press, 1981), 187.

is an engaged person stretching herself toward other persons, hoping to touch them with her ideas and values in order to make them see the world as she sees it. The underlying assumption is that the speaker believes the audience is capable of changing the situation.[7] This is a defining characteristic of speeches: a speaker who invests herself in the cause, trying to change the world by influencing her audience and believing in the potential of change.

So, why do people listen to speeches? They do this because they want to be part of a group. They want to experience and feel—and learn—something together—as a community, or even take action. They want to see speakers in the flesh and sense their presence. They want the speaker to see them—and they want to see each other attend to the speaker. No other form of communication does this as well as speechmaking.

The Power of Making a Case

There are two important features that can allow the speechwriter "make the case" of a point or an issue: narratives and arguments. The use of narratives in a sociological sense is the glue the binds communities. It is not surprising that narratives are very prevalent in rhetorical acts. Speechwriters consider "storytelling" a defining trait of a speech as it is surely one of the most defining traits of oral cultures.[8] Often what really separates the speech from other forms of communication is the coherent and consistent argumentation delivered by an engaged individual, who wishes to induce or increase the adherence of an audience in a direction of a particular viewpoint. The direct physical, situational, and personal meeting between speaker and audience puts the speaker at risk, and this particular constraint differs from mediated communication, where an individual communicates in "safe" distances from the audience.

Arguments in a speech are as important as stories, and speechwriters should be aware of what makes a good argument. We do not mean argumentation in a logical or philosophical sense. Speechwriters have to forward good rhetorical argumentation: They have to be able to provide

---

[7] Lloyd F. Bitzer, "The Rhetorical Situation," *Philosophy and Rhetoric* 1, no. 1 (1968), 1–14.

[8] Cf. Walter Ong, *Orality and Literacy* (London and New York: Routledge, 1982).

compelling reasons. Good reasons do not necessarily appear only as facts, numbers, and deduction; but also as stories, images, and examples. Good reason alone may not be sufficient to construct an argument, as appeals to feelings, emotions, and crucially, appeal to the speaker's credibility are equally important variables in the rhetorical process.

When a speaker wishes, for example, to persuade people that unemployment is a problem, combining a vivid story of the specific unemployed person with the indisputable facts and statistics can provide a stronger reason to solve the problem than economic indices alone. The personal account as a narrative can offer a powerful addition to cold facts and simple logic of cause and effect. Personal stories can add the affective appeal that touches others, hence the concreteness and reliability of an argument and its enhanced appeal.

Arguments in written texts are physically separated from the reader. In a sense it is not someone's argument anymore, it is just an argument in the paper, in the newsletter, or on Facebook. However, when speakers actually stand before an audience they are not just making an argument; but individuals personally reaching out to audience members, trying to touch them with specific ideas and values, hoping that they might be accepted by the auditors. Put differently, seeing the speaker speak is much more powerful than reading a text.

It important to note, though, that a narrative alone cannot carry the case being made. When advocating a position, speakers put themselves on the line and going beyond just telling a story. When making claims, speakers are obliged to back them up, investing in the cause, and leaving the faith of a given cause in the audience's hands. In doing so, speakers take a stand, they willingly run a risk in front of other people by showing character and respect for the listeners, even when failing or being proven wrong; but doing so anyway is an indicator that the speaker believes in the cause and trusts the audience. This is the hallmark of truly great speeches: Speakers investing their reputation in a cause, aiming to change the world by swaying the audience. This was what Neil Kinnock did in his famous speech to the Labour Party Conference in Bournemouth 1985, when he argued that you "can't play politics with people's jobs." This was what John F. Kennedy did with "Ich bin ein Berliner," what Martin Luther King did with "I have a dream," what Margaret Thatcher did with the Bruges speech, and what Barack Obama did with "A more perfect union." This is what speechwriter should aim for.

From Flaming Oratory to Everyday Language

Making a case does not necessarily mean resorting to flaming oratory bursting with rhetorical metaphors or flourishes. In most cases, the time for such appeals is long gone. In both Europe and the USA, the traditional political speech was a dominant form of communication until the Second World War. After the war, political communication moved from speeches at meetings, in big halls and open public squares into conversations and interviews on radio and television. Beginning with the 1950s, American politicians started buying time on television to deliver half-hour speeches. When the short 30 seconds political television commercials became dominant in the USA during the 1960s, the broadcasting of whole speeches largely disappeared from the screen. More recently, citizens view primarily (though not exclusively) short fragments from political speeches often inserted in news programs while the politicians and political action committees (PACS) own television advertising. While the consistent oral argumentation largely disappeared with this fragmentation, the sight of a speaker in front of an excited crowd remains a potent sign of leadership. We encounter the same kind of *ad populum* argument in the visual rhetoric, which began appearing in the beginning of the twenty-first century, where politicians place cheering and applauding crowds *behind* themselves, so that viewers can clearly observe how popular the speaker is. This setting amounts to the scene enhancing the speaker's argument. The presidential election of 2016 offers a reversal of sort of the very claim we just made as we note the extensive time devoted to candidates' speeches and debates, with major television networks providing uninterrupted coverage of primary and presidential debates as well as major speeches, but also giving space to cover tweets and phone-in calls. Whether this is a new trend or an anomaly, time will tell, yet, we are on safe ground when we offer that prior preparations and the importance of speechwriters became quite obvious with one presidential candidate in particular. We also note that political success in the 2016 election was not determined nor based on refined and well-designed speeches, and that, too, is a serious point.

In general, though, both in Europe and the USA, broadcast media has brought speechmaking to move from a flaming oratorical style of yesteryear to a more moderate, natural, and conversational style that appears more appropriate for the screens of today.⁹ This change is most evident in one historical example; the differences between the intense and almost conventionalized variations in the body and voice of Adolf Hitler, and the affable explanations given by President Roosevelt in his fireside chats.[10]

Historically, public communication has moved from a more to a less formal mode of address. Rhetoric scholar Kathleen Hall Jamieson argues that modern speeches are conversational, rather than oratorical: "The old eloquence, which spoke in metaphors of battle and fire, was contentious, passionate, and intense. Today, speakers who still try to conquer and inflame are as anachronistic as the amphitheater and the aqueduct."[11] The conversational style gained ground in the last half of the twentieth century—the age of television—but the change from traditional oratory to a more colloquial mode of speaking had long been coming.

The conversational style is a simulation of everyday speaking: a relaxed vocabulary, colloquial expressions, loosely constructed sentences, and an avoidance of subordinate clauses. When professional speechwriters wish to create a personal style for their clients, they refer to the speakers and their listeners in first-person pronouns ("you", "I"), use informal contractions ("You're", "we're"), and use conjunctions at the beginning of sentences ("And", "But"). The conversational mode is characterized by a subject matter that relates to issues in our everyday life. Reagan refined the conversational style by speaking in a low voice, using self-revelation that displayed feelings in order to come across as a genuine and an empathic leader that people could identify with.[12]

Today, conversational style is a widespread practice in speechwriting. Professional speechwriters use traces of everyday conversation to add "listenability" to a speech and to create a sense of relationship between speakers and listeners. Markers of the conversational mode can be found in most contemporary political speeches, as in a New Year's speech by the Danish Prime Minister, Helle Thorning-Schmidt.

---

[9] Kathleen Hall Jamieson, *Eloquence in an Electronic Age: The Transformation of Political Speechmaking* (Oxford: Oxford University Press, 1988), 45; Max Atkinson, *Our Master's Voices: The Language and Body Language of Politics* (London and New York: Methuen, 1984).
[10] Jamieson, *Eloquence*, 45.
[11] Ibid.
[12] Ibid.

> Good evening. A Thursday in December, I sat on the floor in a living room in Valby. I had Holger, who's six months old, on my lap. I was visiting the mother's group. Is there anything more life-affirming than being pulled in the nose by a curious baby? Children are lovely. They are the most important thing that we have. If we are asked what really matters for us in life, most of us will answer: our children. I certainly will. But our children are not just important to their parents and grandparents. They are our common future[13]

Not only is the prime minister's speaking style very close to everyday language—with short and simple sentences, a loose syntax, and a plain vocabulary—she also makes herself appear motherly caring by telling a personal anecdote and displaying emotion. The banality "Children are lovely" demonstrates just how down-to-earth this chief of state can be or thinks she ought to be.

Undoubtedly, the predominance of everyday language in public speeches reflects a general development of a more egalitarian society. Still, there is a reason to be cautious. While the conversational style may appear more egalitarian and democratic than traditional oratory, appearances may be deceptive. According to Robert Branham and Barnett Pearce, a speaker's allusion to conversational settings and relationships, for instance when she speaks about herself or makes eye contact with individual listeners, creates an illusion of intimacy and conversation, not a genuine dialogue: "The broadly inclusive conversational frame, with all its intimations of intimacy and identification, generally conceals and reinforces power. Because their relations with their audiences are not truly dialogical or egalitarian, the conversational frame serves to obscure, rather than to dismantle, the hierarchical relationships between speakers and listeners."[14]

On a more fundamental level, it is a problem that plain speeches on practical matters have so little power to enthuse an audience. If the public is never exposed to political speeches that enthrall and inspire, they will eventually lose interest in public speaking. Peggy Noonan, speechwriter for Ronald Reagan, is concerned:

> The modern egalitarian impulse has made politicians leery of flaunting high rhetoric; attempts to reach, to find the right if sometimes esoteric quote or allusion seem pretentious. They don't really know what

---

[13] Helle Thorning-Schmidt, New Year's Address, December 31, 2014. Our translation.

[14] Robert James Branham and W. Barnett Pearce, "The Conversational Frame in Public Address," *Communication Quarterly* 44, no. 4 (Fall 1996), 423–439.

"the common man" knows anymore; they forget that we've all had at least some education and a number of us read on our own and read certain classics in junior high and high school. The guy at the gas station read *Call of the Wild* when he was fourteen, and sometimes thinks about it. Moreover, he has imagination. Politicians forget. They go in lowest common denominator.[15]

Despite all its obvious rhetorical qualities, the conversational style is not without problems. Fortunately, it seems that the conversational mode has not quite replaced a more traditional brand of oratory. There is another trend in contemporary public speaking that is characterized by ceremony, complexity in language, and rhetorical figures. These public addresses are composed with an intention of moving the audience emotionally. They are distinctly, though not exclusively, epideictic: They are delivered at ceremonial occasions and their purpose is to praise, blame, memorialize, and reinforce the community by celebrating its core values. Some of the speeches are political speeches, made by politicians or heads of state with the purpose of formulating a future course for the nation.

The speeches of John F. Kennedy are considered among the high points in twentieth-century public speaking. In his inaugural address (1961), penned by speechwriter, Ted Sorensen, he used the rhetorical figure antimetabole (a repetition of words in successive clauses, but in reversed order) to capture the complex political climate as a power struggle that still allowed vision and hope for a better future: "So let us begin anew – remembering on both sides that civility is not a sign of weakness, and sincerity is always subject to proof. Let us never negotiate out of fear, but let us never fear to negotiate."[16]

Another instance of twentieth-century eloquence is Earl Spencer's funeral oration to his sister Lady Diana. Spencer's rhetorical strategy was to transcend Diana's death with the principle of good, in order to both commemorate Diana and blame the British press and royal family. With rhyme and rhythm, he announced her to be "the very essence of compassion, duty, style and beauty." The ceremonious, high style was cultivated in alliterations and parallelism (similarity in the syntactical

---

[15] Peggy Noonan, *What I Saw at the Revolution: A Political Life in the Reagan Era* (New York, NY: Random House, 1990), 70.

[16] John F. Kennedy, Inaugural Address, January 20, 1961. Ted Sorensen considers the American University Commencement Address, June 28, 1963 to be his best speech. Ted Sorensen, *Counselor: A Life at the Edge of History* (New York, NY: Harper, 2008).

structure), and paradox when he called her "a symbol of selfless humanity, a standard bearer for the rights of the truly downtrodden, a very British girl who transcended nationality." And the eloquence was perfected in an intricate a chiasmus (a repetition of concepts in successive clauses, but in reversed order): "only the strength of the message you gave us through your years of giving has afforded us the strength to move forward."[17]

Some of the more recent examples of moving public addresses are less generous in their distribution of rhetorical figures. Instead, their effect seems mainly to derive from the speakers' display of emotions. In 2014, Frans Timmermans, the Dutch minister of Foreign Affairs, delivered a speech in the Security Council of the United Nations. His speech dealt with a plane crash that caused the death of Dutch citizens. The plane was shot down only four days earlier above Ukraine, where a battle had broken out between pro-Russian separatists and the Ukrainian army. At the time of the speech, there was great uncertainty about what was going to happen to the remains of the passengers. Timmerman argued for a swift repatriation of the victims' remains and proposed that the Dutch lead the investigation into who caused the crash.

Timmerman's speech incorporates some of the traces of the conversational style: He begins with a matter-of-fact statement ("We are here to discuss a tragedy") and employs a quiet indignation when he addresses the failure to secure the crash site from thugs. In certain intense passages, he deviates from the manuscript, looks at the listeners, and addresses them directly. The speech is very moving, not because of its stylistic elegance, but because of Timmerman's way of creating empathy with the victims and the surviving relatives. He visualizes scenes from the tragedy and demonstrates in language and delivery how much he is affected by the tragedy: "Since Thursday, I've been thinking: How horrible must have been the final moments of their lives, when they knew the plane was going down. Did they lock hands with their loved ones, did they hold their children close to their hearts, did they look each other in the eyes, one final time, in a wordless goodbye? We will never know."[18]

A similar example of quiet sobriety is found in some of the national eulogies after politically motivated mass shootings. Two days after the massacre in a summer camp for the youth division of the Labor party on

---

[17] Earl Spencer, Eulogy for Princess Diana, Westminster Abbey, September 6, 1997.

[18] Frans Timmerman, Speech in the Security Council, UN, July 21, 2014.

the island Utøya, the Norwegian Prime Minister Jens Stoltenberg spoke in the cathedral of Oslo. Much of the pathos of this brief statement lies in Stoltenberg's enactment of his personal grief. While on the verge of crying, he speaks about a few of the victims that he knew personally. A single chiasmus stands out: "If one man can show so much hate, think about how much love we all can show."[19]

By comparison, following the shooting of Congresswoman Gabrielle Gifford and several members of her audience, President Obama gave a speech that is both long and complex. The speech comes closer to grand oratory in a traditional sense; it begins with a reading from the Bible ("Scripture tells us"), dwells on existential questions, and cautions against polarization of the political debate. Obama also speaks about individual victims, often with a peculiar, touching twist that moves the audience to laugh.[20]

One characteristic of Obama's speeches, here and elsewhere, is the incorporation of narratives, storytelling about his family background: his African father that succeeded in studying in the USA where he met his American mother. The narrative line highlights the time before becoming president in order to create strong identification with many who took it as an expression of the American dream. An example from Obama's speech in Berlin from 2008 is illustrative:

> I know that I don't look like the Americans who've previously spoken in this great city. The journey that led me here is improbable. My mother was born in the heartland of America, but my father grew up herding goats in Kenya. His father - my grandfather - was a cook, a domestic servant to the British.
>
> At the height of the Cold War, my father decided, like so many others in the forgotten corners of the world, that his yearning - his dream - required the freedom and opportunity promised by the West. And so he wrote letter after letter to universities all across America until somebody, somewhere answered his prayer for a better life.

Our point is that Obama's speeches, in general, are considered a counterweight to the general tendency to write more conversational speeches.[21]

---

[19] Jens Stoltenberg, Eulogy Address, July 24, 2015. Our translation.
[20] Barack Obama, Tucson Memorial Speech, January 12, 2011.
[21] See, for instance Barack Obama, Keynote Address at the 2004 Democratic National Convention, July 27, 2004; Night of New Hampshire Primary, January 8, 2008; "A More Perfect Union," March 18, 2008; Election Night Victory Speech, November 4, 2008.

The distinction between traditional oratory and everyday style is no novelty. Ancient rhetorical theories have taught us of the three levels of style: the grand, the middle, and the simple style. Apart from the middle style, there is much resemblance between the old teachings and the modern distinction between eloquence and conversational style. The grand style is characterized by intricate arrangement and complex language. The purpose is to move an audience, either emotionally or to perform some action. The simple style is characterized as ordinary speech common to everyday conversation. According to the old rhetorical theories, colloquialisms and informal language belong to the plain style that is best suited for instruction and explanation. And like the conversational style, the simple style is not only distinguished by language, but also by the topics that are common and belong to the practical, everyday life. The author of *Rhetorica ad Herennium* notes that if speakers are not to bore their audiences, they must combine different stylistic modes.[22]

Both the conversational style and the traditional eloquence are stylistic repertoires that function as available means of persuasion, and may be used productively to the benefit of public speaking. Both stylistic ideals are strategic and purposeful. Both argue and perform. The contrasting of styles is productive because it makes us think about what we do with language and its potential impact on audiences. For contemporary speechwriters, the most important lesson must be that the stylistic spectrum is wide, and that speakers do not have to limit themselves to only one type.

WRITING SPEECHES FOR OUR TIME

Anyone aiming to write good speeches in our time must be aware of the role of speechmaking today *and* of how speechmaking differs from other forms of communication. First, it is important to maintain that the time of speechmaking is not over, and that speechwriting is still an essential tool in the communication of businesses, organizations, and politics. Radio, television, and the Internet have given speeches new possibilities. The media, old and new, are not challenges, but opportunities and potential vehicles for the power of speeches.

Second, in our mediated world, a speechwriter must think of a speech as a two-step effort. The first step is getting the adherence of

---

[22][Cicero]: *Rhetorica ad Herennium* 8, 17.

the audience present in the actual speaking situation. The second is using media to maintain and strengthen this adherence, *and* acquiring the adherence of a wider audience of people not present in the original speaking situation.

Third, since traditional and mediated speeches work in different situations, it is important to be aware of their different rhetorical constraints. Generally, traditional eloquence is best suited for the traditional speech, while the mediated speech often works best with a conversational style. In the same way, traditional eloquence is the better choice for larger crowds, while conversational style is best when addressing smaller groups.

The traditional speech is a situational, physical, and hierarchical event, which unites a group of people in time and space, and directs everyone's attention to the speaker and her cause. This means that speechmaking is uniquely suited to establish community and inspire.

CHAPTER 3

The Beginning of Speechwriting

The art of rhetoric, whether intended for developing speeches and oratory or for a critical assessment of its construction and effects, is grounded in theories that withstood the tests of time. From ancient Greece through the Roman era to the medieval, Renaissance, and into the modern era, theories of rhetoric sought to advance the practice of effective public speaking as well as the critical methods for assessing them. The theories of rhetoric are thus functional and foundational to our development of the speechwriting process.

CLASSICAL THEORY ON RHETORIC AND SPEECHWRITING

In the fifth and fourth centuries BCE, the practice of speaking in public was recognized as an intellectual process that included principles of persuasion that could be taught and reflected upon for centuries to come. The first to theorize about the practice of speaking in public were the sophists, itinerant teachers of public speaking who shaped the practice into a teachable art. Though successful in their influence over the practice of speechmaking, they were also criticized for engaging in a loose approach to ethical public oratory. Their social success was a likely reason for the philosophers' attack on the sophists and their suspect teaching. Socrates and his disciple Plato were particularly effective in challenging the study of rhetoric had it not been for Aristotle's creative approach to finding the agreeable position between the philosophers and the sophists.

© The Author(s) 2019
J. E. Kjeldsen et al., *Speechwriting in Theory and Practice*,
Rhetoric, Politics and Society,
https://doi.org/10.1007/978-3-030-03685-0_3

Aristotle is acknowledged as the great thinker who found the creative way to frame rhetoric—the art of speaking in public—as a counterpoint to dialectic, the principal method of inquiry espoused by the philosophers. He reasoned the importance of individuals addressing the public and the different reasoning processes available to speakers in seeking to persuade others.

Aristotle's treatise *On Rhetoric* stipulates key variables as foundational to the art of rhetoric: the important notions of invention—designing the speech, especially finding the best means (or proofs) of persuasion for a given issue at a given time and with a specific audience in mind; the organization and structure of the speech, its optimal style and preferred delivery, as well as an overall ability to recall the speech when addressing a public such that the speakers' control over it would enhance their credibility. The Roman scholars of rhetoric such as Cicero and Quintilian would add to Aristotle's conception to identify five canons or the key variables in the development of speechmaking: Invention, Arrangement, Style, Delivery and Memory. This model would ground the teaching of public speaking for centuries, and most public speaking textbooks of the past two centuries still abide by this basic framework. In a practical sense, this means that teaching the practice of public speaking has continued to follow a consistent sequence of topics, ranging from the planning of the speech to the selection of the best organizational pattern, determining its style, settling on a delivery mode, and resorting to extemporaneous presentation as the contemporary version of memory and control over the topic addressed. The last canon has gone through significant changes in recent years with the introduction of the teleprompter, allowing for the appearance of memorized speeches, and the complete mastery speakers have over their speeches though they read them verbatim.

Importantly, Aristotle's treatise *On Rhetoric* came about after the philosophers' attack on the teaching of rhetoric for its unethical and manipulative potential. Ethics, then, was the single prompt for the serious undertaking of rhetoric as an area of study that eventually included oratory, public speaking, and rhetorical theory. Aristotle sought to put boundaries on those public speaking practices that did not abide by ethical standards, and the system he proposed was meant to keep rhetoric an honorable and respectable practice. Since history is replete with examples of demagoguery and manipulative speaking, it is important to point out that ethics and rhetoric go hand in hand and that speechwriting must aim at the good, the honorable, and the just.

Aristotle pointed to several reasons why the art of rhetoric carries great value: Truthful rhetoric would always triumph over injustice and lies, rhetoric is essential for convincing audiences not fully versed in scientific or technical knowledge, it can show both sides of an issue in question, and it could provide the best means of defending oneself from accusations. In all, rhetoric is a public art that is flexible, allowing individuals to select the best means of persuasion in a given situation. In doing so, Aristotle outlined three primary artistic proofs the speaker could develop:

1. *Logos*, the selection of the suitable reasoning process for a public presentation. Here, he would suggest the use of signs, examples, the enthymeme, or probabilities to reason a case.
2. *Pathos*, the appeals to emotions and feelings. Here, he would develop a detailed list of emotions and their potential impact on audiences.
3. *Ethos*, the attributes audience members assign to a speaker in terms of credibility, believability, expertise, and overall attitude.

In further developing his rhetorical theory, Aristotle conjured up three primary types of speaking situations, each divided further into two additional options:

1. *Ceremonial, or epideictic speeches*: speeches that seek to praise or to blame a person or an entity. Ceremonial speeches focus on the present and reflect on existing conditions and memories from the past. The objective of ceremonial speaking is honor or dishonor, its substance focuses on virtues or vices, and its audience is usually made of spectators or critics who function as judges of an individual or entity and the values espoused in their action.
2. *Deliberative speeches*: speeches that exhort or advocate a policy and those that oppose it. Deliberative speeches aim at the future as they seek to provide advice regarding a policy, projecting advantages or disadvantages of a given proposal. The substance of deliberative speeches is counsel or advice and its audience is usually an assembly or the general public, and as stipulated by Aristotle, its subjects or topics (topoi) cover issues of ways and means, war and peace, national defense, imports and exports, and legislation.

3. *Judicial speeches*: speeches arguing the guilt or innocence of an individual or an entity. They are designed to accuse or to defend, and their focus is on past events. Their aim is the establishment of justice or injustice, and its audience is usually made of judge or jury. The judgment of guilt or innocence is made against a known and acceptable standard, ruling, or law.

These six speaking occasions are foundational while other speech occasions can be considered as further modifications thereof and aimed at unique settings and occasions to include, among others, a professional presentation, an after-dinner speech, a eulogy, or a commencement address. Once the primary three types of speeches are understood and practiced; other speech types or nuances thereof can be constructed by further development of the basic modal.[1]

The classic perspective outlined here informs us of the key variables in the rhetorical process, allowing us to consider the macro-picture of speechwriting, whereby prior to outlining a suggested sequence of steps, we ought to begin with a focused assessment of the specific topic, a solid understanding of the speaker's persona as well as all related constraints as essential for assessing the merit and direction of a given speech and its rhetorical construction. These prerequisites are important for both speaker and speechwriter who need to assess their strengths and limitations as well as the specifics of a given speech topic. Following such a general assessment of speech and speaker, can the specifics of the speechwriting process be underway.

LOGOGRAPHY IN ANCIENT GREECE: THE AGE OF SELF-REPRESENTATION

Putting the above stipulations in context, we acknowledge that in ancient Athens, oratory was crucial in both public and private life. The Athenian democracy and its political system was based on the participation of all or at least a large number of citizens. All important decisions were made by councils. Whether it was a matter of charting the course for foreign policy or of condemning a citizen to exile, a collective of

---

[1] John H. Timmis III, *A Conspectus of Classical Rhetoric* (Dubuque, IA: Kendall/Hunt Publishing Co., 1977), 38.

citizens made the decision, and the primary means of influencing these decisions was oratory.

The assembly decided the political course and the judicial system depended on private citizens, wherefore the need for well-argued and persuasive speeches was evident. While speeches had been delivered in the courts and in the city council for centuries, Athenians did not begin to write the speeches down until the middle of the fifth century BCE. This practice of writing speeches began in the courts and then expanded to include political speeches as well as other types of oratory, such as funeral orations.[2]

Ideally, all citizens of Athens would participate directly either as judges in the councils or as orators. In reality, however, those belonging to the elite delivered most political and ceremonial speeches. Many of the politicians and officials who had the skill and experience to address large crowds on state matters, were educated by intellectuals who taught rhetoric and philosophy, often grouped together as the "Sophists."[3]

While private citizens rarely had the opportunity to make deliberative speeches in the assembly, nor the opportunity to praise the athletes in the Olympic Games, it was more likely that they had to deliver a speech in court, either because they were prosecuted or because they had filed a suit themselves. The Athenian legal system had no public prosecution, but relied on the private initiative of the citizens. The main form of legal procedure was private cases (*dikai*) between individuals in which the injured party or his relatives brought a suit against the offender. Another major form of procedure was political indictments (*graphai*) in which any citizen could bring a prosecution for wrongdoing.

When citizens were prosecuted, they would have to personally present their defense speech in court. They shared the speaking time with a friend or a relative, but did not hire a lawyer to argue their case. This legal practice was grounded on the idea that amateurism was more democratic than professionalism. If charge and defense were handed over to professional lawyers, the argument went; no amateur would be able to win a case. Yet, citizens were allowed to rely on external aid in writing the

---

[2] Michael Gagarin, "Greek Oratory," in Harvey Yunis (trans.), *Demosthenes Speeches 18 and 19* (Austin: University of Texas Press, 2005), xii.

[3] Mogens Herman Hansen, "Indledning," in Mogens Herman Hansen (trans.), *Lysias Taler* (København, Denmark: Museum Tusculanums forlag, 1980), 17.

speech, and it thus became customary to hire a professional speechwriter: a logographer.

Antiphon (ca. 480–411), who is often associated with the Sophists, was a pivotal figure in instituting the practice of logography. He was interested in the practice of law and began giving general advice to private citizens who were engaged in litigations and had to address the court themselves. Around 430 BC, Antiphon went further and began writing out whole speeches for others to memorize and deliver.[4]

While many forensic speeches were written beforehand by a professional speechwriter who also assisted in giving legal advice, speakers in the assembly seldom relied on a manuscript for the simple reason that speaker did not know in advance the exact topic or issue. Some speeches were later written down when speakers wanted to publicize and preserve their views, or demonstrate their success. Unlike the published text of forensic speeches that were had to be faithful to the speeches delivered in court, political speeches were probably revised before publication. Subsequently, writing and publication gave practical rhetoric aimed at swaying the opinion of Athenians the status of literature—like Pericles' funeral oration written by Thucydides or the intellectual, imaginary speeches by Antiphon and Gorgias (*Helen*).

The thriving rhetorical cultural climate in classical Greece gave rise to many speechwriters and orators, and the canon of ten Attic orators set up by Ancient scholars have made some names particularly known to posterity.[5] On this list are some of the best speechwriters of all times, among them, Demosthenes (384–322) who came from a wealthy Athenian family, but lost his fortune and had to earn his living as a speechwriter. His earliest speeches were composed to prosecute his guardians for mismanaging his inheritance. He later became a prominent politician who addressed the assembly on various political issues himself. One of the most famous speeches *On the Crown* was written as a response to another of the ten Attic orators, Aeschines, who had accused him of not being worthy of receiving an honorary crown.

---

[4] Gagarin, xiii.

[5] Aeschines (ca. 395–322), Andocides (ca. 440–ca. 390), Antiphon (ca. 480–411), Demosthenes (384–322), Dinarchus (ca. 360–ca. 290), Hyperides (389/8–322), Isaeus (ca. 415–ca. 340), Isocrates (436–338), Lycurgus (ca. 390–ca. 324), and Lysias (ca. 445–ca. 380). Gagarin, xiv–xvii.

Another prominent logographers from the Attic canon of orators is Isocrates (436–338) who also came from a wealthy family, but after having lost his property in the Peloponnesian War, became a speechwriter in Athens. He preferred to consider himself an educator and a philosopher, and eventually, he abandoned logography and turned to writing and teaching. Lysias (ca. 445–ca. 380), who was a metic, a non-citizen resident in Athens who could not become a politician or participate in the public life directly, practiced speechwriting and contributed indirectly to Athenian rhetoric. More than thirty speeches in his name have survived, including his vivid narratives and his strategic creation of the speaker's character, ethopoeia.

In ancient Greece, logography was a profession, and the logographers provided a service for pay by clients. As a trade, speechwriting for others carried high fees and its attraction to non-citizen residents did not exactly improve its reputation. However, their custom of charging fees in a culture governed by gift exchange was later interpreted as culturally and economically innovative. Seen in this light, the logographers' fees transformed the value of discourse in a way that is quite consistent with their general pedagogical and social program of demystifying social knowledge and cultural value.[6]

In general, the ancient Greeks had a prejudice against delivering prepared written speeches, preferring instead spontaneity and improvisation. Edwards has pointed out that there existed a "tension in which listeners were at the same time desirous of hearing a polished speech, but antipathetic towards one which was read out or which had obviously been prepared."[7] The critical attitude toward logographers and the written speech can be found in the text *On Those Who Deliver Written Speeches* (also called *On Sophists*), whereby the rhetorician Alcidamas criticizes speechwriters such as Isocrates and argues that the speech delivered extempore is far superior to the written speech. For people who ask for "speedy help in their law-suits," he writes, producing written speeches is too slow.[8] And adding, would it not be ridiculous if when a citizen is asked

---

[6] James Fredal, "Why Shouldn't the Sophists Charge Fees," *Rhetoric Society Quarterly* 38, no. 2 (2008).

[7] Michael J. Edwards, "Antiphon and the Beginnings of Athenian Literary Oratory," *Rhetorica: A Journal of the History of Rhetoric* 18, no. 3 (2000), 227–242, 231.

[8] Alchidamas, *The Works and Fragments*. Edited and translated by John (London: Bristol Classical Press, 2001), 10.

to speak or when the "water-clock in the courts was already running" the speaker "were to proceed to his writing tablet in order to assemble and con his speech?"[9] No, the speaker must be able to appropriately express things on the spur of the moment and make good use of the critical moment, and to do this he must have a "flexible mind and a well-stocked and ready memory ... keen to acquire an ability to make speeches which correspond to the needs of life."[10] As Andersen points out, Alcidamas' horizon is the courtroom or the people's assembly; here, "the speaker needs to respond immediately, discuss unexpected arguments, and in all things to be capable of adapting himself to the exigencies of the moment."[11]

In a more concrete sense, the outlook of the speaker and the audience depended on the specific sites where speechmaking and deliberation took place in ancient Athens. One of the main places was the Agora, the city center. It was a large square on the northwest slope of the Acropolis, where social and religious activities, commerce, outdoor theatrical performances, and athletic contests were held. The Agora was also the heart of the Athenian democracy where most of the administrative and judicial functions and political assemblies took place. Political debate was a central activity in the Bouleterion, a large building in the Agora that served as a meeting place of the 500-member council (*boule*) made up of fifty citizens from each of the ten Athenian tribes, chosen by allotment each year. As a legislative body of the city-state (*polis*), the Council prepared the bills that were voted on in the assembly of all citizens (*ekklesia* of the *Demos*).

Another prominent speaking platform in ancient Athens was the Areopagus, a large rock located below the Acropolis. Later, the apostle Paul is said to have delivered a sermon to the Athenian people from the Areopagus rock. Although the impressive landscape invites the modern visitor to imagine how speakers addressed the audience standing on the top of the rock, we do not know for certain if speakers indeed addressed audiences from high above, or if they stood closer to the audience on the less steep western slope.

The most important site of the Athenian deliberative democracy is the Pnyx, the place where the assembly of the citizens (*ekklesia*) met ten

---

[9] Ibid., 11.
[10] Ibid., 34.
[11] Andersen, 2011, 244.

times a year. A flat stone sculptured from the rock served as the speaker's platform (*bema*), and the citizens were sitting on the ground, perhaps on cushions, or on narrow benches or folding stools.[12] The Pnyx was reorganized several times; the most radical revision was made around the fourth century BC, when the orientation of the open auditorium was reversed and the seating capacity was increased from 5000 to 6000 people. The reversal meant that the audience that had previously been facing the view of the Acropolis, the Areopagus, and the Agora was now placed with their backs to this spectacular scenery. Theories that explain the drastic reversal include the need to avoid the cold Northern wind or to avoid the distraction of the audience have been put forward, but no satisfactory explanation has been given so far.[13] Later a large wall was erected and the seating capacity expanded further to an estimate of up to 13,500 people. Famous orators like Demosthenes, Aeschines, and Isocrates have spoken on the Pnyx. The activities of the Pnyx were later transferred to the Theater of Dionysos on the south slope of the Acropolis.

Finally, speeches were made in honor of the dead in the Keramikos, an important cemetery and the potters' quarter of the city. At the beginning of the "Dromos," the ancient road leading from the main gate in the city wall to Plato's Academy, there was a square 40 meters wide, wherein the Athenians congregated to honor their dead with ceremonies, games, and funerary speeches. On either side of the road, prominent Athenians and those who fell in the city's battles were buried in the public tomb. One of the greatest ceremonial speeches of all times, Pericles' Funeral Oration for the first dead in the Peloponnesian War in 430 BC was delivered here.

It is not difficult to image how rhetorical figures such as *amplificatio* and *antithesis* between "us" and the enemy at "our" gate would be attractive instruments for the speechwriter to hold the attention of the massive crowd. Today, "the medium is the message," dictum is not far from the ancient Greeks whose material surroundings shaped and influenced speeches and speechwriting in ancient Athens. The quality and

---

[12] Mogens Herman Hansen, "Reflections on the Number of Citizens Accommodated in the Assembly Place on the Pnyx," in *The Pnyx in the History of Athens*. Papers and Monographs of the Finnish Institute at Athens, eds. Björn Forsén and Greg Stanton (Helsinki, 1996), 26.

[13] Heiner Knell, *Athen im 4.Jahrhundert v.Chr. – eine Stadt verändert ihr Gesicht* (Darmstadt: Wissenschaftliche Buchgesslschaft, 2000), 56.

expediency of a rhetorical message depends on the specific circumstances and on what persuades the immediate audience. A logographer in ancient Athens would have to consider what particular arguments and rhetorical devices would be effective in a face-to-face society such as the Athenian polis.

LOGOGRAPHY IN ANCIENT ROME: THE AGE OF REPRESENTATION

While an eager market for written forensic oratory in Athens, where *logographers* (e.g. speechwriters) wrote speeches on behalf of clients,[14] the citizens of ancient Rome were allowed to have advocates speak on their behalf in court. Such advocates would speak for defendants, and sometimes also for plaintiffs.[15] Where male Athenian citizens had to speak in court, ordinary Roman citizens could hire an advocate who would speak for them. Advocates, such as Cicero, would craft and deliver the speech. The need for speechwriters who could write in the character and tone of others naturally diminished, especially in the forensic genres. Trials generally took place in public, probably out in the open, under the warm sun. The parties, their lawyers, the president of the court, and a large jury would be present. Surrounding those involved in a trial would be a curious, noisy crowd, hoping for scandal, looking for amusement or indignation. This was especially the case in the criminal cases, where speeches about assault, murder, and treason invited to a grand and gripping kind of rhetoric as well as spectators to please.

Besides the courts, the most important kind of speechmaking was political speechmaking. One kind of political speechmaking was the so-called *contio*, a setting for citizens to hear the message of a speaker. A magistrate summoned the meeting and all could attend with neither a ballot nor any official decision-making process underway. The objective was primarily that of a briefing or persuasion. Often, a meeting was summoned in order to explain decrees adopted in the Senate, at other times a meeting was called in order to persuade the public about cases which were to be voted upon after the meeting. The meetings normally took place in the public rostrum on Forum Romanum, which was a large terrace where the orator could move freely and make gestures. Neither the

[14] Catherine Steel, *Roman Oratory* (Cambridge: Cambridge University Press, 2006), 29–31.

[15] Steel, *Roman Oratory*, 29.

Greeks nor the Romans used a speaker's lectern of the kind as is often used by orators today.

Another important kind of Roman rhetoric was the political oratory in the senate. Most meetings, debates, and speeches were given in the Senate-building at the Forum Romanum. Normally, a magistrate would make a proposal and then ask the people present to offer their opinion. First, the elder and most superior senators would argue for their positions. After this, other individuals were given an opportunity to speak. The less important a senator, the less time he was granted. As speakers were afforded less and less time, the few remaining speakers would only provide their agreement or disagreement. Usually, about one hundred senators would participate. However, during the Republic, the number was raised to 300, and in some periods, it had increased to between 600 and 900 people. It was during these circumstances that the fieriest oratory was delivered.

As in Athens, orators in Rome did not use scripted texts. Speeches were delivered from memory and were mostly written down not before, but *after* they had been delivered.[16] A "written speech", Quintilian writes, in a discussion of the vices and virtues of writing speeches "is merely a record of on that has actually been delivered" (XII.x.51). However, even though both Cicero and Quintilian discussed writing in their works, none of them had said anything significant about writing speeches for others. This can be taken as an indication that logography was not a prevalent practice in Roman oratory.

While citizens and senators had less need for ghosts to write their speeches, we know that at least two emperors used speechwriters. The philosopher and dramatist Seneca (c. 4 BC–AD 65) assisted Nero (37–68) both in writing funeral oration for the Emperor Claudius and with his maiden speech as emperor. We also know that a political speech (a *contio*) by the Emperor Otho (32–69) was written by the politician and orator Trachalus.[17] The transition in Rome from a Republic to authoritative rulers had a negative impact on the art of rhetoric which practically meant putting major constraints on *inventio* while privileging style and delivery. This setback would last till the Renaissance, depriving for centuries people's complete understanding of the art of rhetoric.

---

[16] Robert Morstein-Marx, *Mass Oratory and Political Power in the Latte Roman Republic* (Cambridge: Cambridge University, 2008), 25. Cf. Steel, *Roman Oratory*, 27.

[17] William T. Avery, "Roman Ghost-Writers," *Classical Journal* 54 (1959), 167.

CHAPTER 4

Research and Theory on Speechwriting

While there is a vast amount of research on political communication and some on political speechmaking, there is only a limited amount of research done on speechwriting. Most of the existing research has come from the USA, while Europe[1] and other continents seem to lack behind. Attending only to the USA, Lois J. Einhorn pointed out the lack of research on speechwriting in 1981 and argued that the anonymity of most ghostwriters was "partially responsible for the fragmented nature of the speechwriting literature."[2] Ghostwriters are not as ghostly anymore, some are even famous, and many speechwriters have written memoirs about their time as speechwriters in the White House. Among these are Kennedy Speechwriter Ted Sorensen (*Counselor: A Life at the Edge of History*, 1990), Reagan Speechwriter Peggy Noonan (*What I Saw at The Revolution*, 1990), and George W. Bush Speechwriter Matt Latimer (*Speech-less*, 2009).[3] Scholarly literature on the subject has

---

[1] Cf. Antje Schwarze and Antje Walther, "Redenschreiben Für Den Bundeskanzler: Formulieren, Koordinieren Und Beraten," in *Das Wort Hat Der Herr Bundeskanzler: Eine Analyse Der Großen Regierungserklärungen Von Adenauer Bis Schröder*, ed. Karl-Rudolf Korte (Wiesbaden: VS Verlag für Sozialwissenschaften, 2002), 34.

[2] L.J. Einhorn, "The Ghosts Unmasked: A Review of the Literature on Speechwriting," *Communication Quarterly* 30 (1981), 43.

[3] Other examples are: W.F. Gavin, *Speechwright: An Insider's Take on Political Rhetoric* (East Lansing: Michigan State University Press, 2011); C.R. Smith, *Confessions of a Presidential Speechwriter* (East Lansing: Michigan State University Press, 2014).

grown in the last 25 years; however, the research is still rather sparse and fragmented.

Speechwriting as a craft and profession appears to have gained a new status in recent years. Barack Obama's oratory has been praised, and his speechwriters, such as Jon Favreau, has earned the respect of both communication professionals and citizens across the world. The critical, often pessimistic, ethical perspective that dominated research from the beginning of the 1960s has largely been abandoned, and a new pragmatic attitude has entered the scholarship on speechwriting. Today, the art of speechwriting is seldom seen as a deceiving activity and more often is treated as a form "craftsmanship" necessary in contemporary public communication.

Martin J. Medhurst proposed three types of research into the study of invention, disposition, and style. Rhetorical scholars could study: (1) *"the effect of the writer(s) upon the invention manifested by the speaker,"* (2) *"the inventional resources of a particular writer by tracing that writer's efforts over several different speakers,"* (3) *"the evolution of rhetorical situations by observing the circumstantial forces that motivate change in the speech drafts* and point to matters of audience analysis, rhetorical purpose, personality and policy conflict, and differing interpretations of facts, motives, and outcomes."[4]

At least three trends can be observed in contemporary research of speechwriting: first, more focus on institutional and processual aspects of speechwriting; second, a growing interest in the constitutive aspects of speechwriting, especially regarding ethopoiia and the speaker's character[5]; and third, a combination of qualitative and quantitative research methods in the study of process, content, and reception.

The practice and research of speechwriting is most prominent in the USA. The dominant part of studies on the subject deals with American politicians or business leaders, and the most studied of all is presidential speechwriting. However, speechwriting is also practiced and studied in other parts of the world. Besides the USA, Europe is the place where speechwriting appears to be mostly practiced and studied. These are also the regions that we as authors are familiar with, and hence, the examples we resort to are taken from our own contexts.

---

[4] Martin J. Medhurst, "Ghostwritten Speeches: Ethics Isn't the Only Lesson," *Communication Education* 36 (1987), 247–248.

[5] For example, Bruss, "Writing for the Ear."

We divide the research on speechwriting into the following key categories concerning: (1) in antiquity, (2) in the US White House, (3) in European politics, (4) in ethical implications, (5) in institutional and procedural issues, (6) in speaker style, character, and authenticity, and finally, (7) in research methods as explicated in interviews with speechwriters. Clearly, these issues overlap, as the notion of ethics in speechwriting, for instance, relates to all the other issues.

RESEARCH ON SPEECHWRITING IN ANTIQUITY

Classical studies of ancient Greece and Rome has documented that writing speeches for others is not a new phenomenon. In ancient Greece, logography was a profession, and the logographers provided a service for pay. Logography was in demand because private citizens in court were required to present their case themselves. Instead of having lawyers plead the case for them, citizens had speechwriters formulate their speeches, which they then delivered themselves. The Roman system allowed the use of lawyers to plead a case, and the need for speechwriters in court thus diminished. Thinking about speechwriting in antiquity was done by contemporaries such as Plato, Aristotle, and Quintilian in their general theories on rhetoric. Later, biographers such as Dionysius of Halicarnassus developed a more specific focus on selected speechwriters and orators. The research focus in antiquity was concerned with techniques in composition, evaluating the quality of the writing, and reflecting on the ethics of speechwriting. Modern research into speechwriting in antiquity also elaborated on determining how widespread the practice was, who engaged in the practice, how were practitioners viewed, how was speechwriting performed, and when.[6] We say more about this in Chapter 2: "The History of Speechmaking."

---

[6]For example, Michael J. Edwards, "Antiphon and the Beginnings of Athenian Literary Oratory," *Rhetorica: A Journal of the History of Rhetoric* 18, no. 3 (2000); W.T. Avery, "Roman Ghost-Writers," *The Classical Journal* (1959); Michael Gagarin, "Greek Oratory," in Demosthenes, Speeches 18 and 19, translated and in by Harvey Yunis (Austin: University of Texas Press, 2005); James Fredal, "Why Shouldn't the Sophists Charge Fees," *Rhetoric Society Quarterly* 38, no. 2 (2008); Catherine Steel, *Roman Oratory* (Cambridge: Cambridge University Press); Kristine S. Bruss, "Persuasive Ethopoeia in Dionysius's Lysias," *Rhetorica: A Journal of the History of Rhetoric* 31, no. 1 (2013), 34–57.

Research on Speechwriting in the US White House

Most of the research in the field is on speechwriting in the US White House. Robert Schlesinger's *White House Ghosts* covers the period from Franklin D. Roosevelt to George W. Bush and is based on archival work and interviews with presidential speechwriters. Ritter and Medhurst's *Presidential speechwriting* (2003) covers speechwriting in the White House from Franklin D. Roosevelt to Ronald Reagan. An introductory essay by Medhurst debunks ten myths about presidential speechwriting that plague modern scholarship: (1) Speechwriting is *not* just a modern activity.[7] Since the beginning of the Republic presidents such as George Washington has requested and received assistance with their speeches; (2) Warren G. Harding, *not* Roosevelt, was the first modern president to use speechwriters on a regular basis; (3) the individuals writing speeches were *not* always been called speechwriters and often they have been administrative assistants or policy advisors; (4) presidential speechwriters are *not* always employed as members of the White House staff—at times, presidents have "turned to people outside the official structure for assistance with their speeches"; (5) speechwriters do *not* only ornament and amplify the writing, they also invent ideas and help create policy; (6) presidents are *not* marionettes reading the words that others wrote for them. A speech is thoroughly vetted, and the presidents are involved in the creation of many speeches; (7) the most successful speechwriters do *not* have a passion for anonymity. Many writers are well-known public figures; (8) presidential discourse would *not* be better, and more ethical, if speechwriters were eliminated. On the contrary, speechwriters are good advisors that help both the president and the nation; (9) speechwriting does *not* make it impossible to judge what presidents really believe. Any researcher studying presidential rhetoric must—and should—not study the words alone, but look at the full situation the words is a response to; and finally, (10) speechwriters should *not* be kept from the policy discussions. Speechwriting is and should be an important and integrated part of the policy-making process.

---

[7] Martin J. Medhurst, "Presidential Speechwriting: Ten Myths That Plague Modern Scholarship," in *Presidential Speech Writing: From the New Deal to the Reagan Revolution and Beyond*, eds. Kurt Ritter and Martin J. Medhurst (Texas: Texas A&M University, 2003), 3–20.

According to Medhurst, four enduring issues are paramount in both the practice and the analysis of presidential speechwriting. One key issue is the speechwriter's *access* to the president. Easy access, Medhurst argues, leads to better speeches and serves the interest of the administration best. The most crucial moments of access are those where ideas are conceived, the final draft is composted, and the moments where administration and involved parties "vet" the drafted speech. The enduring second issue is the relationship of *speechwriting and policymaking*. Restructuring of the White House administration, specialization, and bureaucratization had reduced speechwriters' ability to influence policy. Ritter and Medhurst's book, which was published in 2003, does not cover the Obama administration, where speechwriters seem to enjoy a renewed importance. The third issue concerns the *constraints* of the speechwriting process: the attitudes of president and staff toward speechwriting (internal) and the situational constraints for each speech (external) as decisive for the speechwriting process and the way the speeches turn out. The most enduring issue, according to Medhurst, is the relationship of *speechmaking* to presidential leadership. Since the rise of the rhetorical presidency at the beginning of the twentieth century,[8] presidents have engaged directly with their constituencies, the country, and the world through public communication—and especially through speeches. Therefore, it is essential to study the workings and functions of speechwriting in the White House.

Nelson and Riley's *The Presidents' Words* (2010) is based on an oral history conference. It deals with four forms of presidential addresses: Acceptance address, Inaugural address, State of the Union, and the crisis speech. Each form is covered by a chapter, providing historical accounts of the genre and a chapter containing a transcript of contemporary speechwriters' discussion of the genre led by a scholar. In the introductory essay, Nelson[9] distinguishes between three eras of presidential speechwriting. The first era is *the rise of the rhetorical presidency and the professional speechwriter* (1901–1933). In this era, as Jeffrey Tulis has argued, the presidency became rhetorical in the sense that direct popular

---

[8] Jeffrey K. Tulis, *The Rhetorical Presidency* (Princeton, NJ: Princeton University Press, 1987).

[9] Michael Nelson, "Speeches, Speechwriters, and the American Presidency," in *The President's Words: Speeches and Speechwriting in the Modern White House*, eds. Michael Nelson and Russel L. Riley (Kansas, USA: University Press of Kansas, 2010), 1 ff.

appeal and mass rhetoric became a principal tool of presidential governance. Here, it is "taken for granted that presidents have a *duty* constantly to defend themselves publicly, to promote policy initiatives nationwide, and to inspire the population."[10] Since this change required a president to speak frequently in public, it gave rise to the professional speechwriter.

The second era, that *of the speechwriter-adviser* (1933–1969), whereby the speechwriters were "more than literary clerks, they were presidential advisers on matters of substance as well as rhetorical style."[11] Typically, Nelson explains, they were lawyers rather than journalists.

Finally, we have the current *era of the speechwriting specialist*, which began in 1969, and continues. This era introduced the practice of "housing presidential speechwriters in their own unit outside the policy development process."[12] Besides the general separation from policy development, the changes in this period also lead to more professionalization, specialization, and vetting of speeches by different offices. Most important of all, this period leads to an explosion of the number of speeches delivered, increasing by 250% from Ronald Reagan to George W. Bush.[13]

The aforementioned books are representative of the study of presidential speechwriting in the sense that most of this research is historically oriented and describes speechwriting in different administrations. The studies are based on historical research and biographies as well as interviews with former and active speechwriters.

Research on Speechwriting in European Politics

Outside the USA, it seems that most research on speechwriting is done in Northern Europe, for instance, the Netherlands, Germany, and Scandinavia.

In Germany, studies focused on the prime minister's ("Der Bundeskanzler," "the Chancellor's") speeches, such as the Government Declaration (read more about the speechwriting process for this speech

---

[10] Tulis, *The Rhetorical*, 4.
[11] Michael Nelson, "Speeches, Speechwriters, and the American Presidency," 4.
[12] Ibid., 6.
[13] Ibid., 9.

in Chapter 6).[14] It is not surprising that prime minister's speeches receive most scholarly interest. They are not only the most important in politics; they are also the most frequent in use. On average, the Chancellor delivers on average 200–250 speeches a year. This means that speechwriters work on one speech every day, though, at times, they have to prepare three speeches in one day.[15]

A group of researchers in the Netherlands has examined different techniques in speechwriting, such as the use of humor, and techniques for beginning (exordial) and ending (peroration) speeches.[16] While this mainly experimental research does not directly relate to the speechwriting process itself, the research examines the background of speechwriters and the writing process. In examining the "Professionalizing Speech Production," de Jong and Andeweg write that in the Dutch Government, almost all speechwriters (95% in 2001) had a university master's degree. Fifteen percent had pursued a special communication major in rhetoric or journalism, and most speechwriters (55%) have some journalistic experience. Based on interviews with speechwriters, de Jong and Andeweg describe the writing process as frustrating and not contributing to the overall quality of the speeches.[17] One study documents the positions, activity, roles, and developments of speechwriters in Switzerland.[18] In general, research from Northern Europe suggests that speechwriters are well educated and that most of them have degrees in the humanities or social sciences, that some have studied

---

[14] Schwarze and Walther.

[15] Ibid.

[16] Dorien Mieroop, Jaap Jong, and Bas Andeweg, "I Want to Talk About," *Journal of Business and Technical Communication* 22, no. 2 (2008); B.A. Andeweg, J.C. de Jong, and M. Wackers, "'The End Is Near': Effects of Announcing the Closure of a Speech," in *Professional Communication Conference, IPCC 2008. IEEE International, 13–16 July* (2008).

[17] Jaap de Jong and Bas Andeweg, "Professionalizing Speech Production: Changes in 15 Years of Ministerial Speeches," in *Bending Opinion: Essays on Persuasion in the Public Domains*, eds. Ton van Haaften, et al. (Leiden: Leiden University Press, 2011), 160 f.; Jaap Jong and B.A. Andeweg, *De Eersten Minuten. Attentum, Benevolum En Docilem Parare in De Inleiding Van Teospraken* (Katholieke Universiteit Nijmegen, 2004).

[18] Martina Schäfer and Guido Keel, "Redenschreiber in Schweizer Organisationen: Tätigkeiten, Rollen Und Entwicklungen," *Studies in Communication Sciences* 15, no. 2 (2015), 197–206.

journalism and most, especially in recent years, have work experience within journalism, media, and writing.

In Scandinavia, contemporary research and thinking on speechwriting evolved since the publication of studies in the 1990s. Among other things, researchers dealt with the issues of ethics and authenticity,[19] and the process of speechwriting in government ministries.[20] Recently, several graduate student theses have examined speechwriting, specifically examining the speechwriting processes in Scandinavian ministries and parties. These studies teach us that while the actual speechwriting processes may differ significantly across institutions, it is a general trait that processes involve many employees from different departments who are often political appointees as well as civil servants, who all contribute to the speechwriting process on different levels.[21] A speechwriter is necessarily dependent on the knowledge and information of the technical divisions in a ministry, primarily because context, information, and background are needed in order to ensure that speeches are precise and correct. However, the departmental style of expression—the officialese—and the complex, bureaucratic process of approval also tend to disregard and set aside the communicative and rhetorical demands for a good speech.[22]

Research on Speechwriting and Ethics

One of the main areas of contemporary research in speechwriting has been on the issue of ethics both in politics and in corporate communication.[23] In the early 1960s, Ernest G. Bormann argued that the growing

---

[19] Merete Onsberg, "En mand er en mand, og et ord er et ord - men hvis ord er mandens?" in *Retorik Studier* 11. C.A. Reitzels forlag (1998), 24–61.

[20] Pernille Steensbech, "På ministerens vegne. Om taleskrivning i et dansk ministerium," in *Retorik Studier* 11. C.A. Reitzels forlag (1998), 62–81.

[21] Kristin Hald Skåleskog, *Taleskrivningsprosessen i Norge - en undersøkelser av taleskrivningsprosessen i fire norske departementer*. Master thesis. Department of Information Science and Media Studies, University of Bergen, Norway, 2013.

[22] For example, Mette Stoltenberg, Hvem har ordet? En retorisk analyse af taleskrivning for en anden i danske ministerier og kommuner. Master thesis. Department of Comparative Literature and Rhetoric, Aarhus University, Denmark, 2014.

[23] For example, L.A. Riley and S.C. Brown, "Crafting a Public Image: An Empirical Study of the Ethics of Ghostwriting," *Journal of Business Ethics* 15, no. 7 (1996), 711–720; M.W. Seeger, "Ethical Issues in Corporate Speechwriting," *Journal of Business Ethics* 11, no. 7 (1992), 501–504.

practice of speechwriting not only made rhetorical criticism more difficult, it would actually risk destroying criticism: In the tradition of the "speaker-oriented" criticism, researchers view the speech as "an interaction of the speaker with his environment." An evaluation based on this view requires a thorough understanding of the person who wrote the speech, and personal and textual authenticity is vital. However, "when an entire committee has written the speech, the problem of relevant biographical materials becomes so complex as to be almost impossible."[24] Similarly, speech criticism is difficult to carry out when speeches are written by ghosts, because the "ghost has a tendency to be discrete and careful. ... he dilutes the distinctiveness and strength and spontaneity of whatever writing talent he may have."[25] Furthermore, Bormann argues, when speeches are written in a committee fashion, any kind distinctive style or authenticity of the speaker will vanish.

Speechwriting, according to Bormann, not only makes rhetorical criticism impossible, the practice as such is thoroughly unethical. Having someone else write a speech is a deception that corrupts both the speech and the person speaking, because the speech will be a dishonest presentation of who the speaker is: "If the audience is to know a candidate through what he speaks and writes, then he must be honest with them and present himself as he really is."[26] Bormann's position has been criticized for failing to acknowledge that speechwriting is an institutional activity that has carried out since the founding of the American Republic and that a president speaks "simultaneously as a person and as a spokesman of a vast and complex organization known as the federal government ... his voice is the voice of many persons."[27] In Bormann's preferred mode of criticism, the "speaker-oriented" neo-Aristotelian criticism implies attention to the speaker's biography and self in ways that are not on the same wavelength as the more discourse-oriented methods of contemporary rhetorical criticism. We write more about the ethical aspects in Chapter 11.

---

[24] Ernest G. Bormann, "Ghostwriting and the Rhetorical Critic," *The Quarterly Journal of Speech* 46, no. 3 (1960), 284–288.

[25] Ibid., 287.

[26] Ernest G. Bormann, "Ethics of Ghostwritten Speeches," *The Quarterly Journal of Speech* 47, no. 3 (1961), 267.

[27] D.K. Smith, "Ghostwritten Speeches," *Quarterly Journal of Speech* 47 (1961), 418.

Research on Institutional and Processual Issues

Even though research indicates that the activity of speechwriting has become increasingly professionalized, there are also signs pointing the other way. The memoir of speechwriter Matt Latimer (*Speech-Less*, 2009), for instance, paints a picture of the speechwriting in the Bush administration as accidental and dysfunctional. In the parliamentary systems of many European countries, speechwriting has become increasingly valued and speechwriters have been given more central positions closer to ministers and leaders. Ministries have begun to establish explicit guidelines for the speechwriting process. On the other hand, most speechwriters seem to find themselves in the job more or less by accident. There is no formal education for speechwriters, and even though rhetoricians are educated both in the USA and Europe, most speechwriters seem to be educated in other fields such as journalism, composition/literature, political science, communication science, history, psychology, and law.[28] Though the work of speechwriters has increased in importance, it appears to be considered of less importance than other kinds of communication and public relation work, at least in some European countries.

In Switzerland, a large online survey on speechwriting in business, politics, and administration concluded that one cannot tell the activity of a speechwriter from the job description. A speechwriter will normally be active in more than one branch of an organization, will generally be active in first line communication, and more seldom be active in line-functions.[29]

In Germany, the speechwriting process for the government declaration (when a new government declares its policy for the coming period) has been divided into five phases: (1) conception, (2) gathering material and development of drafts for selected passages, (3) writing the rough

---

[28] Martha Stout Kessler, "Corporate Speechwriting," *The Bulletin* 48, no. 1 (March 1985), 18–22; Martina Schäfer and Guido Keel, "Redenschreiber in Schweizer Organisationen: Tätigkeiten, Rollen Und Entwicklungen," *Studies in Communication Sciences* 15, no. 2 (2015), 197–206, 204; Simone Brendstrup, *Taleskrivning i Danmark. State of the Art 2017* [Speechwriting in Denmark: State of the Art 2017] (Fredriksberg: Rhetor - rådgivende retorikere), 8.

[29] Schäfer and Keel, 205.

draft of the manuscript, (4) polishing the final draft, and (5) delivery.[30] We say more about this in Chapter 7 where we provide three case studies of three different speechwriting processes: a German Government declaration, a speech for a Danish Ministry, and examples of speechwriting from the American presidency.

In Scandinavia, researchers, relying primarily on interviews and ethnographic studies, have provided insight into the processes and institutional circumstances of speechwriting in political parties, government ministries, and organization. In spite of some difference between various ministries in the same country as well as between different countries, the speechwriting process seems to be roughly the same. The variations are mostly situational and appear to depend on five factors:[31] (1) the speaker (the speaker's rhetorical abilities, knowledge, personal qualities, and experience); (2) the speechwriter (the writer's rhetorical abilities, knowledge, personal qualities, and experience); (3) the speechwriter's personal knowledge about the speaker (efficiency and success requires intimate knowledge); (4) situation and occasion (in terms of effort and time spent, the process is very different for epideictic speeches, such as speaking at festivals and national ceremonies, or inaugurating a bridge or a building, significant occasion, or for an important "line speech," i.e. a speech that lays out a policy); and (5) timing and time constraints (even though organizations have developed a plan for the writing process, the phases could be curtailed by time constraints).

Some studies suggest[32] that the speechwriting process is characterized by the speechwriter's dependence on the technical or professional knowledge of others (in the ministries' divisions). This information is provided by civil servants with a bureaucratic and juridical background who generally write in an abstract officialese. Because the speechwriter will often

---

[30] Antje Schwarze and Antje Walther, "Redenschreiben Für Den Bundeskanzler: Formulieren, Koordinieren Und Beraten," in *Das Wort Hat Der Herr Bundeskanzler: Eine Analyse Der Großen Regierungserklärungen Von Adenauer Bis Schröder*, ed. Karl-Rudolf Korte (Wiesbaden: VS Verlag für Sozialwissenschaften, 2002).

[31] Kristin Hald Skåleskog, *Taleskrivningsprosessen i Norge - en undersøkelser av taleskrivningsprosessen i fire norske departementer*. Master thesis. Department of Information Science and Media Studies, University of Bergen, Norway. Cf. Steensbech, *På ministerens vegne*, 68 ff., 2013.

[32] For example, Mette Stoltenberg, Hvem har ordet? En retorisk analyse af taleskrivning for en anden i danske ministerier og kommuner. Master thesis. Department of Comparative Literature and Rhetoric, Aarhus University, Denmark, 2014.

be pressed for time and unsure how to process material from various governmental divisions, she will often copy-paste parts of the material directly into the manuscript.

Ethnographic research has also illustrated how ministerial speechwriting in Europe "is first and foremost a question of ministerial identity building" and functions as a bureaucratic mode of knowledge production.[33] This research points out the cultural differences between the ministries as unitary bureaucracies and the political leadership and their spin doctors, and thus addresses the questions of why the ministerial bureaucracies that produce the speeches seem to be uninterested in audiences, why the speeches always sound the same, and why they never produce new insight. The answer to this quandary is that even though a minister speaks, their speeches display the voice of the ministry and represent the entire ministry. A speech then is not "first and foremost expressions of the points of view of particular politicians or instantiations of particular fields, but rather instantiations of the ministry as such," it is, then, "ministerial mode of knowledge productions."[34]

Research on Speaker Style, Character, and Authenticity

One dominant area of study includes the questions of speaker style, character, and authenticity that clearly relates directly to the question of ethics given the reality that writing in a style different from the speaker's "actual style" has been deemed an act of deception. Kristine Bruss has examined the role of style, focusing on how an oral style can be established in writing, and on how to write speeches for unconventional speakers who prefer to improvise. She has also used veteran executive speechwriter Alan Perlman's insights in order to examine how speechwriters may write speeches that perform fitting characterizations ("ethopoeia") of the speakers. These issues, Bruss point out, "calls attention to enduring tensions in characterization – tensions between imitation and representation, effectiveness and ethics,

---

[33] Iver B. Neumann, "'A Speech That the Entire Ministry May Stand for,' or: Why Diplomats Never Produce Anything New," *International Political Sociology* 1, no. 2 (2007), 183–200; Iver B. Neumann, *At Home with the Diplomats Inside a European Foreign Ministry* (Cornell University Press, 2012).

[34] All quotes are from Iver B. Neumann, *At Home with the Diplomats Inside a European Foreign Ministry* (Cornell University Press, 2012), 85.

and dramatic character and trustworthy ethos."[35] One study on style attempted to gauge presidential personality by comparing the style of the speeches of Ronald Reagan before and after he became president of the USA. The finding points to presidential speeches that projected Reagan as more positive and active than his speeches before becoming president.[36]

In a study on the relation between speechwriting and style, Marie Lund distinguishes between two views on style and formation of character in speechwriting (ethopoeia): One considers style as a "the dress of thought," style as something that can be put on like a piece of clothing or an ornament; the other view considers style as the essence of the individual speaker. In this more romantic view, style is identified with the soul or personality of the speaker. Lund proposes a third view on style, which she finds more appropriate for speechwriting: a constitutive view where style and language are seen as a way of creating meaning and identity. Style as a "performative and dynamic process, which allows new choices, direction, new ways of acting."[37]

WAYS SPEECHWRITING ARE STUDIED

The most used method in the scholarly study of speechwriting is undoubtedly interviewing speechwriters[38] and on rare occasions interviewing the speakers themselves. Most interview-based studies approach the interviews in an interpretative, text-analytic fashion, while some studies also apply social science coding and data analysis to the interview

---

[35] Kristine Bruss, "The Art of 'Jesse-Talk': Speechwriting for Governor Jesse Ventura," *Communication and Theater Association of Minnesota Journal* 37, no. 1 (2010); "Writing for the Ear: Strengthening Oral Style in Manuscript Speeches," *Communication Teacher* 26, no. 2 (2012); "Ghosting Authenticity: Characterization in Corporate Speechwriting," *Journal of Business and Technical Communication* 25, no. 2 (2011), 159; "Persuasive Ethopoeia in Dionysius's Lysias," *Rhetorica: A Journal of the History of Rhetoric* 31, no. 1 (2013).

[36] Lee Sigelman, "Two Reagans? Genre Imperatives, Ghostwriters, and Presidential Personality Profiling," *Political Psychology* (2002).

[37] Marie Lund, "Taleskrivning og stil," *Rhetorica Scandinavica* 65 (2013), 25–39; Marie Lund, *An Argument on Rhetorical Style* (Aarhus University Press, 2017).

[38] For example, Robert Schlesinger, *White House Ghosts: Presidents and Their Speechwriters* (Simon & Schuster, 2008); Bruss, "The Art of 'Jesse-Talk': Speechwriting for Governor Jesse Ventura."

texts.³⁹ The use of archival work is especially prominent in historical studies, and the use of biographies and historical research is often used to establish how speechwriting was crafted. Anthropological and ethnographic approaches have been used in order to examine the culture of speechwriting in ministries and their bureaucratic mode of knowledge production, pointing out that the bureaucratic demand for ministerial identity construction through the speechwriting process appears to overshadow the political and rhetorical demand for appealing to the audience with a vivid, interesting speech, presented in a coherent voice that puts the Minister's persona in the foreground.⁴⁰

While the study of speechwriting traditionally has been a humanistic, qualitative endeavor, the last two decades have shown an increase in quantitative studies. Among these are for instance the use of survey-based study indicating that respondents recognize and accept the use of speechwriters in certain circumstances.⁴¹ A social science-oriented content analysis quantified the speechwriter-policy advisor conflict and found that speechwriters had more influence on a speech by President George H. Bush than his policy advisers.⁴² A study of speechwriting in Switzerland conducted a large online survey of the 100 largest Swiss employers, all Government ministries, the administration in the ten biggest cities and 26 cantons (municipalities), the seven biggest parties, and eight scientific federations.⁴³ The aim was to examine the activity, context, profile, and roles of speechwriters in Swiss organizations (cf. Part 5 above in this chapter).

Interviews and focus groups studies are sometimes preceded by questionnaires. These may be intended to just provide some practical information, but the use of questionnaires may also aim at establishing the

---

[39] E.g Moniza Waheed, et al., "Values in Un Speeches Understanding the Speechwriters' Perspectives," *International Communication Gazette* 75, no. 7 (2013).

[40] For example, Iver B. Neumann, "'A Speech That the Entire Ministry May Stand for,' or: Why Diplomats Never Produce Anything New'." *International Political Sociology* 1, no. 2 (2007), 183–200; Iver B. Neumann, *At Home with the Diplomats Inside a European Foreign Ministry* (Cornell University Press, 2012).

[41] Stuart C. Brown and Linda A. Riley, "Crafting a Public Image: An Empirical Study of the Ethics of Ghostwriting," *Journal of Business Ethics* 15, no. 7 (1996), 711–720 (Netherland: Kluwer Academic Publishers).

[42] Justin S. Vaughn and José D. Villalobos, "Conceptualizing and Measuring White House Staff Influence on Presidential Rhetoric," *Presidential Studies Quarterly* 36, no. 4 (2006).

[43] Schäfer and Keel.

reliability of certain tendencies using scientific measuring tools such as Likert scales. This was done in a Dutch study of the beginning of speeches, which also examined the background of speechwriters in the Dutch government and their view on the functions and technique in speech introductions.[44] In another study, the authors, Jaap de Jong and Bas Andeweg, assembled a corpus of ministerial speeches from 1988 to 1989 and 2003 to 2004 in order to compare rhetorical changes. The results indicate that professionalizing of the speech production occurring from the beginning of the 1990s has led to better speeches in the sense that they are shorter, use shorter sentences, and incorporate more figures of speech.[45] Another corpus-based study examined 434 speeches by Ronald Reagan to examine whether he sounded like the same person before and after he became president. The Dictionary of Affect in Language (DAL) computer program and social scientific regression models were used to score the speeches on the rhetorical dimensions of *activity* and *positivity* continuum. The results suggest that Reagan appeared more active and positive as president.[46]

---

[44] B.A. Andeweg and J.C. de Jong, *De eerste minuten. Attentum, benevolum en docilem parare in de inleiding van toespraken* [The First Minutes: Attentum, benevolum en docilem parare in the Introductions of Speeches]. Den Haag: Sdu-uitgevers. Dissertation Radboud Universiteit Nijmegen (www.deeersteminuten.tudelft.nl/Bijlagen/summary.pdf), 2004.

[45] Jong and Andeweg.

[46] Sigelman.

CHAPTER 5

The Rhetorical Canons of Speechwriting

All speechwriting must engage in three tasks. Whether one is writing a speech for a business leader, a politician, or a president, one must (1) identify argument and content, (2) organize the parts of the speech, and (3) create persuasive language and style. These tasks are the first three of the rhetorical canon of speechwriting since antiquity, also referred to as inventio, dispositio, and elocutio. The last two tasks in the ancient canon are memorizing the speech (memoria) and preparing a convincing delivery (actio). Since contemporary speechwriters are mostly engaged in the three first of these canons, we will give an account of the most important issues concerning content, organization, and language.

FINDING CONTENT AND ARGUMENTS

Former White House Chief Speechwriter Robert Lehrman has said that sometimes he thinks that his real title is not speechwriter, but speech *researcher*.[1] Writing speeches is as much about finding ideas, examples, and arguments, as it is about putting them in writing. Lehrman points to three main things political speechwriters need to explore in their research: the event, the ideas, and the poetry. Exploring the event means thinking about the audience, the place, and the aim of the event.

[1] Robert Lehrman, *The Political Speechwriter's Companion: A Guide for Writers and Speakers* (Washington, DC: CQ Press, 2010), 41.

Sources that a speechwriter may use to examine these topics include other staffers in the company, group, party, or organization, the essential information regarding the group addressed (for instance, their Web site).

When researching ideas, Lehrman advises, one should not start from scratch but begin with memos or white papers already in existence, as well as consulting with staffers who know from the top of their heads pertaining information. Lehrman suggests four sources for researching ideas: other staffers, old speeches, online resources, and a speech conference with the speaker.

Researching poetry does not mean writing poems, but making speeches vivid, inspiring, exciting, and able to move people. Finding the right story, detail, image, or anecdote is as important as finding the arguments—and often it is the same thing. Sources that work for vividness and poetry can be attained by a personal contact with the speaker, searching Web sites, books on anecdotes, quotes and jokes, daily papers, TV late-night shows, and other speeches.

The good speechwriter will create her own file on her speaker, so that content, arguments, examples, stories, and details will be readily available sources.

The traditional rhetorical term for Lehrman's "sources" is *topoi*, which means places (in the singular *topos*; in the latin loci/locus). A topos, or a source, is a place you turn to looking for content and arguments. The ancient rhetoricians worked with a kind of topical thinking in order to find arguments. It resembles brainstorming; however, it is more structured in order to ensure that the speaker will find certain, useful arguments. In his book *Institutio Oratoria*, for instance, the world's first professor of rhetoric, Quintilian (35–100 AD), explains the topical system with an analogy[2]:

> For as all kinds of fruits are not produced in all countries, and as you will be unable to find a bird or a beast if you are ignorant where it is usually produced or makes its abode, and as among the several kinds of fishes, some delight in a smooth and others in a rocky bottom of the water, while particular sorts are confined to particular regions or coasts, and you could not attract the ellops or the scarus to our shores, so every kind of argument is not to be got from every place and is consequently not everywhere to be sought. Otherwise, there would be much wandering about, and after enduring the utmost labor, we should not be able to find, unless by

---

[2] Quintilian, *Institutio Oratoria*, 5, 10, 21–22.

chance, that for which we should seek without method. But if we ascertain where particular arguments offer themselves, we shall, when we come to the place where they lie, easily discern what is in it.

Therefore, in order not to wander about, we should structure our search for arguments. As White House Speechwriter Lehrman knows, the necessity of a structured method of researching, which is why he first divided the search into the general places (topoi) of event, ideas, and poetry and then made subdivisions—lists really—of different topoi that belonging to these three.

Clearly then, even though the method of topoi is ancient, it is still useful. Researchers and practitioners have proposed systems of topoi for different kinds of speaking, be it in a court of law or in political setting. One example of a topical system for finding arguments deals with corporate speechwriting.[3] It proposes nine topics (places or sources) to help examine an issue. The three main topics are definition, comparison, and consequences, which are each divided into three sub-topics allowing the speechwriter to ask relevant questions that can help finding the proper and most persuasive arguments:

I. Definition
  A. Negative definition
     Can I "circle in" on what it *is* by stating what it is not?
  B. Restricted definition
     Do the circumstances of my speech require me to state my own specialized definition?
     Can I describe something by describing its *actions*?
     Can I define something by defining its *qualities*?
  C. Division
     Is it useful to define a term by dividing it into its constitutive parts?
II. Comparison
  A. Similarity
     Can I draw an analogy or relate to a similar circumstance?
  B. Dissimilarity
     Does a contrast help my point?

[3] Craig Kallendorf and Carol Kallendorf, "A New Topical System for Corporate Speechwriting," *The Journal of Business Communication* 21, no. 2 (1984).

C. Partial resemblance
      Can I clarify my argument by identifying points of comparison and contrast in the same reference?
III. Consequences
   A. Necessary results (cause and effect)
      What is the *necessary* effect of a given case, or the *necessary* cause of a given case?
   B. Probability
      What are the probable consequences of this action?
      What is the probable cause of an observable effect?
      What are the short-term probable effects?
      What are the long-term-probable effects?
      Are there similar examples of probability in the past?
      Can I suggest a chain of probable consequences?
      If a less common thing occurs, won't a similar but more common thing also probably occur?
      What motives probably caused this action?
   C. Possibility
      If the harder of the two things is possible, isn't the easier thing also possible?
      What are the possible consequences?

While such topical list may look complicated at first sight, they are easy to follow in practice and provide a structured method of researching an issue. Analysis of a subject through the topics, the authors of this list argue, makes it easier to generate ideas that are relevant to the given thesis:

> For example, the topic of definition might lead the speaker to select a restricted definition of health care costs which would include all expenditures for preventive care, treatment, and health insurance. By defining the subject in this way, the speaker makes the problem seem as acute as possible, thereby bolstering the argument. The topic of cause and effect might suggest a consideration of how the Medicare program has contributed to increasing health care costs. And the topic of probability might lead to a prediction of what proportion of the Gross National Product expenditures for health care would represent at various points in time.[4]

---

[4] Kallendorf and Kallendorf, "A New Topical System," 11.

Among the advantages such topical lists have for the speechwriter is not only the structured research method that helps find relevant arguments supporting the claim or thesis of the speaker, but also that such a method is easier to do, is less time-consuming, and is more effective than unstructured brainstorming.[5]

While acknowledging the value of such topical lists as sources of content and arguments, allowing the speechwriter to examine an issue, it is equally important to see people as sources—human topoi, one might say. As Lehrman's account suggests, talking to other people is one of the most important ways of finding content and arguments. Medhurst, for instance, points out that the common wisdom concerning rhetorical invention holds that a speaker often discovers ideas and lines of argument "with the assistance of a topical system or through resort to commonplaces."[6] Unfortunately, he argues, this tells us very little about how speakers find content and arguments. The most important inventional choice for a president, for instance, is not a system of topoi or a handbook of commonplaces, but the choice of speechwriters.[7] The crucial choice is not one of ideas, but of people. In a similar fashion, the most important inventional resources for a speechwriter in a government ministry is the (technical) divisions of the ministry and the civil servants with the expert knowledge of the field and area the ministry is dealing with.

For a speechwriter, of course, the content of a speech to be found is not only in locating arguments and information about the issue. One of the most important kinds of content is material about the speakers: vivid stories from their lives, their thoughts, memories, and feelings, their likes and dislikes. This is both an important part of a speech's content and an essential way for the speechwriter to create the character of the speaker. We address this in more detail in Chapter 7 "Characterizing the Speaker," where we offer ideas for interview questions in the preparation of speeches and the creation of speaker guides.

---

[5] For example, Dominic A. Infante, "The Influence of a Topical System on Arguments," *Speech Monographs* 38 (1971), 125–128. Cf. Kallendorf and Kallendorf, "A New Topical System," 11, 14, n. 9.

[6] M.J. Medhurst, "Ghostwritten Speeches: Ethics Isn't the Only Lesson," *Communication Education* 36 (1987), 241.

[7] Ibid., 242.

Organizing the Parts of the Speech

When organizing the speech, it is essential that the speech is coherent. The speechwriter needs to ensure that the audience is able to follow the line of argument and consider the need and location of an emotional appeal and the need to generate audience attention. Rhetorical theories since antiquity have proposed a number of ways to arrange oral messages. Some have suggested that the speech be divided into two parts; others have suggested three and even as high as nine parts. For example, one rhetorical textbook offers specific patterns of organization, such as chronological, causal, climatic, or anti-climactic order.[8]

Yet, following a structural model slavishly does not guarantee a well-structured speech. When writing a speech, attention must be made to the particulars of the rhetorical situation, and the different parts must be considered carefully in the light of the overall purpose of the speech. The speechwriter may choose to order the parts according to some pattern, for instance a causal order, but she/he may also follow it more loosely, include some aspects and let others go. The important thing is to keep in mind is how the specific techniques relate to the aim of the speech and to the persuasion of the audience. Therefore, in order to arrive at a suitable arrangement of the speech it needs to reflect the function of the parts.

The most tenacious principle of disposition in rhetoric is the four-part speech: *introduction, narrative, argument*, and *epilogue*.[9] This division is the framework of both a great deal of Attic oratory and contemporary public address, such as President Nixon's Vietnamization speech from 1969.[10] According to Aristotle, the only parts essential to a speech are the proposition and the argument; he admits, however, that most speeches also have an introduction and an epilogue. He accounts quite elaborately for the function of all four parts and stresses that with minor

---

[8] James McCroskey, *An Introduction to Rhetorical Communication: A Western Cultural Perspective* (Boston: Allyn and Bacon, 2006), 165–176.

[9] Michael de Brauw, "The Parts of the Speech," in Ian Worthington (ed.): *A Companion to Greek Rhetoric* (Oxford: Wiley-Blackwell, 2010), 187. The Greek terms are *prooimion, diegesis, pistis,* and *epilogos,* the Latin are *exordium, narratio, probatio,* and *peroratio.*

[10] Forbes Hill, "Conventional Wisdom—Traditional Form. The President's Message of November 3, 1969," *Quarterly Journal of Speech* 58 (1972), 373–386.

variations this is the structure of both epideictic, deliberative, and forensic speeches.

The first part, the introduction, has three functions: It must *inform* the audience, capture the *attention* of the audience, and win their *goodwill*.[11] The goal of informing the audience is to enhance their understanding, and the most common means are to present the essence of the matter, or announce the main points in a *partitio*, a "table of content." Modern speeches sometimes present a definition, or make a so-called funnel opening where they proceed from a general perspective to the more specific case. Speechwriters are well advised to return to the *partitio* throughout the speech in order to meta-communicate to the audience where the speech is heading. For example: "As you can see, the case for legalizing marijuana as pain release is compelling. But the political arguments are of little significance if we lose sight of the individual perspective. Therefore, I am now going to take you back to the summer of 2016 when a friend of mine was recovering from."

The function of the introduction is to capture the interest of the audience. To this end, speechwriters employ a variety of techniques: They stress the importance of the subject, literally ask for attention, promise to be brief, and use humor, telling an anecdote, or offering a challenging statement. Many consider the anecdote—a short story about a true or fictitious incident, often with an amusing and a moral twist—the safest way to draw attention. Opening with a brief and relevant story has different functions, such as drawing and focusing attention, making the audience identify with the subject, and stimulating memory. Even though professional speakers, speechwriters, and writers of handbooks in oral presentation prefer the anecdote to draw attention, in practice, a provocative statement, a question, or a metaphor will often prove to be more efficient.[12]

---

[11] De Brauw, "The Parts of the Speech," 191. The data on how modern speeches apply the specific techniques according to function is provided by Jaap de Jong and Bas Andeweg, "Professionalizing Speech Production. Changes in 15 Years of Ministerial Speeches," in Ton van Haaften et al. (eds.): *Bending Opinion: Essays on Persuasion in the Public Domain* (Leiden: Leiden University Press, 2012), 164.

[12] Bas Andeweg and Jaap de Jong, "Start with a Story: Theory versus Practice of the Anecdote as Speech Introduction Technique," in Paul Gillaerts and Philip Shaw (eds.): *The Map and the Landscape: Norms and Practices in Genre* (Berlin: Peter Lang, 2006), 183.

Finally, the speaker must win the goodwill of the audience. While a good relationship between speaker and audience must be displayed throughout the speech, it is crucial that it is established as early as possible. In order to make the speaker appear sympathetic, speechwriters rely on different techniques such as presenting the speaker as credible, or taking away prejudices against the speaker. Also, the speaker can make the impression that she is improvising, or take the underdog position. Another option is to have the speaker appear benevolent via praise, compliments, or stressing common experience with the audience. A modern invention is the gesture of thanking the introductory speaker. While asking for understanding for making an inadequate speech or making self-belittling remarks can be efficient, *captatio benevolentiae* techniques work when performed with humor and elegance; too much flattery and commonplaces like "I am not much a speaker," should be avoided.

According to Aristotle, not every speech needs an introduction, and it is common to omit an introduction in political speeches when the audience is already familiar with the case at hand. This is what the Dutch Minister of Foreign Affairs Frans Timmermans did when speaking at the UN Security Council *in media res*: "We are here to discuss a tragedy." Aristotle qualifies this advice by noting that the speaker may choose to add an introduction to call attention to aspects of the case that the audience may not be aware of.

Let us consider how the British author of the Harry Potter-series J.K. Rowling began her Harvard Graduation Speech in 2005:

> President Faust, members of the Harvard Corporation and the Board of Overseers, members of the faculty, proud parents, and, above all, graduates.
>
> The first thing I would like to say is 'thank you.' Not only has Harvard given me an extraordinary honour, but the weeks of fear and nausea I have endured at the thought of giving this commencement address have made me lose weight. A win-win situation! Now all I have to do is take deep breaths, squint at the red banners and convince myself that I am at the world's largest Gryffindor reunion.
>
> Delivering a commencement address is a great responsibility; or so I thought until I cast my mind back to my own graduation. The commencement speaker that day was the distinguished British philosopher Baroness Mary Warnock. Reflecting on her speech has helped me enormously in writing this one, because it turns out that I can't remember a single word she said. This liberating discovery enables me to proceed

without any fear that I might inadvertently influence you to abandon promising careers in business, the law or politics for the giddy delights of becoming a gay wizard.

You see? If all you remember in years to come is the 'gay wizard' joke, I've come out ahead of Baroness Mary Warnock. Achievable goals: the first step to self improvement.

Actually, I have wracked my mind and heart for what I ought to say to you today. I have asked myself what I wish I had known at my own graduation, and what important lessons I have learned in the 21 years that have expired between that day and this.

I have come up with two answers. On this wonderful day when we are gathered together to celebrate your academic success, I have decided to talk to you about the benefits of failure. And as you stand on the threshold of what is sometimes called 'real life', I want to extol the crucial importance of imagination.

These may seem quixotic or paradoxical choices, but please bear with me.[13]

Although Rowling is a successful author with a significant ethos, she makes quite an effort to capture the goodwill of her audience of Harvard graduates and their relatives. Her humorous thanks to Harvard for enabling her to lose weight makes the audience pay attention, and she strikes the same self-deprecating note with the Baroness Mary Warnock-anecdote reminding the audience how insignificant and unmemorable such commencement speeches can actually be. These instances of *captatio benevolentiae* are designed to make Rowling appear human and benevolent to her audience. Still, the Gryffindor's allusion reminds the audience that she is, indeed, the author of the Harry Potter series—and the fact that they get that strengthens the identification between the speaker and the audience. Besides, Rowling praises and offers compliments, and she even asks for understanding for making an inadequate speech ("bear with me"). Finally, Rowling includes a *partitio*, informing the audience that she will talk about the benefits of failure and the crucial importance of imagination.

According to the four-part division of the speech, the second part is the narrative. It is usually a mini-story that sometimes imbeds a proposition to be confirmed by the argument, but it also has some more

---

[13] J.K. Rowling, "Harvard University Commencement Address," *The Harvard Gazette*, June 5 2008.

specific functions, such as informing the audience of events past, setting the scene, and revealing the speaker's character in the most favorable way. Narratives in both ancient and modern speeches clearly have a constitutive function: They are used to tell the speaker's side of the story, offer a counter-narrative, and gain terminological control. A narrative of past events and of the speaker's past actions functions as a persuasive construction of character, which may indeed be a substantial part of the argumentative strategy.

The third part of the speech is the proof section where the speaker puts the substantive arguments forward. In ancient rhetoric, the term for the third part was *pistis*, though *pistis* also refers to argument or means of persuasion in general. Arguments are often, but not always, placed in that section.[14] According to Aristotle, we persuade the audience by three means, by appealing to their reason (*logos*), the speaker's character (*ethos*), or to their emotions (*pathos*). The main forms of *logos* arguments in rhetoric are the enthymeme and the example. The enthymeme is a kind of imperfect syllogism, which produces persuasion based on probability. The example is an inductive form of argumentation where the speaker argues from the particular, something that has happened before, to the general. In the above section "Finding content and arguments," you can read more about how to construct a relevant and powerful line of argument.

To make the audience react favorably to the speaker's words and arguments, the speechwriter must pay careful attention to *ethos*, the rhetorical construction of the speaker's personality. Aristotle says that the speaker must appear to be a person of sound sense (*phronesis*), high moral character (*arête*), and benevolence (*eunoia*). The speechwriter strengthens good sense by making the speaker seem competent and knowing about the themes discussed, someone who is able to interpret a situation wisely and knows and observes valid reasoning himself. When the speech respects the community's accepted moral standards, it adds to the speaker's credibility. Finally, the speaker must display goodwill toward the audience. Besides the three appeals to the audience, the trustworthiness of the speaker's appropriate style can also enhance credibility.[15]

---

[14]de Brauw, "The Parts of the Speech," 195.

[15]Edward P.J. Corbett, *Classical Rhetoric for the Modern Student* (Oxford: Oxford University Press 1990), 80 ff.

In Chapter 7, you will find a more specific description of characterization in speechwriting for others (*ethopoeia*).

Emotions are displayed through the speaker's character and stirred up in the audience in response (*pathos*) to specific appeals, such as anger, pity, or pleasure. *Pathos* is a state of mind induced into the audience by rhetorical language, or the deliberate art for the construction of shared public emotion.[16] Subsequently, *ethos* and *logos*—the speaker's way of conducting herself, managing her perceived character, and the use of language—persuade the audience into experiencing certain emotions strategically suitable for changing their opinion regarding a given issue. In this way, the speaker is able to influence her audience to pass judgment on the issue in question in accordance with her own advocacy. But the dynamics between reason and emotions entails that what appears to be reasonable and rational is actually regulated by publicly shared emotions, or *pathos*. The point here is that premises of enthymemes are drawn from generally accepted opinions and from shared emotions of the audience that *precede* the logic of enthymemic reasoning.[17]

In practice, persuasive appeals are not limited to one part of the speech or another; the speechwriter must use persuasive appeals in the entire speech where they seem fitting. As a rule, it is desirable that the speaker's *ethos* is established in the introduction to give the speaker a basis from which to argue, and that *pathos* appeals are placed in the epilogue to create a collective sentiment that the audience may carry with them when the speech is over.

The closing of the speech, or the epilogue, must get the attention of the audience, evoke the audience's emotions, and recapitulate the main points of the speech.[18] It is common practice among modern speechwriters to make the speaker gain the desired attention by simply announcing the close of the speech. To evoke emotions, speakers tend to strike a positive and constructive note enticing audiences to action, forward words of thanks and encouragement, flatter, praise and strengthen a sense of cooperation and togetherness. Classical closing commonplaces such as appealing to pity

---

[16] Lawrence Green, "Pathos," in Sloane (ed.): *Encyclopedia of Rhetoric* (Oxford: Oxford University Press); Celeste Michelle Condit, "Pathos in Criticism: Edwin Black's Communism-As-Cancer Metaphor," *Quarterly Journal of Speech* 99, no. 1 (2013), 3.

[17] Marie Lund and Carsten Madsen, "Følelsernes rolle i retorik," *Rhetorica Scandinavica* (2018).

[18] de Jong and Andeweg, "Professionalizing Speech Production," 165.

or arousing negative feelings seem not to have survived into contemporary public speaking. In recapitulating the speech, modern speechwriters have added the technique of a circular closing to the traditional summary of main points.

Returning to Rowling's Harvard commencement address, she makes her audience pay attention when she announces the ending:

> I am nearly finished. I have one last hope for you, which is something that I already had at 21. The friends with whom I sat on graduation day have been my friends for life. They are my children's godparents, the people to whom I've been able to turn in times of trouble, people who have been kind enough not to sue me when I took their names for Death Eaters. At our graduation we were bound by enormous affection, by our shared experience of a time that could never come again, and, of course, by the knowledge that we held certain photographic evidence that would be exceptionally valuable if any of us ran for Prime Minister.
>
> So today, I wish you nothing better than similar friendships. And tomorrow, I hope that even if you remember not a single word of mine, you remember those of Seneca, another of those old Romans I met when I fled down the Classics corridor, in retreat from career ladders, in search of ancient wisdom:
>
> As is a tale, so is life: not how long it is, but how good it is, is what matters.
>
> I wish you all very good lives.
>
> Thank-you very much.

In the epilogue, Rowling returns to earlier points and themes with a circular closing. She revisits the Classics corridor, hints at the opening anecdote, and makes another humorous allusion to the Harry Potter-universe. The feelings she evokes in the audience are those of friendship and togetherness, as she sends them off with good wishes and encouragement that their friendships will last as long as her own.

Far from the classical four-part division, the majority of speeches vary in their construction because of the practitioners of the trade, from the logographers of ancient Greece to today's practices. Speechwriters for CEOs or politicians, all seem to agree that when it comes to arranging the speech, the most important thing is to compose a focused and coherent speech suitable to the specific arguments, the specific case, and the specific persuasive goals.

Creating Persuasive Language and Style

When writing a speech, the words selected and the construction of sentences shape the meaning and the argument therein. Thus, when a speaker claims "there are only two ways to see this problem," the logic of the antithesis structures the content of her message. When a politician uses the metaphor of "tax burden," she forwards an implicit evaluation of the economic model being described. In classical rhetoric, word selection was the third of five rhetorical canons. *Elocutio* followed *inventio* and *dispositio* and was succeeded by the more practical tasks of memorizing and delivering the speech, *memoria* and *actio*. According to the classical model, language choices are something we consider quite late in the work process, after having found the arguments and after structuring the speech. Contemporary rhetorical and linguistic theories concur that this view is problematic, since content and arguments cannot be separated from discourse. Today, language and style are recognized as vital to the construction of meaning.

Similarly, metaphors and rhetorical figures have often been described as stylistic devices that can be used to apply beauty, feelings, or strength to a message. But modern theories of rhetoric and language have argued that rhetorical figures do much more than adding feelings or quality to an otherwise unaltered speech. Instead, we view rhetorical figures as discursive choices with various purposes. Rhetorical figures are formulations that shape the meaning and value of the speech, and they should therefore be considered relative to their rhetorical function. The significant functions of rhetorical figures are

- To create a feeling of communion between the speaker and an audience;
- To create presence;
- To frame a topic by using a word, concept, or metaphor that implies an attitude or a perception;
- To structure and constitute meaning;
- To be memorable;
- To facilitate comprehension;
- To engage the body; and
- To induce feelings in the audience.

The list is not exhaustive, and items overlap, but this is exactly the point. In fact, more often than not, the persuasiveness of a rhetorical figure is the result of overlapping functions. When a speaker uses the rhetorical figure *paronomasia* to state, "a bad child is really a sad child," the repetition of similar-sounding words implies a huge difference in meaning. But the pinpointed formulation that replaces just one letter not only changes the perception of the child's behavior, it also appeals to emotion and memory.[19] When a speaker says that "the communiqué seems to be deliberately designed not to communicate," the rhetorical figure *polyptoton*—a repetition of words derived from the same root—articulates a critique that is supposed to cause indignation in the audience.[20] The contrast of content in a "communiqué" and a message deliberately designed "not to communicate" is stressed by the etymological closeness of the terms. The epitomized wording of the *polyptoton* not only makes it apt and memorable, it also displays the mockery therein.

Speechwriters may use language, style, and rhetorical figures strategically to create such effects. In their choice of words and articulation, they are able to create communion among members of an audience, to constitute meaning, or to appeal to emotions. Below, we present basic principles of rhetorical style: appropriateness, clarity and vividness, and rhetorical figures.

We do not claim that there is one correct way to speak. That decision depends on the entire situation: the speaker, the audience, the topic, and the occasion. Ancient rhetoricians knew the importance of appropriateness, and to them, it was not only a matter of rhetorical efficacy, but it also involved an ethical consideration of what is proper or decent to say. The Greeks referred to this stylistic ideal as *to prepon*, while the Romans called it *aptum* or *decorum*.

Clearly, the language must be appropriate for the speaker, and what is fitting for a CEO to say is not necessarily fitting for a university student. Rhetorical scholars and speechwriters know that some speakers are able to speak generally about a topic, while others are only allowed to speak from their own experience. The speechwriter needs to consider how the

---

[19] Jeanne Fahnestock, *Rhetorical Style: The Uses of Language in Persuasion* (Oxford: Oxford University Press, 2011), 129. Fahnestock prefers the term *agnominatio* to *paronomasia*.

[20] Bono, "More Leaders Slipping Up Than Stepping Up for Africa at This Year's G8," August 6, 2007.

words will sound in the mouth of the speaker: The same argument has different strength depending on the person who makes it.

Ostensibly, the language must be fitting to the audience. The speechwriter will have to adapt the style, for instance specialized words or technical terms, to the likely level of the audience. More importantly, the speechwriter needs to consider the constitutive aspect of rhetoric in the way she inscribes the audience. She must be careful not to characterize the audience in ways they do not identify with or find respectful. She must be careful not to refer to individuals or groups in terms that exclude them from the discursive community created by the speech. Moreover, she must pay attention to the way she constitutes the relationship between the speaker and the audience, especially how she uses the personal pronouns "we," "I," and "you."

Finally, the style and language of the speech must be fitting to the topic and the occasion. Classical rhetorical theories distinguish between three levels of style: the grand, the middle, and the simple style. The grand style, used primarily in ceremonial occasions, is characterized by complex language and rhetorical figures. The simple style fits topics that belong to the practical, daily life and is known as ordinary speech common to everyday conversation. The middle style lies somewhere in between. The theory of three levels of style may appear rigid in the eyes of contemporary speechwriters, but the general idea that language needs to be adapted to the situation still holds: The more formal the occasion, the more serious the tone, the more subtle the humor, the more elaborate the sentences, and the greater the number of rhetorical figures.[21]

Oral, everyday language is characterized by a loose structure and a plethora of phrases, commonplaces, and dead metaphors. An obvious advantage of having a written manuscript is that it enables speakers to avoid the mundane and, instead, communicate orally with focus and precision. The speechwriter must strive for a language that is clear and concrete, and seeking to avoid clichés that are so common in public speeches. A speaker is much more likely to make an impression on the audience if she speaks in a vivid language with a varied sentence construction. Therefore, the speechwriter must take the trouble to write in a language that, at least occasionally, uses the full specter of the vocabulary, combines words, and constructs sentences in ways that are new and

---

[21] Jo Sprague, Douglas Stuart, and David Bodary, *The Speaker's Handbook* (Wadsworth, 2013), 237.

interesting. Also, to maintain the attention of the listeners, the speaker needs to meta-communicate the direction of the message via signposts, summaries, and previews to ensure comprehension by making organization clear. We address this topic in Chapter 7, when discussing how to write for the ear.

One of the ways to make language interesting, precise, and memorable is to use rhetorical figures. Rhetorical figures are formal and ideational patterns that can be used by speechwriters to obtain desired effects. Rhetorical scholars have identified almost two hundred rhetorical figures, but the speechwriter will certainly need less. Below, we describe some of the functions of rhetorical figures.

One function of rhetorical figures is to enhance a sense of communion between the speaker and an audience such as allusion, quotation, or rhetorical question.[22] When alluding or quoting, the speaker bonds with the audience by referencing a shared experience between speaker and audience. When George W. Bush in his 2001 State of the Union Address alluded to "one Sunday in 1941," he counted on the American people to recognize that he was comparing 9/11 to Japan's attack on Pearl Harbor in the Second World War.

Although an agreement is implied and the audience is not supposed to advance an answer, a rhetorical question is a slightly more forceful way to engage an audience. In his Berlin speech in 1963, for instance, Kennedy asked rhetorically, "Freedom is indivisible and when one man is enslaved who are free?" The implied answer was "none," and since it would probably have been too bold to present this idealistic idea as a straightforward proposition, the rhetorical question seemed a better strategy.

Communion may also be obtained by quotations, such as "Failure is an orphan, but success has a hundred fathers" or "A journey of a thousand miles begins with a single step," some of many Chinese sayings in John F. Kennedy's oratory.[23] One of the functions of quotes is to include the audience in a community of like-minded people. When members of the audience understand the meaning of the quote in the new context, they are rewarded with feelings of pleasure that they were able to appreciate

---

[22] Ch. Perelman and L. Olbrechts-Tyteca, *The New Rhetoric: A Treatise on Argumentation* (Notre Dame: The University of Notre Dame Press, 1969), 177–178.

[23] Ted Sorensen, *Counselor: A Life at the Edge of History* (New York: HarperCollins, 2008), 134.

the value or truth of the quote. Quotes may have other functions as well such as providing backing to a claim or associating the speaker with the author's wisdom and eloquence.

Irony, too, can create a sense of intellectual kinship between speaker and an audience. However, when the speaker utters something by saying the opposite, only those who get the intended meaning are included, and even they might feel the danger of having failed. The negative undercurrent of irony makes it a risky strategy for a speechwriter to use in a speech. In fact, humor in general seems to have the ability to both unite and divide.[24] While humor can loosen up a tense atmosphere or bring about a sense of relief, it can also be used to divide the audience from a defined group of political opponents or ethnic, religious, or historical minorities.

Quite often humor performs both functions at the same time. When the Danish Prime Minister Lars Løkke Rasmussen made a toast to President Obama and his wife in May 2016, the laughter in the room was at the expense of the likely Republican presidential candidate and his many supporters: "I'm very fond of Donald, too. I support him as a president. He's really smart. Shows great leadership skills. A true visionary … and I am, of course, talking about Donald Tusk, our Polish president of the European council." In another example, and with subtler malice, the Danish crown prince Frederik in his speech to his parents at their 25th wedding anniversary addressed his father, prince Henrik: "Papa, they say that if you spare the rod you will spoil the child. We never felt spoiled." In the last example, humor was used to divert the press from a political inconvenience. When the Danish population voted against a proposal to adopt a EU treatise at the same time that the Danish national football team won the European championship in 1992, the Foreign Minister Uffe Ellemann-Jensen used humor to change the subject and save face: "If you can't join them, beat them."

Some rhetorical figures such a metaphor, antithesis, or *antimetabole* have the potential of structuring the argumentation in ways that constitutes a new perception. For instance, it was Winston Churchill's introduction of the metaphor "iron curtain," that made the division between

---

[24] John C. Meyer, "Humor as a Double-Edged Sword: Four Function of Humor in Communication," *Communication Theory* 10, no. 3 (2000), 310–331.

Western and Eastern Europe real.[25] When using a metaphor, words taken from another semantic field are brought into a new experience. Persistent metaphors to discuss the European Union have been vehicles of transportation, such as a high-speed train, an express bus, or a supertanker. The argument in these metaphors is that EU is moving fast in the direction of unity, and that individual member states cannot risk missing out on this progress. In stark contrast to the much older iron curtain metaphor, the speed metaphors are now worn out clichés that have lost most of their persuasiveness among member states.

Another rhetorical figure that has a structuring function is the antithesis. In a campaign video for the Labour Party to the British general election in 2015, the actor Martin Freeman constructs his argument as an antithetical choice: "I think, in the end, it's simple. It boils down to a choice between a Labour government or a Conservative one. But it isn't just a choice between two different plans, two different ways of getting the deficit down. It's a choice about two completely different sets of values, a choice about what kind of country we wanna live in." While the antithesis has certainly been tried out before in political campaigns, the recurrent *paralipsis* (or *praeteritio*) which is the rhetorical device of giving emphasis to a subject by professing to say little or nothing of it is less common. With mild irony, Freeman both mocks the generic predictability of the campaign speech and playfully enacts the antithetical scheme: "So yeah, I *could* tell you that Tories would take us on rollercoaster of cuts while Labour would make sure the economy works for all of us - not just the privileged few, like me. But it's not just about that. I *could* tell you that."[26]

The *antimetabole* (when two words are repeated in reversed order) and the *chiasmus* (when semantic or syntactic grammatical constructions or concepts are repeated in reversed order) are perhaps the rhetorical figures that most people associate with high oratory. In Kennedy's Inaugural Address penned by Ted Sorensen, an *antimetabole* was succeeded by a *chiasmus*: "And so, my fellow Americans, ask not what your country can do for you; ask what you can do for your country. My fellow citizens of the world, ask not what America will do for you, but what, together, we can do for the freedom of man." The eloquence is a result

---

[25] Winston Churchill, 1946. Jeanne Fahnestock, *Rhetorical Style: The Uses of Language in Persuasion* (Oxford: Oxford University Press), 107.

[26] https://www.youtube.com/watch?v=JbHNVtsAD2M.

of complexity and elegance in both the syntactic structure (a-b-b-a) and the ideas it gives rise to; yet at the bottom of this elegant reversal is a crude antithesis.

A speechwriter also needs to consider the perceptive frame of particular words and concepts. No words are neutral or objective, and some terms are framed politically. If a political opponent uses terms like "peripheral region" or "ghetto" for certain areas, or describes old citizens in terms of the "old age dependency rate," a political speechwriter needs to be aware that repeating such politically biased terms might give the opponent an advantage. Instead of using words or concepts that are framed by the political adversary, the speechwriter needs to refer to the topics in words that favors—or are at least not unfavorably to—the speaker's political agenda. Largely, what is rhetorically possible in these situations depends on what the public is willing to accept.

Considering the orality and presence of speeches, perhaps the ability to create a bodily resonance through rhyme and rhythm is the most important effect of rhetorical figures. Sometimes referred to as figures of sounds, rhetorical figures such as *assonance*, *alliteration*, and *onomatopoeia* appeal to the senses and thereby enhance memorability in the audience and in the speaker. The *assonance* is a repetition of similar vowel sounds in the stressed syllables of adjacent words that has a rhyming effect. Consider the first sentence of Franklin D. Roosevelt's declaration of war against Japan in 1941: "a date *which will live in infamy*," or "the *strong* and *murky current*" of Senator Edward Kennedy's Chappaquiddick address (1965).

A rhythmic effect is created by the *alliteration* which is an occurrence of the same consonant sound at the beginning of closely connected words, as in Earl Spencer's funeral speech to Diana (1997): "we managed to contrive to stop the ever-*present paparazzi* from getting a single *picture* of her." Similar rhythmic effects are produced by devices such as *isocolon* (phrases of equal number of syllables) and *anaphora* (the repetition of the first part of the sentence). Martin Luther King (1963) has provided the most famous *anaphora* of all times: "*I have a dream* that my four little children will one day live in a nation where they will not be judged by the color of their skin but by the content of their character. *I have a dream* … etc."

The rhetorical figure *onomatopoeia* is defined as a word that imitates the sound of the thing, such as "rustling leaves" or "splash of water." A sensual communicative strategy here makes the audience feel or experience the topic, rather than merely understanding it. As with rhyming and rhythmic effects, the primary rhetorical function is to create presence: to make the object of discourse present to the mind of the audience.[27]

Rhetorical scholars of centuries past have invested passion and labor in classifying and categorizing rhetorical figures, but contemporary speechwriters are often reluctant to consult the comprehensive compendiums available. Speakers and speechwriters seem to agree that the most important stylistic ideal in speechwriting is to be close to daily language and the speaker's natural way of speaking. Hence, in order to avoid a pompous and artificial style, many speechwriters tend to hesitate using rhetorical figures. As illustrated above, this is, however, a misunderstanding. Rhetorical figures have a number of functions, all of which are a means to writing vivid and eloquent speeches in a varied language. Rhetorical figures structure the argument, appeal to the senses and emotions, and facilitate understanding and memory. When disregarding rhetorical figures, speechwriters miss an important resource in speechwriting and risk writing dull speeches.

---

[27] Ch. Perelman and L. Olbrechts-Tyteca, *The New Rhetoric: A Treatise on Argumentation* (Notre Dame: The University of Notre Dame Press, 1969), 174.

CHAPTER 6

Genres of Speechwriting

At times, speechwriters feel that they begin from scratch with every new speech. One solution is to cut and paste from previous speeches, sometimes bringing in material that really belongs to a different situation than the one addressed in the speech at hand. Some situations, however, are similar in the sense that they share the same kinds of constraints and seem to ask for the same kinds of answers—answers that draw upon similar kinds of content and expression. Similar situations can condition similar responses: speeches that are alike. Similar speeches constitute genres, and familiarity with genres is necessary for understanding the overall rhetorical plan when writing. Knowledge of genres are also necessary in order to prevent the practitioner from beginning anew with every writing task. In this chapter, we examine the genres of US politics and presidential speeches, genres in European political speechwriting, and business and organizational speeches.

Genre of Presidential Speeches

In their important study *Deeds Done in Words*, Karlyn K. Campbell and Kathleen H. Jamieson stipulate the various genres or types of presidential speeches and the unique features of each. The typology they have identified though is not fixed but rather fluid, allowing presidents a flexible approach to understanding the framework of a given speech as well as allowing audiences to come to a given rhetorical exchange with some prior knowledge and expectations thereof. In this sense, almost every presidential speech can be categorized as responding to a specific situation, and hence, it follows some known and expected pattern of guidelines. More than two hundred years of experimenting with such genres has produced memorable and great speeches but also weak and poorly constructed speeches. The understanding of the specific genre has often been the marking line that separates strong from weak speeches.

Before describing the key speech genres presidents resort to, it is important that we explain the significance of this perspective. A generic perspective of rhetorical acts assumes that most speeches address known and repeatable occasions and that speechwriters as expert advisors to speakers can refer to these genre and discuss them with the speaker in order to secure agreement over how a speech topic fits a given audience and setting. Importantly, the discussion here is meant to draw larger implications as they relate to settings outside the presidential preview and their common practices even in non-political contexts.

Rhetorical genres were initially stipulated by early rhetoricians. Aristotle, for example, considered three primary genres: ceremonial (epideictic) speeches that either praise or blame, deliberative speeches that argue the merits of a policy, usually in terms of support or opposition, and judicial (forensic) speech that seeks to establish a person's guilt or innocence. These genres are instructive as they cover most speaking situations and the descriptions Aristotle provided are helpful in understanding how to construct them. For Campbell and Jamieson, presidential genres allow for comprehending the pragmatics of speech types and assisting rhetors in comprehending rhetorical genres via their "substantive, stylistic, and strategic similarities."[1] What allows a genre to emerge is the recognition that a given speech type carries an internal dynamic and that it has been adopted over some period and thus can offer a sense of stability and familiarity.[2] An important caveat here is that the genres are helpful as they provide guidelines. However, their adherence to form opens the door to other speech types, helping both speakers and audience members enter a rhetorical situation with some expectations of the forthcoming speech.[3]

---

[1] Karlyn K. Campbell and Kathleen H. Jamieson, *Deeds Done in Words: Creating the Presidency* (The University of Chicago Press, 2008), 9.
[2] Ibid., 10.
[3] Ibid.

The primary presidential genres such as the *Inaugural Address*, national eulogies, *State of the Union Address*, *Veto Messages*, and *Farewell Address* among others have stood the test of time often for their flexible and elastic applications *The Inaugural Address* as ceremonial speech functions as the symbolic entry into office, commences the new presidency, and invokes the office's trapping. It tends to emphasize the connection between the past and the future vis-à-vis the incoming president's rhetorical performance. Often an elevated and dignified speech seeks to "affirm or praise the shared principles that will guide the incoming administration."[4] The speech is "a rite of passage," whereby the new president rehearses national values and symbolically performs the transition from the outgoing to the incoming administration.[5]

National eulogies are also ceremonial speeches, and they, too, require strong performance that can do much to enhance the speaker's perception by others.[6] A national eulogy seeks to make sense of the death of a person or persons, such as the tragedy of 9–11, or John F. Kennedy's assassination. Its objective is to ensure the people that the nation is safe and than those who died are transformed into "symbols of national resilience," allowing the president to assure the nation that such a tragedy will not happen again.[7] Death and continuity are the extreme poles of this speech, seeking to offer a spiritual rebirth after a tragedy or trauma.[8]

The *State of the Union address* is perhaps the weakest of all genres of presidential rhetoric given the great variations among them though some threads can be identified as consistent. The objective of this speech is to report to the nation on its status on various fronts. This speech often seeks to meditate on national values, offering an assessment of the nation's primary issues at given intervals and making policy recommendations.[9] Under the Aristotelian generic stipulations, this is a policy or a deliberative speech, meant to review accomplishments or lack thereof and propose a future course of action. This speech is often the cumulative efforts of various cabinet secretaries, and as such, it is a stitched speech constructed by input of various department heads, mandating

[4] Ibid., 29–30.
[5] Ibid., 36.
[6] Ibid., 75.
[7] Ibid., 84, 87.
[8] Ibid., 102–103.
[9] Ibid., 139.

that the speechwriter(s) turn the draft into a coherent speech. The writing challenges are greater here than in the previous two genres that are, by definition, more cohesive and thematic.

The *Veto Message* as a unique genre is the prerogative of the president who decides to send back to Congress legislation already approved by it and in so doing, refuse to sign and implement it. It is, in essence, a rejection decision that is accompanied with a message that justifies the opposition to the legislation. The veto is invoked over major issues and is often situated in a great controversy.[10] The veto then puts the president and Congress in conflict and by default, allows the executive to maintain the upper hand over the legislative branch. The grounds of the veto are important to consider as they stipulate either a constitutional reasoning or expediency as the two primary reasons for rejecting a policy voted by the majority.

The *Farewell Address* is the final address of the president seeking to end the term in office with a speech whose primary objective is to provide counsel to the nation. Upon departure, the president is in a position to look back and reflect, spell out a legacy, and impart words of wisdom acquired during the time in office. As the mirror effect of the *Inaugural Address*, the president has the final opportunity to address both continuity and change.[11] What began four or eight years earlier when a new presidency was ushered in has now come to an end and though the president is vacating the office and returning to the role of a private citizen, the nation is told that it will withstand the change and its future secures if it heeds the warnings therein. The essence of the *Farewell Address* as a ceremonial speech is that of contemplation and meditation on the nation's values, and as such, it calls for fusing style and content to produce an eloquent speech with memorable lines, that kind that will leave strong impressions.[12]

The stipulations of the various genres are important to speechwriters not necessarily for general knowledge of the American presidency but importantly for understanding that most speeches of the same type resemble other settings and expectations that lie outside the presidential preview. In short, presidential genre can inform speechwriters of the

[10] Ibid., 165.
[11] Ibid., 307–308.
[12] Ibid., 310, 333.

parameters of specific occasions and expectations thereof. For example, an incoming university president or a chief executive officer of a corporation may be expected to deliver the inaugural address upon entry into the new position or be asked to eulogize the passing of important individuals. The titles of such speeches will likely not resemble those that US presidents deliver but generically they can be rather similar. Likewise, speakers may be asked to present that state of the organization at some regular intervals or reject a major proposal that necessitates a formal presentation that explains the decision. It is also conceivable that upon stepping down from a leadership position, a presiding officer will be asked to deliver a departing speech.

Given the reality that most of the speeches are ceremonial with some fusion of deliberative aspects, the emphasis on style and content becomes paramount, calling for well-written speeches with both substantive strength and stylistic strength that leave a meaningful impression on audiences. To a lesser degree, these generic speeches call for deliberative speeches. Here, the need for well-crafted policy proposals requires a pragmatic speech that is persuasive and factual but not necessarily push the persuasive aspect too strongly as not to create the boomerang effect of turning against the speech.

SPEECHWRITING IN AMERICAN PRESIDENTIAL POLITICS

Speechwriting in the American political system is as old as the Republic. Alexander Hamilton drafted George Washington's speeches and messages,[13] and Andrew Jackson had close aides clean, edit, and finalize extensive drafts of important messages he initially wrote himself. William Seward was consulted by Lincoln over the writing of several speeches.[14] Nathaniel Hawthorne likely drafted his friend Franklin Pierce's *Inaugural Address* though they were at the opposite ends of the political spectrum. Modern presidents such as Franklin D. Roosevelt continued this long-standing tradition of relying on close aides who, for the most part, remained elusive and unknown to the public, writing some of

---

[13] H.W. Brandt, *Andrew Jackson: His Life and Times* (New York: Anchor Books, 2005), 432.

[14] Kurt Ritter and Martin J. Medhurst, *Presidential Speechwriting: From the New Deal to the Reagan Revolution and Beyond* (College Station: Texas A&M University Press, 2003), 4.

the most inspiring and memorable rhetorical lines. Few knew that Ray Moley wrote Roosevelt's 1933 *Inaugural Address* and that the speech was written over several months. Dwight Eisenhower, who was a speechwriter for General Douglas MacArthur, often consulted his brother when finalizing his own presidential speeches. John F. Kennedy had Theodore Sorensen function not only as a speechwriter but as his alter ego. Lyndon B. Johnson's important *American Promise* speech in 1965 about voting rights was written by several individuals with very little input from the president.[15] Recent presidents have expanded the role of speechwriters though Calvin Coolidge was the first president to have used the formal title of speechwriter among his staff members.[16] Presidents such as Ronald Reagan were quite astute about the speechwriting process and the careful management of producing effective speeches and engaged more heavily in the process. Other presidents such as Jimmy Carter or George H.W. Bush had little appreciation for the spoken word and the work of speechwriters was much more complicated if not altogether frustrating.

The overall picture is that of a long but inconsistent tradition of the speechwriting process in the political arena in the USA, especially in presidential politics. For the first century and a half, speeches were drafted, edited, and finalized by an array of aides, most of them trusted confidants who assisted the president in the process. Only since the mid-twentieth century has the process began to involve more speechwriters working in a more or less structured executive and often removed from the speaker-president. Yet, despite this inconsistent experience among different presidents and over more than two centuries, much can be discerned from this practice. The process of speechwriting is still quite informal with different presidents at different times employing a varied assortment of aides to handle speechmaking, resorting to more or less a structured approach to the speechwriting process, and approaching the importance of speechmaking with different levels of appreciation and understanding. A picture, though, thus emerges of strong and great presidents who were also effective speakers and astute users of good speechwriting practices. The reverse is also true that less effective presidents were also less appreciative of the rhetorical features of the office and hence also the practice of speechwriting.

---

[15] Garth E. Pauly, *Lyndon Johnson's American Promise: The Voting Right Address* (College Station: Texas A&M University Press, 2007).

[16] Ritter and Medhurst, *Presidential Speechwriting*, 5.

The process of speechwriting was and still includes the initial ideational phase that begins with the president and close aides, having to deliver a speech or assessing a situation as necessitating one. However, as Medhurst correctly reminds us, invention when speechwriters are involved is not the same as speakers developing their own speech idea, strategies, and venues.[17] Initial thoughts or points are drafted by not just the president but the advisors, speechwriters, and councilors and not always in a very methodical way. Even designating an audience is contemplated relative to the topic at hand, political calculations of maximizing advantages and minimizing setbacks. Some presidents would draft more points than others with early presidents often drafting complete speeches in rough form. Speechwriters would take initial points as guidelines and draft a speech and even engage in editing it. Other individuals entrusted with the speech assignment would further develop and edit it with some completely rewriting speeches, while others suggesting some changes as well as editing it for style before bringing it back to the president for a final review, edit, and sometimes even an early read-through. Indeed, the entire gamut from *Invention* to *Arrangement, Memory, Style,* and *Delivery*, to use the Roman canons of rhetoric, has been practiced inconsistently by different presidents. While several presidents have used speechwriters for the development of the speech ideas or direction all the way to its stylistic quality, others have limited the function of speechwriters to that of wordsmithing. Some presidents such as Eisenhower and Reagan worked closely with their speechwriters, possessing that rare quality of understanding the function of words in the political contexts. Other presidents lacked such an appreciation and have minimized their importance often by physically separating speechwriters from political and policy advisers.

It is important to note that the modern presidency, especially those from the 1950s onward, has given many more speeches than their predecessors and are expected to address the public and the media at a much higher frequency, sometimes even on a daily basis. Their counterparts in the nineteenth century gave few speeches though when they did, they presented much lengthier ones. In his eight years in office Andrew Jackson delivered, for example, two Inaugural Addresses, eight annual messages to Congress which were written documents and not

---

[17] Martin J. Medhurst, "Ghostwritten Speeches: Ethics Isn't the Only Lesson," *Journal of Communication Education* 36, no. 3 (1987), 241–249.

orated, two primary veto messages, a key proclamation, and a Farewell Address most of them delivered in written form and widely distributed in the press. By comparison, Gerald Ford, who was president for about two years, delivered hundreds of speeches during a two-year presidency. Clearly, the high frequency of delivering speeches since the television age has complicated the work of presidential speechwriters.

The ethical aspect of presidential speechwriting is also important to contemplate. At the basic level, the obvious issue is the notion of whose ideas are expressed in public. Indeed, one can easily find faults in taking a speech by a president as uttering the words written by someone else, unknown to the public. At the heart of the issue is our basic assumption that individuals own their words and the thoughts and ideas therein. The help of others, especially once revealed a la Cyrano de Bergerac, could change our perception of who is actually speaking to us and even more critically, where we locate issues of knowledge, intent, and trust. Yet, and as we have already discussed, in most if not all things rhetorical, be it a term paper, a public speaking class, a group presentation, or a public hearing, rehearsing our public statements is often accomplished by seeking and receiving the input of others. We do so to modify points thereafter, even revising argument, re-reframing an earlier perspective, changing initial plan, or being told to sound more formal than our daily conversation with friends. In short, others are often involved in helping us become more proficient presenters. The role and function of speech-making in the political arena are perhaps its most crucial activity. One can argue that a president's primary job is to communicate, sometimes in public, sometimes in close settings, consulting and listening, talking on the phone, and even tweeting. The decision-making process, which is what the executive is all about, begins and ends with rhetorical acts, and as such, their importance is critical and their effectiveness is often on the line. It is not surprising then that special care has been taken over more than two centuries to ensure that public addresses and statements are focused, effective, proper, adaptive to the audience at hand, and that they generate the objectives set. Just as a given president has advisors on a host of issues such as military, economics, domestic, and foreign issues, the public address variable is no different and it too requires assistants, advisors, editors, and expert help.

The formalization of speechwriters in the White House as a profession and a position in the twentieth century coupled with the significant increase in the number of presidential speeches has also added to the realization of a growing distance between speaker and speech. That speakers-presidents are, for the most part, not the authors of their speeches is a much more understood if not altogether an accepted notion today, hence the growing revelation of who wrote a particular address. In January 25, 2015, on the eve of President Obama's State of the Union Address, the *New York Times* included an article on the president's speechwriter and his process of writing the address delivered later in the evening.[18] With contemporary research tools, especially those relying on archival material, it is rather easy to find out who drafted a speech, even historical ones, who inserted what paragraph and the extent to which a given president has had little or heavy hand in inputting and editing a given speech. We know the names of prominent politicians and lesser-known consultants and advisors and most importantly, the public knows of the speechwriters in a given administration. All of this is to suggest that speechwriters have become a formal position and a necessary one but also that what was once a behind-the-scene process of speechwriting is now much more transparent. Yet, with the mystery gone, so has the reverence for presidential addresses that were construed as an art form in yesteryears and attributed, at least by the public at large, to the president's own authorship and penmanship. The seeming distance between a president and speechwriters also suggests a diminished reverence for the rhetorical art.

An effective speechwriting process does not begin with the cleaning of a speech draft and editing it for stylistic proficiency or adding elegant language; it begins at the inventional phase, whereby ideas and thoughts about what a speech should be about are framed, arguments are selected, direction is identified, and the respective audience (or audiences) is contemplated. Yet, speechwriters have been employed by presidents over a wide range of purposes ranging for the limited objective of adding only prose, while others have been involved in the entire rhetorical process. Indeed, the more involved speechwriters are in the process, the more they are bound to be part of the policy-making apparatus and the potential for greater frictions with those whose formal responsibility is to formulate policy. At the heart of the issue of employing speechwriters is the

---

[18] http://www.nytimes.com/2015/01/20/us/politics/cody-keenan-obamas-hemingway-draws-on-friends-empathy-and-a-little-whisky-for-state-of-the-union.html?hpw&rref=politics&action=click&pgtype=Homepage&module=well-region&region=bottom-well&WT.nav=bottom-well&_r=1. Accessed January 25, 2015.

erroneous assumption by some that words can be separated from actions and that two entities can work off each other without acknowledging the other. This erroneous assumption is often at the root of difficult speech-writing processes and less-than-effective speeches.[19] The better presidential speeches, and by implication, general speeches, are those written by policy advisors with a penchant for good writing. The reverse is also true, whereby good speechwriters with knowledge of policy-making can write good speeches. The principle idea forwarded here is that ghostwriting that is limited to stylistic flourishes and devoid of knowledge or understanding of policy issues could result in grand speeches that have little to suggest. The opposite is the desirable result—that of effective speeches that have tangible things to say even if they are not of the grand style or of elevated prose.

Genres in European Political Speechwriting

Like American presidential genres, the genres in European political speechwriting allow for comprehending national addresses via their substantive, stylistic, and situational similarities. When European leaders of state make annual addresses to the people, or when they make a declaration of war, their speeches are responses to specific situations, and they carry an internal dynamic that has been adopted over time, offering a sense of stability and familiarity to rhetors and audiences alike. Over the past decade, terrorist attacks on European cities and religious sites have brought European leaders to engage in *National Eulogies* that mourn the dead and ensure the people that core, democratic values of Western societies such as freedom of speech and freedom of religion are still intact and will be guarded in the future.

In several European countries, the government gives an annual report of the state of the nation in a speech that marks the formal start of the parliamentary year. In the Netherlands and the UK, this is done in the *Speech from the Throne*, where the monarch reads out a speech outlining the government's agenda to the members of parliament. Though it is read by the monarch, the speech itself is prepared by the government, similar to the American *State of the Union Address* as well as its likely precursor. In other countries, this rhetorical

---

[19] Ritter and Medhurst, *Presidential Speechwriting*, 12–14.

duty has passed on to the prime minister. Thus, the Danish Constitution of 1953 demands that the prime minister on the first assembly of the Danish Parliament each year "renders an account of the general state of the country and of the measures proposed by the Government."

Campbell and Jamieson's outline of the three elements that are constituent of the American State of the Union Address can be transferred to the European address opening the parliament. The function of the speech is (1) to assess of information and issues, (2) give policy recommendations that follow from the assessments, and (3) rehearsing national values. According to Campbell and Jamieson, the State of the Union Address often establishes a link between the two first elements: the president's interpretation of problems and political propositions thereof. The speech gives the president the opportunity to launch a comprehensive narrative and, on this basis, chart a course for the nation.[20]

A similar generic texture can be found in the addresses opening European Parliaments. The purpose of the Opening Address is to account for existing problems and construct a collective narrative that may serve as the ideational point of departure for future initiatives. The Danish Opening Address, for instance, is characterized by a meditation on values with stock topics such as praise of the Constitution, praise of Danish democracy, and praise of the collaboration of the Danish Parliament. These epideictic elements are used to reflect on and re-interpret what it means to be Danish, and they have an argumentative function. The Opening Address is first and foremost a political speech, and the construction of a national collective identity is used to back political propositions.[21]

One example of how the construction of a national collective identity warrants political dispositions can be found in the social democratic Prime Minister Jens Otto Krag's Opening Address of 1972. The Address was given the day after the Danish election, when a majority of Danes approved joining the European Economic Community (later EU). In the speech, Krag inscribed the Danish history in a narrative of a unique European identity. To account for the purpose of the Danish membership of the European Economic Community, he re-established European

---

[20] Karlyn Kohrs Campbell and Kathleen Hall Jamieson, *Presidents Creating the Presidency: Deeds Done in Words* (Chicago: University of Chicago Press, 2008, 139).

[21] Marie Lund, *An Argument on Rhetorical Style* (Aarhus: Aarhus University Press, 2017), 117.

kinship by drawing connections with the cradle of democracy: "We want to maintain and develop the democracy as it was born in the European continent, and as it was developed differently according to the will and thoughts of the nations and of the people. [...] Let us make use of the new Europe to create a continent that unites the best of European culture, from ancient Hellas and Rome to the modern times that we live in ourselves."[22]

Another major speech in European political speechwriting is *The Prime Minister's New Year's Speech* on TV. The New Year's speech is a ceremonial speech that fuses epideictic and deliberative aspects, and more than the Opening Address, it must rise above the ideological differences of practical politics and interpret national values and ideas, such as democracy, freedom, tolerance, and human rights. The prime minister has the opportunity to create a sense of communion and common past in the audience and give the direction for the future.[23]

In some European democracies with constitutional monarchy, the monarch has an important rhetorical role to perform in the televised annual address to the nation. The function of the speech is to continue and reinterpret the narrative of the collective national identity and its values. The New Year's speech confirms and rhetorically enforces both the sense of community and the boundaries of the Kingdom.[24] Although the speech is not supposed to express political opinions, formulations of values may indeed come close to and be interpreted as such. At a garden party on the 25th anniversary of his and Queen Sonja's regency, the Norwegian King Harald spoke of what it means to be Norwegian. His speech was both praised and criticized for the inclusion of minorities and that subsequently, prompted a national debate: "Norwegians are

---

[22] Jens Otto Krag, "Opening Address," October 3, 1972. http://danmarkshistorien.dk/leksikon-og-kilder/vis/materiale/jens-otto-krags-s-tale-ved-folketingets-aabning-1972/?no_cache=1&cHash=c90ba371e59c1de84015c20fcd07050a. Accessed January 31, 2017.

[23] Esben Bjerggaard Nielsen, "Statsministerens nytårstale, 1940–," http://danmarkshistorien.dk/leksikon-og-kilder/vis/materiale/statsministerens-nytaarstale-1940/?no_cache=1&cHash=20806eeb62a7a629709eb340d9f6e1b0.

[24] Carsten Madsen, "Magtens repræsentation af danskhed. Konstitueringen af nationalidentitet i Dronning Margretes nytårstaler," *Passage* 76 (2016), 129–143.

girls who like girls, boys who like boys, and girls and boys who like each other. Norwegians believe in God, Allah, the Universe, and Nothing."[25]

Other important speeches in European political speechwriting are the ceremonial, yet political speeches made in some countries on annual celebrations of the Constitution Day or the Labor Day on May 1. Contrary to the New Year's speeches and the opening speech, no one has monopoly on these speeches. In the *Constitution Day Speech*, politicians and personages from the cultural life put forward their opinions on democracy, freedom, and national values.[26] In the *Labor Day Address*, especially left-wing politicians and members of trade unions and political organizations demand better wages and increased rights for the working class.

In the UK, for example, speeches by government officials are not limited to policy issues but include speeches to party gatherings as well. In fact, speeches at party conferences often set the prime minister's platform and the government policy agenda. One prominent case is that of Margaret Thatcher's famous speech to the Conservative Party Conference in 1980. Against the backdrop of colleagues who predicted that once becoming prime minister, Thatcher would revert to the consensus policy of the Conservative governments of the 1970s known as the "U-turn." Thatcher mounted a strong advocacy against such a disastrous turn stating, "to those waiting with bated breath for that favourite media catchphrase, the U-turn, I have only one thing to say. You turn if you want to. The lady's not for turning. I say that not only to you, but to our friends … and also to those who are not our friends." Her primary speechwriter practiced the line with the prime minister several times "to get the intonation right," seeking to put the emphasis on the "you" in the "you turn," as a take on the "U-turn" phrase. The right intonation on the first "you" was key to the success of the line and the entire speech. It succeeded, yet the most memorable line from the

[25] King Harald, "Speech at the Garden Party (2016) (Our Translation)," http://www.kongehuset.no/tale.html?tid=137662&sek=26947&scope=27247.

[26] Sofie Horskjær Madsen, "Grundlovstaler, 1849–," http://danmarkshistorien.dk/leksikon-og-kilder/vis/materiale/grundlovstaler-1849/?no_cache=1&cHash=29db-b620a3dd00020ae6edd8971fbee1.

speech, "The lady's not for turning," was not the one the speechwriter expected to stick. But it did.[27]

European politicians speak most frequently to the public when there is an election to one of the different councils, the national parliaments, the municipal councils, or the EU Parliament. In political parties, there are annual speeches at the political conventions, notably the speech of the party leader. Election nights may be the occasion when political leaders make victory speeches or if defeated, deliver a farewell address.

Besides these rather formalized genres of political speeches, speechwriters are involved in a host of everyday communication assignments for European politicians. When local politicians inaugurate a cultural event, open a public swimming pool, or speak at local community meetings, a professional speechwriter has often written or drafted the speech in advance. Speechwriters prepare the arguments and suggest a style when politicians appear in debates on public meetings on radio and television. They also write letters to the editor and assist politicians' presence in the social media.

BUSINESS SPEECHES AND ORGANIZATIONAL SPEECHES

Compared to political speechmaking and speechwriting, business and organizational speech are astonishingly under-researched. In 1981, Einhorn had only nine references to corporate speechwriting in her survey of speechwriting types.[28] Thirty years later, the situation seemed to be the same. In 2010, Dale Cyphert noted that the complete published rhetorical analysis of US business speakers is so limited that she was able to fit a comprehensive bibliography into a single footnote.[29] This continued lack of research into this field is surprising, considering the vast amount of corporate speeches delivered every year. Cyphert advocates that rhetoricians give more serious attention to "rhetorical analysis and criticism of the public discourse of business leaders, in particular, contemporary

---

[27] Andrew S. Crines, Timothy Heppell, and Peter Dorey, *The Political Rhetoric and Oratory of Margaret Thatcher* (London: Palgrave Macmillan, 2016), 90.

[28] Einhorn, "The Ghosts Unmasked," cf. Martha Stout Kessler, "Corporate Speechwriting," *The Bulletin*, March 1985, 18–22.

[29] Dale Cyphert, "The Rhetorical Analysis of Business Speeches," *Journal of Business Communication* 47, no. 3 (2010), 346–368, 361.

corporate officers."[30] Such studies of business speakers, she argues, would enhance the disciplinary aims of business communication scholars, and focus on rhetorical theory within business communication can provide a richer understanding of business speakers. Cyphert proposes nine questions of rhetorical importance in the study of the business speech.

1. *What is the canon of excellent business speech?* Providing a body of literature to define and explain examples of speeches is necessary to "identify common patterns of technique, content or responsiveness to an audience or situation that might form a theoretical basis" for understanding the business speech. Research into business speeches should catalog failed business speeches along with the mediocre and the eloquent, in order to provide "a baseline from which to develop both critical and theoretical insight."[31]
2. *Why is business speech absent from the study of rhetorical communication?* While there is a considerable body of knowledge about business communication in general, there is very little research into the many thousand influential speeches delivered by business speakers. Why, Cyphert asks, is "the collective 'voice' of a corporate public relations effort deemed more theoretically relevant than the public discourse of an individual, high-profile corporate leader?" The answer, she suggests, lies in academic presuppositions about the business speech, which leads to the following questions.
3. *What is the rhetorical role of the business speaker?* Several assumptions in rhetorical research seem to preclude the inclusion of the business speech in the scope of rhetorical discourse. First, rhetoric is understood in terms of public communication, whereas business is "idealized as an aggregate of private, self-interested transactions." While rhetoric traditionally focuses on the messenger, most public relations theory focuses on the corporate message. Second, a business speaker is generally framed as the voice of a collective, corporate entity, which is difficult to position within a rhetorical theory that "privileges the autonomous, individual author as the proper subject of study." Third, there is an implicit assumption that a corporate leader is always a mouthpiece for corporate

---

[30] Cyphert, "The Rhetorical Analysis," 347.
[31] Ibid., 48. The quotes in the following sections 2–9 are from pages 348–359.

identity and action. Rhetorical thinking that values individual voice and discourses that conform to the norms of rhetorical literature may "simply dismiss the corporate speaker as arhetorical."
4. *What is the rhetorical impact of mundane discourse?* Rhetorical studies of speechmaking, especially political speechmaking, is generally justified by the impact it makes and the social change it creates. However, even though business speeches may have effect on economic events or outcomes, most corporate and business speeches are often mundane day-to-day communication that do not appear to create any immediate and important change. Furthermore, the rhetorical study of exemplary speeches, Cyphert suggests, has largely been for pedagogical purposes. The mundane speechmaking in the corporate world does not lend itself easily to such studies of exemplary instances of rhetoric. A rhetorician studying business speech should attempt to "recognize those areas where the rhetoric of business is uniquely situated to answer questions of theoretical interest, not merely illuminating the rhetoric of business, but also expanding the understanding of rhetoric more generally."
5. *Is there a discernible scope of business rhetoric?* The scope of rhetoric has been discussed for two millennia, so defining the scope of business rhetoric requires more than just gluing the terms business and communication together. The challenge, Cyphert argues, is to "move beyond a simplistic observation that business people behave rhetorically and go on to ask how the rhetoricity of business practices informs our understanding of rhetoric."
6. *Is there a discernible style of business rhetoric?* While there is consensus that business discourse is rhetorical, the question of the distinctive rhetorical style of business rhetoric and corporate speeches is still unanswered. Research should pay more attention to the examination of a discernible style of business rhetoric, because it could lead to "a host of questions about the moral character, epistemological presumptions, and social relationships inherent in the business community."
7. *What method of rhetorical criticism is suitable for the study of business rhetoric?* While this is a "trick question," Cyphert puts it forward, in order to point to possible ways of critique that rhetorical theory offers: close textual analysis, Burkean analysis, postmodern critique, stylistic examination, and classical theories.

8. *How does the study of business speakers inform rhetorical theory?* Business and management studies have much to learn from rhetorical theory, but such theory may also be informed through the application of corporate rhetoric and business speech. Douglas Ehninger[32] has suggested three systems of rhetoric: the *grammatical* in the classical attention to rhetorical rules, the *psychological* of the eighteenth century that focused on the psychology of the speaker and audience, and the *sociological* of contemporary focus on rhetoric as socially constructed. However, "the corporate speaker functions in ways that simply cannot be fully explained," by these three systems.[33] The corporate speaker, Cyphert argues, is still subject to "rules, psychology, and social influences, but is also a functioning part of a complex corporate entity that itself has the ability to perform rhetorically."
9. *How can rhetorical theory illuminate the relationship of business to society?* This is the final question: how can we "more accurately describe, understand, and evaluate the role of business within the larger realm of human society?"

Already in 1985, Kessler stated that virtually all America's large corporations use speechwriters. The demand for corporate speechwriters increased about 30% a year from 1975 to 1989, and the number is arguably even greater today.[34] CEOs and leaders of business and organizations frequently deliver speeches both internally and externally. Given the busy schedules of such leaders, most seek assistance in writing these speeches. Based on qualitative interviews with corporate speechwriters, Kessler distinguishes between six types of external speeches with the following aims: (1) promoting the cooperation within the business community; (2) lobbying on behalf of the company before regulatory agencies, legislative committees, and similar institutions; (3) influencing course of events by speaking out on specific issues that affect their particular company or industry; (4) defending the company or themselves in reaction

---

[32] Ehninger, Douglas, "On Systems of Rhetoric," *Philosophy & Rhetoric* 25 (1992), 15–28.

[33] Cyphert borrows this argument from: Richard E. Crable, "'Organisational Rhetoric' as the Fourth Great System: Theoretical, Critical, and Pragmatic Implications," *Journal of Applied Communication Research* 18, no. 2 (1990), 115–128.

[34] Martha Stout Kessler, "Corporate Speechwriting," *The Bulletin*, March 1985, 18–22.

to events; (5) promoting themselves as individuals; and (6) speaking at invited events such as business conventions, college convocations, and seminars. Successful leaders, for instance, are frequently invited to do inspirational and motivational speeches.[35]

In addition to the external addresses, business leaders increasingly deliver speeches internally, talking to their own executives, managers, and employees. This may involve ceremonial speeches celebrating anniversaries or accomplishment, and it may involve delivering difficult messages dealing with hostile takeovers, downsizing, or layoffs.

A special kind of business speech is the product launch, which was perfected by Steve Jobs and Apple. While presentation tools such as PowerPoint and Keynote often put the speaker in the background and orient the audience toward the slides instead, Jobs used slides in a way that simultaneously supported his ethos and made the product stand out. These presentations not only functioned as product launching but also as identity creating and brand-promoting rhetoric.

---

[35] Ibid. Cf. Robert J. Myers and Martha Stout Kessler, "Business speaks: A Study of the Public Speaking of America's Corporate Leaders," *The Journal of Business Communication* 17 (1980), 5–17.

CHAPTER 7

How Speeches Are Written

Working with Other People: Ways of Writing Speeches

In her memoirs of her time as a speechwriter for Ronald Reagan (*What I Saw at the Revolution*, 1990), Peggy Noonan describes the frustration that arises during the attempt to write a good speech when several individuals are involved in commenting and vetting the text. "It was a constant struggle over speeches," she writes, "over who was in charge and what would prevail and which group would triumph. Each speech was a battle in a never-ending war."[1] In her assessment of the damage committee-writing can do to a speech, she writes:

> Think of a bunch of wonderful, clean, shining, perfectly shaped and delicious vegetables. Then think of those old-fashioned metal meat grinders. Imagine the beautiful vegetables being forced through the grinder and being rendered into a smooth, dull, textureless purée.[2]

Even though this image describes writing in the US White House, European speechwriters have expressed similar concerns with the speechwriting process. The process of writing speeches within the institutional settings of governments, ministerial departments, and similar organizations

---

[1] Peggy Noonan, *What I Saw at the Revolution: A Political Life in the Reagan Era* (New York, NY: Random House, 1990), 72.
[2] Ibid.

is probably the most determining constraint of how a speech would finally turn out. This chapter provides accounts of speechwriting processes and case studies of how speeches are written in political organizations.

While the speechwriting process in the White House has been extensively described in both research and speechwriter memoirs, there is no discernible pattern to describe individual presidencies and their speechwriting process. Andrew Jackson (1828–1836) delivered more addresses, vetoes, and proclamations than his predecessors and even many of those who followed him, yet he outlined and drafted most of his public addresses. He outlined his First Inaugural Address and drafted an eloquent address only to see two more versions that were deemed stronger. Yet, one of his biographers considered the draft superior to the final address. At the other extremes are presidents who allowed others to engage in all the drafting and got involved only when a final version of the speech was ready. Such was the case of Lyndon Johnson and his major address on the Civil Rights Act (1964). In between these cases are variations on the same theme—of more or less involvement of the president in the working of a speech. Some prefer to work on a draft before finalization, such as Franklin D. Roosevelt sitting with Raymond Moley to finalize the First Inaugural Address, while others, such as Jimmy Carter, receive final drafts with little or no input.

The inconsistencies described here are relative to the rhetorical sophistication of a given president and their appreciation, or not, of the rhetorical perspective in politics. This point is important as it brings us full circle to the essential dilemma facing speakers and speechwriters. Do they believe in the power of speeches as a tool in the hand of politicians to carve a path, to direct people, and to move them in a given direction? The speechwriters vary in their background and experience. There is no specific profession or expertise that is detrimental to the profession of speechwriters as lawyers and writers are considered equal in their "knowledge" of rhetoric and speechmaking. Even a successful dabbling in writing a speech may be sufficient for hiring one as a speechwriter. In short, any individual with peripheral practice in wordsmithing is often sufficient for being hired as a speechwriter. Yet, over the past several decades, speechwriters as a unit have emerged in the White House as a recognizable administrative unit. We know less about such processes in the parliamentary systems of Europe.

In Europe, most speechwriters work in government ministries. How speechwriting is carried out differs not only from country to country, but also from ministry to ministry in each country. Generally, speechwriters are not hired as speechwriters, but instead as advisors, communication officials, or in similar positions as civil servants. They not only do speechwriting but perform a wide range of advice and communication tasks: writing letters to the editor, columns, and produce online material. In general, a speechwriter in a European government ministry is a civil servant that will keep the job after a government changes. Some speechwriters, however, may be political appointees and would leave the office with the departing Minister. Dealing with communication strategy in general, these speechwriters normally function as more than just speechwriters, and they are often referred to as spin doctors.

In the last couple of decades, communication and speechwriting have increased in importance, and speechwriters have more centrally been placed in the ministries. In Northern Europe, for instance, the last couple of decades have shown a trend toward moving important parts of the writing from the technical divisions to specifically assigned communication professionals working closer with the ministry's State Secretary (US: undersecretary) or Secretary General ("Statssekretær" and "departementsråd"). There is also a more direct contact with speechwriter and cabinet ministers. The organization of speechwriting differs not only between countries, but also between ministries of the same government. In some ministries, the initial phase of writing a speech is left to the technical divisions, and others in the same government may leave all the speechwriting phases to a designated group of communication professionals, sometimes specifically organized and named as a speechwriting group. In spite of the increased ministerial attention to speeches in recent decades, however, speechwriting still generally seems to be considered of less importance than other communication tasks.

It has been claimed, sarcastically, that sometimes speechwriting by civil servants in the Netherlands consists of nothing more than inserting the phrases "Ladies and gentlemen" and "Thank you" to existing written documents.[3] Recent research, however, does not support this assumption. Generally, speechwriting in European politics and administration seems to have achieved a new level of professionalism during the last 15–20 years. In spite of this professionalization, there still seems to be more attention given to correctness of facts than to making speeches vivid and compelling. At the Dutch Ministry of the Interior, for instance, a policy of finalizing a document by putting one's initials on it was very strictly maintained. As in the case of Peggy Noonan's meat grinder

---

[3] J. Mulder, "Het anonieme schrijverschap: ghostwriting," *[Tekst]blad* 2 (1995), 16–20

metaphor, the result was a very long and frustrating writing process that did not contribute to the quality of the speeches: "The speeches became dry because so many people wanted their own opinions reflected in it."[4] According to de Jong and Andeweg, the same culture of finalizing documents exists today:

> The difference between then (the end of the 1980s) and now is that speechwriters today, especially in the case of occasional speeches, employ 'backdoor methods' to discuss speech drafts with the speaker at an earlier stage, resulting in a kind of official approval before all the other supervisors in the organizational line approve the document. In practice, the level of contact between speechwriters and speakers varies according to the speaker.[5]

The importance of checking and finalizing can also be found in other European countries, where some ministries have up to ten steps of approval, where rhetorical considerations are disregarded to the benefit of bureaucratic and institutional demands.[6] These bureaucratic procedures of approval are sometimes referred to as "the line," because they take the revision of the speech through a strict "line of command." While such elaborate procedures of approval may be rhetorically inexpedient, they make sense from an institutional perspective, because the words of a Minister will reflect back on the party of the Minister, the ministry, the civil servants, the government, and in some instances, even on the nation. The words spoken may create changes in policy or advance new policies that must be carefully vetted, especially in the field of foreign affairs. In the multiparty systems of European countries, the most institutionalized speechwriting processes are performed in the government ministries. The phases of the speechwriting process of several

---

[4] R. Kagie, "Schuren en schaven. De souffleurs van de nieuwjaarstopraken," *Vrij Nederland* II January 8–11 (1992).

[5] Jaap de Jong and Bas Andeweg, "Professionalizing Speech Production: Changes in 15 Years of Ministerial Speeches," in *Bending Opinion: Essays on Persuasion in the Public Domains*, ed. Ton van Haaften, et al. (Leiden: Leiden University Press, 2011), 160 f.

[6] For example Denmark, see Mette Stoltenbergm, *Hvem har ordet? En retorisk analyse af taleskrivning for en anden i danske ministerier og kommuner*. Master thesis. Department of Comparative Literature and Rhetoric, Aarhus University, Denmark (2014), pp. 39, 78.

Norwegian ministries seem similar to most of the speechwriting in other European ministries.[7]

1. *Invitation to speak is evaluated and accepted or declined.* The process often begins with an invitation to the Minister or the State Secretary to give a speech. The political staff, sometimes the political adviser, or the cabinet minister will then decide whether to accept or decline the invitation. If the offer is accepted, then information about the event, audience, aim, and so on will be provided to the speechwriter, who must also contribute to the initial plan.

2. *The work is organized and information is gathered.* If the ministry has one or more people acting specifically as speechwriters, one or more of these are assigned to write the speech. Some ministries have specific speechwriters; some even include a speechwriting group, while others have one or more communication officers taking care of all forms of communication, including speechwriting. In some cases, the task of a given speech is assigned directly to the relevant department or division. The assigned speechwriter will first contact the organizers of the event where the speech is to be delivered and will then gather content and information from the divisions dealing with the subject matter. Generally, the writer will also have one or several short meetings with the State Secretary or the Minister, depending on the importance of the speech. How this phase proceeds depends much on the importance of the speech. The so-called line speeches are those that put forward (new) policies. Such speeches are considered important and will allow more contact with the political staff (e.g., State Secretary and Minister), and provide the opportunity to make *commissions* ("bestillinger") to the departments. A commission is a request for information addressed to the Director General of the department (a civil servant), who will then delegate the work within the department. The request could be for

---

[7]The following part on the general speechwriting process is based on Skåleskog, Kristin Hald, *Taleskrivningsprosessen i Norge - en undersøkelser av taleskrivningsprosessen i fire norske departementer.* Master thesis, Department of Information Science and Media Studies, University of Bergen, Norway (2013); Mette Stoltenberg, *Hvem har ordet? En retorisk analyse af taleskrivning for en anden i danske ministerier og kommuner.* Master thesis, Department of Comparative Literature and Rhetoric, Aarhus University, Denmark (2014); Maria B. Waade, *Med blanke ark og taleskriver til. En kvalitativ stuidie av taleskrivning i tre små norske opposisjonspartier.* Master thesis, Department of Information Science and Media Studies, University of Bergen, Norway (2016).

information about the rhetorical situation (the event, organizer, audience, etc.) or about the subject or for relevant content or arguments.

Sometimes the speechwriter will ask for information and then develop a draft thereafter; at other times, the speechwriter will ask the department to write a draft. Following, is an actual example of a speechwriter's *commission* for a draft from an employee in a department[8]:

> Hi
>
> I don't think we need a meeting for this. But please come by if you want to.
>
> I agree that the script for the parliamentary debate is a good point of departure, but remember that the Minister does not need a full script.
> - Write bullet points with the arguments connected
> - The title for the Minister is: [Title of speech]? (A weird title, perhaps, or does it make sense?)
> - Important that the Minister really connects with the audience (shake hands with the audience). The Minister wishes to be in tune with the audience. Check who will be present - list of participants.
> - They call it a consultative conference - it seems that there will be a lot of short presentations from experts and users with experience. Important that the Minister recognizes this in the beginning
> - In brief, what is the main message that the Minister wants to convey (the key takeaway)
> - Build up the main message with 3–4 themes - preferably numbers and examples
> - Create a good closing that connect the threads and points forward.
>
> Can you hand in something on Friday, April 5th?
> Greetings [name of speechwriter]

3. *The text is structured (dispositio) and formulated (elocutio)*. Getting information and drafts from various divisions will often take weeks, especially with important speeches. Sometimes the speechwriter will receive a draft, other times only general information, often of a technical and professional character. The job of the speechwriter then is to organize the information and to formulate it in a way that fits the speaker and is understandable to the audience. Generally, much thought goes into

---

[8]This example is from Kristin Hald Skåleskog, *Taleskrivningsprocessen i Norge [The Speechwriting Process in Norway]* (2013).

adapting to situation and audience, for instance, by working on an appropriate beginning. While the administrative divisions provide facts, policy, and technical information, the speechwriter normally is the one who must obtain the rhetorical material that may make a speech personal and vivid: anecdotes and personal stories from the speaker, the use of quotes, literature, and cultural references. The main challenge is to unite the demand for technical information and correctness with the rhetorical need to craft a poignant, vivid speech that is written in a coherent voice that is true to the speaker.

4. *Check and approval.* Check and approval may occur at several stages of the speechwriting process. However, the most important time is when the speech nears completion. Normally, a speech is sent to the political staff, such as the political adviser and the State Secretary, *and* to the technical division and civil servants, including the Director General. The political staff ensures that the speech accords with policy and the wish of the Minister and with the civil servants and the divisions checking professional and technical references. Thereafter, the speech is returned to the speechwriter with suggested changes. The speechwriter often finds herself in a negotiating position trying to create the best possible speeches while simultaneously negotiating contradictory instructions from the political and the professional side. One speechwriter expresses it in this way:

> The divisions and the Minister often disagree. They have different approaches to an issue, or the divisions do not want the Minister to say something in this or that way, and the Minister, perhaps, do not understand why the division makes everything so complicated.[9]

The process of check and approval can have the speech go forth and back between the parties several times. With important speeches, even the Minister may be involved. The Minister may also be involved in changing formulations so that words and expression fit his style. When the speech is deemed finished, the last phase consists of preparation for delivery and the delivery itself.

5. *Preparation and presentation.* In most cases, the speechwriter's job is over when the script is finished. Often, a cabinet minister will get the

---

[9]Quote is from interview by Skåleskog in Skåleskog, *Taleskrivningsprosessen i Norge* (2013), 60.

speech just before the speech is delivered. Often ministers read through the speech when it is finished and then reread it in the car on the way to the event. Sometimes the Minister will see the speech for the first time in the car or at the event. On the way to the event, the Minister may ask his advisors about terminology or the event and sometimes rehearse by reading the speech out aloud. At other times, a minister will rehearse the speech well in advance, especially if it is a "line speech." Generally, the speechwriter is not involved in rehearsing and preparing delivery; however, there are instances with important speeches where speechwriters and other advisors help the Minister work on delivery sometimes doing so thoroughly and weeks in advance.

When the speech is delivered, a speechwriter or another advisor will often be present. This will give the writer a sense of what works or does not work, for both the speaker and the audience. Being present helps the speechwriter with future speeches. The speaker will often stray from the manuscript, leave elements out or add material, such as short anecdotes, or reference the audience. It is valuable to note these instances as well as the speaker's presentational style and delivery. Furthermore, since a Minister's speeches are published in written form and often online, it is important then to authenticate them before publication. In some rare cases, the delivered version would become the official record of the policy. This policy statement will then go back into the system and be handed the next time a speechwriter makes a *commission*.

Three Case Studies of Speechwriting

Case Study 1: Writing the Government Declaration for the German Bundeskanzler

A Government Declaration is the speech where a new government announces its policy for the coming term. The prime minister delivers the speech to parliament at the outset of its new term. The audience includes members of parliament, the national media, and the public. The objective of the speech is to inform government officials and cabinet bureaucracy about policies and aims of the new government. The speech can be compared to the Inaugural Address of US presidents.

In the case of a coalition government, which is the most common in Europe, the speech will naturally be a compromise, attempting to accommodate the wishes of all parties involved in the government. The prime minister, who used to speak for his or her party, must now address the whole nation on behalf of a national government, which often consists of two or more parties. Following, we provide a short account on the production of the speechwriting process for the German government declaration as it is described by Antje Schwarze and Antje Walther in their chapter on speechwriting for the German prime minister ("Bundeskanzler").[10]

As in the case of American presidents and other European prime ministers, the German prime minister may organize the speechwriters differently from previous administrations. Generally, the organization is informal and relies on personal constellations of trust. Mostly, speechwriters are directly connected to the Prime Minister or her office. One or two individuals would function as chief speechwriters, and a total of five to ten people could be involved in the writing process.

While speechwriters draft different kinds of speeches without much participation from the prime minister, he or she is actively involved in the crafting of the Government Declaration. For this speech, an ad hoc group of loyal, reliable people is designated. Generally, the members will have extensive political experience and some may have previously worked with the Prime Minister. Besides the speechwriters of the Prime Minister's office, the group may consist of trusted members of government and party, as well as external personalities such as scientists, journalists, or intellectuals.

While the working out of the content is done by a team of five to seven persons, the actual wording is taken care of by a group of two to three persons, led by the chief speechwriter. Depending on the prime minister, the chief speechwriter may be an official position or may hold this position unofficially. Schwarze and Walter describe the crafting of the Government Declaration as an exceptional case that completely breaks the normal framework for the speechwriting process:

> Drafts are edited, passages are put forward to mutual discussion, preliminary written out and sent on to other participants.

---

[10] Antje Schwarze and Antje Walther, "Redenschreiben Für Den Bundeskanzler: Formulieren, Koordinieren Und Beraten," in *Das Wort Hat Der Herr Bundeskanzler: Eine Analyse Der Großen Regierungserklärungen Von Adenauer Bis Schröder*, ed. Karl-Rudolf Korte (Wiesbaden: VS Verlag für Sozialwissenschaften, 2002). Our description of the speechwriting process for the German Government Declaration is an elaborate summary of the account provided by Schwarze and Walter.

The divisions ("Fachabteilungen") of the PM's office and the press office ("Bundespressamt") put forward case documents and background information. In contrast to other speeches, the divisions in the department will contribute directly, since these divisions have not yet been properly adjusted to the new government. In the final phase, the work will carry on both day and night. Through the multiple and thorough working through of the speech the original draft achieves a strong and thought through condensation.[11]

The production of the speech does not follow a standard plan; however, Schwarze and Walter describe five main phases for work:

1. *Conception*. The prime minister briefs a few selected associates about ideas and wishes for the speech. The main point of the speech is fleshed out, and it is decided which experts, divisions, scientists, political allies, and intellectuals should be involved. It is decided which members of the team will be responsible for which parts of the speech. The participants do an analysis of situation, audience, and aim. In some cases, the chief speechwriters may have had a short brainstorm meeting in advance without the Prime Minister, discussing specifics with the department chiefs ("Abteilungsleitern") and other involved persons. Thereafter, the main concept of the speech is developed, which is then discussed with the PM. At this point, the Prime Minister may have already been thinking about the speech for months and would seek additional feedback from others such as social groups and parties.

2. *Gathering of material and development of drafts for selected passages*. The foundation for the Declaration is the coalition agreement, the party program propositions from its partners, and accounts from the divisions. Inspiration for the speech may be sought in previous declarations and in inaugural addresses of American presidents. The speechwriters from the government team and from the divisions develop drafts for selected passages. The beginning and the end are generally the last phrases to be written.

3. *Creating the rough draft of the manuscript*. As soon as all the major draft passages are completed, they are worked together into one rough draft. At this point, only two or three people are involved. As soon as the first draft is considered finished, it is sent to different departmental divisions, ministers, and advisers for comments. Here, as in all the phases of the writing, the prime minister will discuss different aspects

[11] Ibid., 41.

with members of the team and comment on issues such as sequence of themes, content, formulations as well as provide directions about additional further revision. The draft is often discussed with other speechwriters and team members, and sometimes the prime minister will present the first full coherent draft to members of the cabinet and coalition partners in order to secure adjustments that accommodate the whole coalition. Ministers will have access to parts related to their office and may propose changes. After the many revisions and controls, the proposals from the involved parties (divisions, ministers, speechwriters, advisers and coalition partners, etc.) are worked into the final draft. Then, a process of editing and shortening of the speech begins. Finally, language is repeatedly worked through to ensure it is adapted to the style of the Prime Minister, facts and numbers are checked, the remaining instances of officialese are removed, and language is checked for possible misunderstandings.

4. *Polishing the final draft*. In an intensive final round with the Prime Minister and the closest advisers, the last stylistic changes are made and the text is proofread. The first and last sentences of the speech are often worked on until the last minute.

5. *Final manuscript and delivery*. In some cases, the final manuscript is worked on until minutes before the delivery. For the Declaration of Prime Minister Konrad Adenauer (1878–1967), the last pages were handed in while he was delivering the speech. This was a special case, while, in general, the prime minister only has limited time to prepare the delivery. When the prime minister goes to the podium, the job of the speechwriter is more or less done. Each speech, as one speechwriter told Schwarze and Walter, is a "play that is only performed once."[12]

Case Study 2: Speechwriting in a Danish Ministry

Like many European government administrations, and to a certain extent the US administration, the Danish central administration is characterized by a hierarchical chain of command where speechwriters rank below technical experts and department heads. Because of speechwriters' general subordinate position, they must submit to the commentaries, inputs, and changes that higher-ranking public servants consider

---

[12] Schwarze and Walter, "Redeschreiben," 45.

improvements of the speech. They have to pick their battles in a government administration largely run by government officers and specialists who value factual accuracy and diplomacy higher than audience-friendly communication.[13]

Most speechwriters in Danish municipalities and government offices are public servants, and it is their professional duty to aid any current mayor or Minister in a truthful, legal, and loyal manner. The speechwriter must be politically neutral and assist the leader in power to perform her official duties, but unlike a spin doctor, the speechwriter is not allowed to give political strategic advice in, for instance, political campaigns.

Generally, speeches are not as valued as exposure in the mass media. A TV debate or a newspaper interview is considered more valuable to a Minister or local councilor than a speech often heard by only the immediate audience. Perhaps this is also why actual cooperation with the politician, praised in every manual on speechwriting, rarely takes place in Danish speechwriting processes. For most political leaders, time is in short supply. Even so, the last 5–10 years has seen increased attention paid to communication and speechwriting, and today, speeches are often the responsibility of appointed speechwriters rather than shifting civil servants.

Mette Stoltenberg Hansen's study of the speechwriting process in Danish ministries and municipalities shows that there are multiple procedures to follow. Rigid hierarchy is, however, a dominant characteristic. Like many other European countries, the Danish administration of ministries and departments is based on a strict hierarchical structure, which involves the right to give orders downward in the system and the obligation to take orders from higher-ups in the system. This means that the speechwriter is subject to an extensive, bureaucratic process of revision and approval, where government officials, civil servants, assistant secretaries, and heads of sections must control and approve the speeches. The following case study is illustrative of such a process.

A government speechwriter is informed that the Minister has accepted an invitation to speak to an audience of scientists. It is one month before

---

[13] The case study is based on Mette Stoltenberg Hansen's investigation into the speechwriting process in Danish ministries and municipals: "Hvem har ordet? En retorisk analyse af taleskrivning for en anden i danske ministerier og kommuner." Master thesis, Aarhus Universitet (2014).

the occasion. The speechwriter meets with the chief consultant who is responsible for the political and legal aspects of the speech, and they agree to order expert input from two different offices. Two weeks later, the speechwriter receives the expert briefs. The following paragraph is from one of the briefs:

> The first assessment report from IPCC was completed in 1990 and served as the basis for The United Nation Framework Convention on Climate Change (UNFCCC), which was signed by 154 countries in Rio de Janeiro in 1992. The treaty aims to stabilize atmospheric concentrations of greenhouse gases at a level that would prevent dangerous anthropogenic climate changes.

The language is distinguished by numbers ("1990," "154," "1992"), technical terms ("atmospheric concentrations of greenhouse gases"), and abbreviations ("IPCC," "UNFCCC"). The general impression of the language is that it is complex, factual, and technical. Even though the audience is familiar with climate and environmental politics, such heavy academic language would be unfavorable to use in a speech where the audience's perception depends on the clarity of the oral communication. Furthermore, the language is characterized by stiff, hypotactic syntax with passive constructions ("was completed," "was signed") and relatively long sentences.

Both briefs are written in officialese; they have a high level of abstraction, are heavily loaded with information, and are much closer to traditional bureaucratic and written genres resembling more a bill or the technical report than a speech manuscript. Danish speechwriters in the central administration admit that when pressed for time, they are sometimes tempted to "borrow" directly from a written brief. Many civil servants use the copy/paste function too often to produce a poor speech out of a good brief. Subsequently, government speeches often sound like a reading from the Public Records Act or the economic statement.[14]

The speechwriter's first draft is indeed close to the briefs with a direct import of key terms like "science," "challenges," "political," and "point at." However, the speech is developed around the idea that science and politics are interdependent, with science inscribed as an active agent.

---

[14] Kristian Madsen, *Skriv gode taler. Taleskrivning som strategisk kommunikation* (København: Gyldendal, 2012), 73.

Also, some examples of how scientific data contribute to a political agenda are quoted almost verbatim from one of the briefs: "In Denmark we are close to the 40% reduction in CO_2 emissions that science says we should make before 2020 to stay below a 2 degree rise in temperatures." However, to facilitate the audience's understanding, the speechwriter has left out the rather technical formulation "relative to 1990" which refers to the fact that all reductions in CO_2 are measured in relation to a 1990 level.

Subsequently, the draft is sent to the chief consultant who is legally and politically responsible for the speech. He makes some changes to avoid frictions with the involved parties. Besides, he reinserts the conversion to a 1990 level because it is the correct terminology for such measurements. He inserts one more political objective that adds to the overall impression of the manuscript as a detailed, written text loaded with information.

In the second draft, the speechwriter makes a series of changes to turn the manuscript into oral communication. The long, hypotactic sentences are now composed as main clauses with active verbs. The shorter sentences now have only one piece of information which makes them easier for the audience to listen to and absorb. The language is made rhythmic through repetitions and rhetorical figures, such as anaphors and epistrophes (respectively beginning or ending a series of lines, phrases, clauses, or sentences with the same word or words). These changes simplify and clarify some of the aspects that made the earlier version appear complex and abstruse.

The second version is sent to the person responsible for the speech, but in his absence, the speech is transferred to another who adds some changes of her own. Beside a series of technical adjustments, she finds it inappropriate to name two scientists who have written a feature about sustainability in a newspaper. Whereas the speechwriter used them as an example to concretize an abstract topic, she thinks it is indelicate to praise some scientists and not others. The speechwriter meets her request halfway: He keeps the example, but in vaguer wording.

From here, the speech is approved at a higher level in the hierarchy by the office manager who has no comments. It is then sent to the next level, the national head of department who notes that all reductions of CO_2 must be mentioned and relative to the 1990 level. He also adds new information about a future bill. The paragraph about the bill is written in abstract language with several technical terms and no examples to illustrate to the audience the value of the bill. Additionally, the extra paragraph obstructs the overall composition of a list of three, now making it into a list of four items. The speechwriter incorporates the changes since they come from a high level in the hierarchy and are therefore not debatable.

By now, there are three days to the delivery of the speech, and the speechwriting process is so advanced that the speechwriter has no time to work on the manuscript. The speech is sent to the Permanent Secretary and the Minister who both find it inappropriate to name the two scientists. Although the speechwriter at an earlier stage in the process has fought for these names as concrete examples, they are finally omitted from the speech.

Experienced speechwriters in Danish ministries report that they often copy from their own earlier speeches that have already been approved. This is not just about saving time, but also about writing speeches that stand the chance of getting them approved by higher levels in the system. From her own time as a ministerial speechwriter, Pernille Steensbech Lemée has observed how speechwriters are silently and unnoticeably disciplined into writing speeches that will get accepted by the superiors.[15] The phenomenon was described by Ernest Bormann as early as 1960: "The ghost has a tendency to be discreet and careful. He weakens adjectives and tones down the strength of statements. He knows the punishment for a misstatement or a careless word."[16]

Case Study 3: Speechwriting for US Presidents

Several case studies from the practices of the USA can illustrate the varied experience of speechwriting and the presidency. Franklin D. Roosevelt's radio address *On the Banking Crisis* of March 12, 1933 (later dubbed the *First Fireside Chat*), was an effective if not a crucial speech altogether. Devoid of metaphors, high eloquence, or even memorable lines, it was a practical speech about how banks operate and why the nation's banks were depleted of their gold reserve. There could not be much that was exciting about this speech, yet it was among the

---

[15] Pernille Steensbech Lemée, *Med andres ord—ghostwriting i praksis* (København Ø: Handelshøjskolens Forlag, 2005), 14.

[16] Ernest Bormann, "Ghostwriting and the Rhetorical Critic," *Quarterly Journal of Speech* (1960), 46, 287.

most successful speeches in American history as it salvaged the banks from collapse and the US' economy from disaster.[17] The actual speech is rather dull but effective. It was direct, minced no words, and made no attempt to inspire anyone. Its strength was in the message it sent— that banks would resume solvency once people return hoarded money and gold to the banks and that president made it a priority to restore financial stability. The speech was about confidence, instilling trust in the actions the president had taken. Eleven hours later when the banks reopened after being closed for several weeks, many re-deposited their hoarded money and gold. Bank solvency resumed with a matter of days. The speech was successful because it was about clear ideas and a reasonable path to recovery. As for the speech preparations, one person drafted the speech based on an initial outline and three more individuals with knowledge of banking and currency listened with Roosevelt reading the initial draft before editing it and finalizing it. The point made here is that presidential speeches need not be grand or elevated, that specific objectives and clear arguments are necessary for its development, and that the work of speechwriters is essential in all phases of the speechmaking process. Equally important is the fact that the speechwriter wrote a speech that was in line with Roosevelt's speaking style.

The background of speechwriters who wrote for American presidents is rather varied. The person who drafted Roosevelt's *First Fireside Chat*, Arthur A. Ballantine, was Hoover's Assistant Secretary of Treasury. Roosevelt employed different speechwriters for different topics as needed and would finalize each speech with the speechwriter who drafted a given speech, often lying on a couch and reading or reviewing a speech and finalizing it. One person, who wrote speeches for Adlai Stevenson, was a young campaigner who knew Ted Sorensen as both were debaters in college. Sorensen recommended this person as a speechwriter. Another one of Stevenson's speechwriter worked for the Director of the Office for War Mobilization and Reconversion and when this individual became an assistant to President Truman, he took his aide to the White House with him.[18] All three speechwriters for the three different politicians had no training in speechwriting and no keen understanding of the difference

---

[17] Amos Kiewe, *FDR's First Fireside Chat: Public Confidence and the Banking Crisis* (College Station: Texas A&M Press, 2007).

[18] Lois J. Einhorn, "The Ghost Talk: Personal Interviews with Three Former Speechwriters," *Communication Quarterly* 36, no. 2 (1988), 94–108.

between writing for the ear and writing for the eye, yet they produced good speeches. Writing for Roosevelt required astute knowledge of the topic or policy, a careful assessment of the audience intended, and a strong sense of how Roosevelt imagined the specific address. Writing for Stevenson meant little editing from the presidential candidate who had little time for careful reading and editing of the many speeches he gave on the campaign stump.[19] Writing for President Harry Truman was altogether a different process as it was primarily a group effort.[20] After an initial discussion between Truman and one key advisor over the position to be taken, a team of speechwriters and staff members familiar or involved with the topic at hand would join to discuss the parameters of the speech, outlining it and dividing portions of the speech to different team members. After written portions were finalized, the team would meet again to read each other's speech portions, providing feedback and reviewing sometimes three or four drafts before being satisfied with the speech. When a speech was important, Truman would call for a meeting to review the speech and give his final decision over it.[21]

The experience of one speechwriter for Richard Nixon sheds a different light on the relationship between speaker and speechwriter. William F. Gavin writes years later of his experience as one member of the speechwriting team and not among the more prominent among them. Yet, Nixon appreciated his input and had specific tasks that Gavin was uniquely able to provide. Gavin's observations are revealing as he considered Nixon a gifted speaker with a "buttery baritone" voice, and though not an orator, he was nonetheless a good speaker. His speeches did not include ornamental flourishes. Instead, Nixon considered his speeches a tool, even a weapon, to be used when solving problems.[22] Gavin also notes that one of Nixon's difficulties "was his inability to convey sincere emotion without appearing mawkish or, worse, deceitful," and that as his speechwriter, he helped Nixon overcome this deficiency in one key

---

[19] Einhorn, "The Ghost Talk: Personal Interviews with Three Former Speechwriters," 97.
[20] Ibid.
[21] Ibid., 97–98.
[22] William F. Gavin, "Source Material: His Heart's Abundance: Notes of a Nixon Speechwriter," *Presidential Studies Quarterly* 31 (2001), 358.

speech.[23] Knowing of Nixon's account of his childhood hearing a distant train at night as symbolic of big dreams about the world beyond his small town, Gavin wrote a passage describing a child laying in bed at night and listening to the sound of a distant train and a little boy—Nixon—dreaming "of faraway places he would like to go to." Nixon liked the passage and its rhetorical work that made him appear as possessing emotions as well.[24] The speechwriter dug into the speaker's biography to produce the narrative line that the speaker appreciated.

Beyond Nixon's appreciation for attaching some emotional appeals to his seemingly cold character, Gavin tells us, the president repeatedly requested his speechwriters that "the speeches needed anecdotes, little *parables*, something with *heart*."[25] Nixon sought to convince his speechwriters that he knew he was right in making this request and that anecdotes, parables, and writing for the heart are needed because they work and because they move people. Nixon reacted to his critics and in turn asked his speechwriters to prove them wrong. He also wanted short lines and something "meaty and quotable and should be material I can easily work into a stump speech, even if I am speaking outdoors without a podium … . Don't be cute or gimmicky—just hit hard with crisp one-liners whenever they are appropriate." Ever the fighting president, Nixon, Gavin opines, wanted "to make language do the job."[26] Nixon, then, had a limited view of speeches, whereby they were taken as means to political objectives and that words, and often words alone, could save the day.

On a very short notice, President Ronald Reagan had to address the nation shortly after the space shuttle *The Challenger* exploded seconds after takeoff. For the nationwide televised event, observed live on television by many and especially by school children seeing the first teacher go into space, the explosion was a horrible site. The exigency of the event necessitated a national address. Reagan had six hours to assemble a speechwriting team that would write a fitting address to the nation. One speechwriter, Peggy Noonan, wrote the initial draft, and for the most part, the final speech was heavily reliant on her writing. The early

---

[23] Gavin, "Source Material: His Heart's Abundance: Notes of a Nixon Speechwriter," 359.
[24] Ibid., 360.
[25] Ibid., 362.
[26] Ibid., 363.

discussion of the speech had Reagan suggest a "life must go on" theme but it was discarded and replaced with the need to comfort the nation and build the speech around the theme of space exploration as part of the nation's pioneering history and the frontier metaphor.[27] Noonan completed the first draft at 1:00 p.m. with a second draft submitted half an hour later and with only minor tweaking.[28] At 3:30 p.m., the speech was almost done with few added paragraphs including the one about Francis Drake, the early sea explorer, allowing for an analogy of one disaster with another. The important implications of this speechwriting case are that the usual speechwriting process, which in the Reagan White House took some six to seven days to construct, was compressed to six hours and yet the result was a first-class speech. Also important is the reality that the initial drafter of the speech can quickly lose control over the content of the speech, as was the case with Peggy Noonan who had to accommodate the input of others.[29] Crucially, Reagan had little input over the speech yet the speechwriter wrote a speech that for many was vintage Reagan. She understood him, his visions, and views as well as his style and ways of speaking and wrote a speech that sounded as if he was the one to write it.

Unlike Reagan, speechwriting in the Obama administration is described by the speechwriters as highly cooperative. The speechwriters worked closely with the president and the president, in turn, was highly involved in the speechwriting process.[30] The speechwriters went through "countless drafts and rewrites, late nights, and last-minute edits from the motorcade." Speechwriter Jon Favreau describes the September 9, 2009, address to a joint session of Congress on health care and centering on the line "What we face … is above all a moral issue; at stake are not just the details of policy, but fundamental principles of social justice and the character of our country." This was not the president's line, states Favreau, but that of Senator Ted Kennedy. The speech was conceived as necessary to rally support and it was timed to be delivered a week prior to the vote on it. While Favreau finalized the draft, President Obama

[27] Mary E. Stuckey, *Slipping the Surly Bonds: Reagan's Challenger Address* (College Station: Texas A&M Press, 2006), 61–63.

[28] Stuckey, *Slipping the Surly Bonds: Reagan's Challenger Address*, 67.

[29] Ibid., 80.

[30] https://medium.com/@ObamaWhiteHouse/in-review-president-obamas-top-speeches-as-chosen-by-his-speechwriters-712780fdd58e#.uzextgbde. Accessed March 21, 2017.

heavily edited the draft. Struggling to find a fitting end to the speech, Favreau was handed a letter written by Ted Kennedy to Obama after being told of his terminal illness. In it was the phrase "the character of our country," that "jumped out at me," and with that, he found the concluding phrasing. In the meantime, the President also noticed Kennedy's phrase and used it as inspiration for his own ending: "our ability to stand in other people's shoes; a recognition that we are all in this together, and when fortune turns against one of us, others are there to lend a helping hand." The happenstance of speechwriting cannot be discounted. Speechwriters often struggle with an entire speech or a portion of it and help and even inspiration can come for the least expected source.[31]

Another speechwriter, Terence Szuplat, assisted President Obama in writing the speech for the April 18, 2013, interfaith service for the victims of the Boston Bombing. Once the bombing occurred, the speechwriting team knew it would have to write a speech. The sermon-like speech began with the line "On Monday morning, the sun rose over Boston," painting the picture of how "a beautiful morning ... was shattered by the bombing." The president received the first draft the night before the service and worked on it and improved it. Among his editing input was the insertion of the biblical verse "God has not given us a spirit of fear and timidity," to function as the theme of the speech and added another biblical phrase, "run with endurance" as a bookend for the speech. Szuplat, a Bostonian himself, states that he wrote the speech not with the larger Boston community in mind but with the image of an uncle, also a Bostonian, who embodied the spirit of the city's defiance and pride. With this image in mind, the speechwriter wrote the line "If they sought to intimidate us, they picked the wrong city." After the speech was over, the unidentified uncle called his nephew to tell him that the president "did good." What we can take from this particular episode is how one person stood for the collective audience and how the concrete individual who embodied the character and spirit of an entire city was a sufficient image for the speechwriter's inspiration. Both the speechwriter and the president had a heavy hand in the writing of the speech and its final version was a fitting response to a particular event at a particular location and necessary for the success of the speech.[32]

[31] Ibid.
[32] Ibid.

Jeffrey Tulis in his seminal study on the Rhetorical Presidency notes that though every president has relied on ghostwriters to write their speeches, much has changed in the practice since the early days of the Republic and that today's speechwriters are tasked with the talent of translating "the political policies of others into persuasive prose."[33] Since the president can access the public directly and in great frequency, speechwriters have become indispensable with the need to produce speeches, articles, proclamations, and press releases. Yet, notes Tulis, most speeches are planned in advance and that the commitment to speak often precedes the actual content of the speech, whereby speechwriters write speeches to fit settings already selected, and looking for material or issues that fit the speech in question.[34] Tulis is also concerned with the increasing tendencies of speechwriters to encroach on policy issues. He tells the story of James Fallows, President Carter's head speechwriters who had to arbitrate between Secretary of State Cyrus Vance and National Security Advisor Zbigniew Brzezinski, and their respective draft statements on foreign policy, and when he advised the president that these differences could not be solved by rhetorical means, Carter simply "stapled the drafts together and delivered the speech."[35] Indeed, the key lesson here is that rhetoric is meant to assist in articulating a policy but it cannot salvage the incoherent or the under-developed policy. In short, realizing the limitations of speechwriting face and the potential obstacles presented by speakers is essential to understanding its functions and objectives.

Forms of Collaboration

As it is clear so far, speechwriting can be organized in many ways and take several forms of collaboration. The Speechwriter Susan Jones, who has worked for both political and corporate speakers, distinguishes between two models of speechwriting.[36] In the US *White House model*, "speechwriters tends to work on words already on paper, crafting and refining the president's speeches. The team is kept in seclusion. For reasons of

---

[33] Jeffrey Tulis, *The Rhetorical Presidency* (Princeton University Press, 1987), 184.
[34] Tulis, *The Rhetorical Presidency*, 184.
[35] Ibid., 185.
[36] Susan Jones, *Speechmaking: The Easy Guide to Writing and Giving Speeches. New Edition* (London: Politico's, 2008), 143.

security they may not be told the important parts of the speech." In the UK *Whitehall model*, producing speeches for cabinet ministers is mostly a collaborative process. It involves the minister, policy officials, press advisers, political advisers, and a speechwriter. The speechwriter functions primarily as one of the officials or advisers. The speechwriters are "closely involved with the speaker and the policy at all stages. They are as concerned with content and purpose as with style. They are anonymous. Many chief executives and directors in business and other non-government organizations are in a similar process."[37] The organization and forms of collaboration in the speechwriting of both Whitehall and the White House may vary, depending on the minister or the president. Some speakers prefer to work closely with one aide, others delegate to a speechwriting group, and yet others are dependent on, or obligated to, letting the speech go through the command line of cabinets and advisers. This is common for many ministerial departments and for a variety of US presidential speeches. We may call these three forms for the counselor, the group, and the line.

The counselor is an individual that is close to the speaker, often someone who has worked with the speaker for a while and who has established a strong relationship with the speaker. Ted Sorensen as John F. Kennedy's alter ego is such an example. The counselor and the speaker work closely and are hesitant to involve others equally much in the process. The counselor may also be a close aide but the duration of the work is limited as did Ray Moley who worked with Franklin D. Roosevelt on his First Inaugural Address for several months but left the White House shortly thereafter. In European ministries and departments, this model is relatively rare, where speechwriting generally involves a broad spectrum of advisers and bureaucrats. In political parties, however, especially in smaller parties, it is more common that the party leader has a trusted aide who works as designated speechwriter.[38]

The group. The more common speechwriting process has several individuals involved with the writing tasks, often providing the speaker with a final or near final product. Some speakers would engage in heavy editing, while other speakers would take a more minimal approach. While Franklin D. Roosevelt preferred the working of one individual on a given

---

[37] Ibid.
[38] Cf. Waade, *Med blanke ark og taleskriver til.*

speech, Barack Obama worked with a team of speechwriters, often with one speechwriter coordinating the work of a given speech.

While *the line* (see below) is the most traditional and common in speechwriting in European ministries and departments, the last decades have shown a rise in other ways of organizing the speechwriting process. One of those is *the group*. The Norwegian Ministry of Trade and Industry, for instance, changed the organization of the ministry in 2009 and established a communication and speechwriting group of three people (initially four). For each speech, one person from the group was appointed as the responsible coordinator and writer; however, other group members would also provide help and advice.

The line. As previously described, *the line* involves a process of many steps of input, revision, and approval from internal bodies in the ministry or organization. This kind of hierarchical and bureaucratic process, however, can also be found in some US presidential speeches. The annual State of the Union Address, for instance, proscribed in the Constitution, follows to a great degree the line feature of speechwriting. Here, the input of various cabinet secretaries and their respective units calls for individual input that reflects the work, objectives, and summaries of each governmental department. Once the disparate input is assembled, the speechwriter takes the input and "stitches" them together to ensure a coherent address. The work of speechwriters here is rather convoluted as style, and focus varies between different departments and their speechwriters, yet once all input is in, another speechwriter has to ensure the coherency and consistency.

The hired gun. While ministries, departments, political parties, and big organizations and corporations have employees, communication departments, and even designated speechwriters, other speakers and organizations will need to hire writers externally to help them compose and deliver their speeches. They may get assistance from communication companies or from individuals making a living as speechwriters.

In Denmark, the rhetoric consultancy company *Rhetor* has carried out an investigation of the speechwriting profession through 55 qualitative interviews.[39] They talked to speechwriters from ministerial departments, bureaucratic and political offices in municipalities, political

---

[39] Simone Brendstrup, *Taleskrivning i Danmark 2017: State of the Art* (Frederiksberg: Rhetor - rådgivende retorikere, 2017).

parties, and organizations and businesses. The report identifies six basic models for cooperation in speechwriting.

1. The duo: Speaker and one speechwriter work in close collaboration, similar to the model of *the counselor* mentioned above.
2. The dedicated speechwriter: One speechwriter is responsible for the speech and has access to the speaker.
3. The speechwriter team: Several speechwriters in a team distribute the responsibility among themselves and generally discuss and involve each other in all speeches. The team has access to the speaker. This is similar to the model of *the group* mentioned above.
4. The project: Collaboration across different offices, where several experts work together on the speech from beginning to end. One person in the project group functions as coordinator or chief responsible person. The group may or may not have access to the speaker.
5. The speech coordinator: One person has the responsibility of the speech and may revise it or work it through toward the end. However, the main writing is done by the experts (for instance in the divisions of a ministerial department). One variant of this is the speechwriter functioning as a consultant for the person in the bureaucracy responsible for writing the speech. Generally, the writer does not have access to the speaker, but the speech coordinator may have.
6. The standard bureaucracy: One speechwriter is responsible for speeches, which are ordered, written, and handed in. The speechwriter does not have access to the speaker.

Of course, there are many variants of these basic models. In some instances, several models are used at the same time, each fitting a given speech type.

Another distinction between forms of collaboration, especially in ministerial departments, is between the *speechwriter as writer* and the *speechwriter as editor*. When functioning as a writer, the speechwriter does the writing and only uses the experts, divisions, or civil servants as consultants. They provide input, information, and facts, and they comment on the text and propose revisions; however, they do not write in any substantial way. When the speechwriter functions as an editor, a selected person from the most relevant division or office in the organization will carry out the writing. The speechwriter then, does not write, but will mainly contribute relevant information about the speaker and improve the draft rhetorically, by revising during the work, and especially the finished draft.

The assessment of a particular form of collaboration between speechwriter and speaker ultimately depends on the quality of the speech and how effective it could be with the intended audience. Some speakers prefer to work with one speechwriter, while others prefer the work of several individuals before a speech is finalized and ready for the speaker's review. Some even prefer the work of two competing speechwriting teams so that they can select the best speech. Yet, some guidelines are possible nonetheless. When time pressure is the issue, the work of one speechwriter may be advantageous. A crucial speech, on the other hand, may benefit from the work of several speechwriters. Some speeches, by default, are the product of multiple departments such that they could benefit from the line of speechwriters, advisors, and civils servants. When comparing the various forms of collaboration, we believe that for a given speaking situation, one key or central speechwriter ought to function as the individual who is most familiar with the speaker, who organizes the work of other speechwriters, and who finalizes the speech and gets it ready for the speaker review and final editing.

The central idea advanced here is that familiarity with the speaker is essential and that one speechwriter who knows the speaker is in the best position not only to write the fitting speech but also to advise the speaker about position, phrasing, and warranted advocacies.

CHAPTER 8

Characterizing the Speaker

It is a public secret that many speakers are aided by professional speechwriters. Even so, the speech must always appear to be the speaker's own. A speech is a performance, but it is a performance of what must appear to be the speaker's own words and ideas. After all, public speaking is not a drama, nor is it any other work of fiction. It is a rhetorical act aimed at influencing individuals and inducing action in the social world, and the public rightly holds speakers responsible for the words they utter. This chapter is devoted to the craft of *characterizing the speaker plausibly*. After having defined this particular aspect of speechwriting, we introduce a method for creating a believable character.

Offhand, writing speeches for others seems to differ little from speechwriting in general; the tasks of choosing apt words and finding the most persuasive arguments are common to all branches of rhetorical composition. However, when writing a speech for someone else, the speechwriter must also consider how the speech reflects the speaker's personality. In contemporary rhetorical theories, this is sometimes referred to as characterization. In ancient rhetoric, the term was *ethopoeia*—an aspect of rhetorical composition that is singular to the practice of logography.

Ethopoeia is a combination of the Greek words *ethos* (character) and *poiein* (to make) meaning character making.[1] Although related to the

---

[1] Kristine S. Bruss, "Ghosting Authenticity: Characterization in Corporate Speechwriting," *Journal of Business and Technical Communication* 25, no. 2 (2011), 159–182, 160.

more familiar rhetorical concept *ethos*, it must also be distinguished from it. While ethos is tied to persuasion and the creation of a favorable impression of the speaker through the display of wisdom, virtue, and goodwill, *ethopoeia* is a creation of character suitable to the speaking person. *Ethopoeia* is sometimes described as the creation of dramatic character, which means that the speechwriter will have, if not to weave into the speech the actual character of the speaker—then at least keep him from saying things that are completely foreign to him.[2]

The device known as *ethopoeia* is not just another aspect of rhetorical composition. The concern for characterizing the speaker's personality pervades the entire speechwriting process, and it influences the speech as a whole, especially its style, argumentation, and orality, anticipating and obliging the rhetorical delivery. Instead of searching for good arguments and vivid language, the speechwriter needs to consider these qualities in an individual light: How does *this* speaker tend to argue? What is the style of *this* particular speaker? What is the voice and body language of *this* speaker? How can the speechwriter's manuscript facilitate a persuasive rhetorical delivery? To constitute the speaker's character plausibility, the speechwriter must take a more personalized approach.

Believable Characterization

In order to write a speech that fits the speaker, the speechwriter needs to get to know the speaker and become familiar with her voice and gesture, way of building up sentences, style of language, and sense of humor. The speechwriter should also be acquainted with the speaker's public persona—the strategic image of the person, constructed over a long period. Yet for several reasons, characterization is not reached through an idea of authentic representation of the speaker's personality. First of all, authenticity is based on a notion of identity as whole and stable—a notion defined by the main stream of rhetorical and cultural theories over the last 40 years. Today, we usually consider human identity to be in some way dynamic, fluctuating, and formed by social and discursive processes. Thus, striving to represent a speaker's true personality in language would be futile.

On a more pragmatic note, representations of the speaker's character are available in observing previous speeches, which ought to be studied

---

[2] George Kennedy, *The Art of Persuasion in Greece* (Princeton, NJ: Princeton University Press, 1963), 92.

in order to uphold a dialogue with earlier representations of character. However, if the speaker is a public figure, earlier speeches have probably also been written by speechwriters. The inscribed character in these speeches is therefore to be considered a rhetorical construct based on a negotiation between speaker, political advisers, and speechwriters. Thus, the new speechwriter often meets his rhetor through the eyes and pen of others.

Finally, *ethopoeia*, the fitting description of the speaker's character, needs to be balanced against other needs. Most importantly, the speechwriter should never lose sight of writing a speech with the power to influence an audience. Even if the speechwriter comes to know the speaker as a dull pedant, and that person is very well represented in her long-winded and tedious speeches, it will, of course, be rhetorically unwise simply to reproduce such a boring persona. After all, persuasion is a tenacious goal of rhetoric, and the speechwriter should always aim at making the speaker appear most favorable in their rhetorical acts.

For these reasons, authentic representation of the speaker's true self is not to be considered the goal of rhetorical characterization. It seems more productive to view character making as a rhetorical construct dynamically formed by the speaker's own input, political advice, the speechwriter's suggestions, and narratives shared by the audience. Viewed in this light, it will be possible for the speechwriter to draw on the speaker's usual speaking style without fully reproducing it. While the speech must plausibly appear as to be the speaker's, the speechwriter is allowed to interpret and improve. As the following example shows, the speechwriter often needs to balance multiple considerations.

For her exam in a speechwriting course, a student was asked to write the bishop's speech for the occasion of the Danish queen's annual New Year's reception. The overall purpose of this ceremonial address was on behalf of the Danish bishops to wish the royal family a happy new year. The bishop was well versed in manuscript writing and public speaking, and because of his seniority, he had been writing the speech for the last five years. Having studied his previous speeches, the student, however, noticed that some of the distinctive features of the bishop's style were not entirely desirable. For instance, he had a tendency to compose rather long and complicated sentences that he had difficulties in delivering. Also, his frequent quotations from the Bible as well as works of fiction, and poetry, books that he contended had shaped who he was seemed excessive (in a speech delivered the previous year, he managed to refer to no less than Shakespeare, H.C. Andersen, and the Nobel-prize winning author Henrik Pontoppidan in 6 lines!). When the student wrote her speech for the bishop, she was careful to preserve the distinctive features of his style, but she also made some adjustments. In order to improve his oral delivery, she maintained a varied length of sentences, but avoided abstruse syntax. She made two references to kindred spirits of the bishop, and in order to strengthen the unity of ideas, she made a direct connection between the two.[3] In this case, it would not be expedient for the speechwriter simply to imitate the speaker's earlier speeches. Rather, the example shows that while paying with regard to the speaker's usual speaking style and the speaker's sense of how his style reflects his personality, the speechwriter manages to enhance a rhetorical focus on unity, clarity, and oral style.

In particular, the speechwriter must be careful to obtain some consistency in the speaker's voice. It may stain a speaker's credibility if her speaking style moves in opposite directions. Often a formal speech is succeeded by questions from the audience and the press, and in these situations, it is important that the speaker does not acquire two different personae when delivering the speech and improvising later on. Similarly, a speechwriter must make sure that a public person speaks consistently in different situations. Neglect of consistency in a speaker's delivery may turn out unfavorably. Indeed, John F. Kennedy's inclination to speak in a base style on less formal occasions drew unfortunate attention to the fact that the magniloquence of his public addresses was crafted by professional speechwriters.[4]

ETHOPOEIA IN ANCIENT RHETORIC

Classical rhetorical theories built the description of character on social typologies such as family, profession, native town, and age. His lot in life and social experience determined a speaker's style. As Aristotle argues, a rustic and an educated person would not speak in the same manner.[5] Similarly, on the rhetorical exercise in *ethopoeia*, Hermogenes advises his

---

[3] Jannie Damkjær Jensen, "Taleskrivning til Aarhus' biskop Kjeld Holm. Tale til nytårskur på Christiansborg Slot d. 7. Januar 2015," Unpublished assignment, Aarhus Universitet.

[4] Kathleen Hall Jamieson, *Eloquence in an Electronic Age: The Transformation of Political Speechmaking* (Oxford: Oxford University Press, 1988), 177.

[5] Aristotle, *Rhetoric* 3.7.6–7.

students to "preserve what is distinctive and appropriate to the persons imagined as speaking and to the occasions; for the speech of a young man differs from that of an old man, and that of one who rejoices from that of one who grieves."[6] In ancient Greece, speechwriting was primarily rooted in the court system relying on the initiative of the ordinary citizens, as there was no public counsel for the prosecution. In contrast to Roman citizens, represented by lawyers at court, Greek citizens were supposed to conduct their own cases in front of the judges. They were, however, allowed to share their speaking time with a friend or a relative, and it was accepted to consult a *logografos*: a speechwriter who helped the clients think out the arguments and write the speech. In many cases, he also practiced with the client to ensure a persuasive rhetorical delivery during the court procedure.

Lysias' speechwriting is often highlighted in the history of rhetoric by classical as well as modern rhetoricians.[7] Dionysius of Halicarnassus, for instance, characterizes Lysias in this way: "He often makes us believe in his client's good character by referring to the circumstances of his life and his parentage, and often again by describing his past actions and the principles governing them. And when the facts fail to provide him with such material, he creates his own moral tone, making his character seem by their speech to be trustworthy and honest."[8] George A. Kennedy accentuates Lysias' two great contributions to Greek oratory: the prose style and his ethopoeia that differed from the trite and stereotyped techniques recommended in the contemporary handbooks.

Lysias wrote judicial speeches for Athenian citizens involved in cases conducted at the people's court or at the council of Areopagus, a kind of senate that passed sentence in case of homicide on Athenian citizens. The *ethopoeia* of Lysias' speeches stands out because of uniqueness and subtle rhetorical strategy: Lysias was able to characterize his speaker as an individual personality who at the same time could be considered persuasive by the judges during the court procedures. The defense speech *Against Eratosthenes*, delivered by the Athenian citizen Eufiletos, is an illustrative example. Eufiletos had caught his wife's lover Eratosthenes in her

---

[6]G.A. Kennedy (trans.), *Progymnasmata: Greek Textbooks of Prose and Composition* (Atlanta: Society of Biblical Literature, 2003), 85.

[7]See, for instance George A. Kennedy, *A New History of Classical Rhetoric* (Princeton, NJ: Princeton Paperbacks, 1994), 65.

[8]Bruss, 174.

bedroom and killed him. According to the Athenian law on adultery, this was a legal punishment of an adulterer who was caught in the act. The relatives of Eratosthenes, however, accused Eufiletos of having thought out a cunning plan. They suspected that Eufiletos had another motive for the murder, and that he merely used his wife to entrap Eratosthenes. The character description of Eufiletos, primarily embodied in the *narratio*, is crucial to the defense.[9] Lysias makes Eufiletos speak in an ordinary and simple way employing the rhetorical figure *polysyndeton*, where conjunctions such as "and" and "or" are used in closed succession, thus creating an image of Eufiletos as credulous and harmless. He is represented as a thoughtful husband handing over the lower floor to his wife to ease her nursing of their newborn child. However, overlooking signs of his wife's infidelity for quite a long time makes him appear naïve and easy to deceive. Direct speech, *sermocinatio*, and dramatic presence add drama to the chronological development and ensure the judges' attentiveness. The rhetorical effect of the *narratio* seems obvious: A man like Eufiletos would never plot and play such an underhand game.

CHARACTERIZATION IN CONTEMPORARY RHETORIC

Today, it is a common practice for speechwriters to have an individualized take on the notion of characterization. Rhetorical critics sometimes resort to the metaphor of *customization* in order to explain how style and arguments must be made to fit the individual speaker. More frequent still, rhetorical critics have used the saying "style is the man" to express the idea that the style of the speech should reflect the speaker in his unique personality.[10]

In the following, we present a method of characterization. The method is based on the notion that character formation depends both on a careful study of the speaker's usual language, voice, and body language, *and* is a constitutive act negotiating existing perceptions of speaker and audience aiming at producing persuasive rhetoric.[11]

[9] *Lysias' Taler*. Translated and commented by Mogens Herman Hansen (Museum Tusculanums forlag), 27–36.

[10] The saying alludes to Comte de Buffon's dictum from 1753 "Le style est l'homme même." Marie Lund, "Taleskrivning og stil," *Rhetorica Scandinavica* 64 (2013), 25–39; Marie Lund, *An Argument on Rhetorical Style* (Aarhus: Aarhus University Press, 2017), 37–38.

[11] Our method is a revised version of a model offered by the American speechwriter for business leaders Alan Perlman. Kristine S. Bruss, "Ghosting Authenticity." Alan Perlman, *Writing Great Speeches: Professional Techniques You Can Use* (Boston, MA: Allyn & Bacon, 1998).

We suggest that the four topics of analysis: style, argumentation, intellectual horizon, and physical capacity, are not approached as a process in four steps, but are considered facets that sometimes overlap and all contribute to nuance and sensitivity in the portrayal of character.

STYLE

Style refers to the speaker's distinctive way of using language, for instance a certain fondness of particular words or a preferred way of constructing sentences. To observe distinctiveness in language and style, the speechwriter must either study the speaker's earlier speeches or encounter the speaker in person. The speechwriter must observe the speaker's syntactical preferences: Does she speak in long or short sentences? Does she usually have a varied sentence length? Other peculiar features must be outlined as well: Does she have a large vocabulary? Does she use technical terms? Or, are there any expressions that she seems particularly fond of? The purpose of this analysis is to concretize the speaker's individual style and to the extent that it is advantageous to imitate or to draw on it in future characterization of the speaker.

However, constructing a personal style has other functions than just suggesting the speaker's authorship and ownership. A more general stylistic aim of characterization is to make the speaker appear human. To this end, classical rhetorical sources recommend a style that is clear, precise, and vivid, whereas modern rhetorical criticism has provided a more specialized repertoire of "conversational style." In her study of Ronald Reagan's rhetoric, Kathleen Hall Jamieson outlines the features of a conversational style that has the formal characteristics of everyday speaking: a relaxed vocabulary, colloquial expressions, dead metaphors, truisms, simple syntax, loosely constructed sentences, and an avoidance of subordinate clauses.[12]

Similar strategies are employed by professional speechwriter Alan Perlman for creating the personal style that he favors in his speeches, such as liberal references to the speakers and their listeners in first- and second-person pronouns ("I", "you"), informal sounding contractions ("You're"), simple syntax, conjunctions at the beginning of sentences ("And so I thought I might help you..."), and colloquial expressions.

---

[12] Jamieson, *Eloquence in an Electronic Age*, 166, 172.

In Perelman's view, these traces of everyday conversations add "listenability" to a speech and enhance a sense of relationship between speakers and audience.

The rapprochement to everyday conversation prevents the speechwriter from producing what Perlman calls "speech speech," a term for phrases that exist in political speeches, but nowhere else, for instance "We must," and "Our challenge in the twenty-first century is," etc.[13] Mechanical and worn out expressions are useful reminder to the speechwriter of the need to avoid clichés that make the speaker appear stiff and detached.

Argumentation

By argumentation, we refer to the rhetorical techniques that speakers use to prove and support claims. In order to identify the speaker's preferred way of arguing, the speechwriter must understand the speaker's argumentative stance. Does the speaker present her argument explicitly? Does she appeal to values that are already shared by the audience? Or, does she like to make her point by provoking her listeners? The speechwriter must observe how the speaker provides backings to her claims. Does she present her audience with quality supportive material? Perhaps, it is a distinctive feature of the speaker that she often refers to experts or authorities. Or perhaps, she uses facts, numbers, and statistics to prove her point. She may also inductively enable her audience to draw the conclusion.

Furthermore, the speechwriter must pay attention to the way the speaker gets her points across. When she needs to explain abstract issues, does she use metaphors? When she wants to illustrate something, does she use examples or prefers an anecdote? Does she have a sense of humor? Would she be comfortable telling a story with an emotive appeal? Would she disclose things about herself and draw on her own personal experience?

In order to provide the speaker with a manuscript that makes her argue persuasively, the speechwriter must consider how arguments and appeals match the speaker's personal abilities. After all, not all speakers can tell a joke. And if some of the people in the audience know the speaker or have heard her make a public appearance, the speechwriter must also try to adapt to their expectations.

---

[13] Ibid., 176.

Intellectual Horizon

To write about issues and topics that are appropriate for the speaker to talk about, the speechwriter must have a sense of the speaker's intellectual horizon. The speechwriter needs information about the speaker's education, interests, and reading habits. He needs access to the speaker's cultural, historical, political, philosophical, and religious repertoires. However, the aim of the analysis is not so much to display the speaker's actual knowledge, as it is to interpret it. The speechwriter wants to get a sense of what the speaker could plausibly talk about. If the speaker is known for quoting Winston Churchill, he could also make her refer to Kennedy's speeches as well. If the speaker has read a biography of Margaret Thatcher, the speechwriter could also quote a passage from Germany's Chancellor, Angela Merkel' biography.

References to poetry, music, science, historical events, or political biographies may be used actively in the character making of the speaker. A speaker's ample display of knowledge about hip hop lyrics and recent Internet controversies suggests that the speaker is a person up to date with popular culture and the media landscape. Quotations from the great works of literature and philosophy may portray the speaker as a knowing and sensitive mind. A speaker, whose speech has a recurring motif of scientific landmarks, appears inquisitive and innovative.

Constructions of knowledge can also prove too bold. When the Danish Prime Minister Helle Thorning-Schmidt presented a political reform of the public school system, she spoke with great enthusiasm about the practical use of Pythagoras' theorem.[14] Media bantering soon revealed that her knowledge of the theorem was limited to the example she applied; besides measuring out the right angles when building a bird table, she could say nothing else about the formula. Early in his career as a speechwriter for Kennedy, Ted Sorensen wrote an article in the Harvard alumni magazine about the famous Widener Library, about "gazing at the Library while walking across the Harvard campus," only to learn later what every Harvard graduate knows: At Harvard, the campus is called "the Yard."[15] Some topics are so dear and close to the speaker that a speechwriter must be aware of them. For example, when President

---

[14] Helle Thorning-Schmidt: Opening Address 2012.

[15] Ted Sorensen, *Counselor: A Life at the Edge of History* (New York, NY: Harper, 2008), 134.

Obama addressed the need for greater control over the sales of guns on January 5, 2016, he was emotional and shed tears, reminding the American people of how he feels about young people gunned down in his hometown of Chicago.

PHYSICAL AND PSYCHOLOGICAL CAPACITY

When portraying character, it is important for the speechwriter to assess the speaker's voice and body language. The writing process is facilitated if the speechwriter is able to meet with, interview, and observe the speaker's communication.

It is, for instance, important to be able to measure the speaker's breathing capacity, so that sentence length can be individually adjusted. Some speakers suffer from asthma and are only able to deliver relatively short sentences. If the phrases are too long, the last syllables will be stated with an overstrained voice without sufficient sound, which has a negative impact on the representation of character, and the speaker might start feeling uncomfortable and dizzy because of over-exertion. Furthermore, the speech may not audible to all in the audience. Speakers with vocal experience (e.g., studying drama or singing) will on the other hand often be able to support longer phrases. To oblige the vocal potentials of these clients, the speechwriter may use a broader style and include, for instance, quotations from favorite writers in order to create a poetic and literary persona.

If the speaker has an accent or a dialect, it might be used deliberately as part of the portrait. In the introduction to Bill Clinton's speech in Church of God in Christ, Memphis 1993, his southern dialect, which seemed to be enforced in his rhetorical delivery, helped to create *consubstantiality* with his concrete audience—a concept which was introduced by Kenneth Burke describing the process of identification.[16] Moreover, a dialogue between form and content was made, when Clinton, for instance, paid tribute during a barbeque for a local bishop. In that way,

---

[16] Kenneth Burke defines consubstantiality in this way: "To identify A with B is to make A "consubstantial" with B. Accordingly, since our *Grammar of Motives* was constructed about "substance" as key term, the related rhetoric selects its nearest equivalent in the areas of persuasion and dissuasion, communication and polemic." See, Kenneth Burke, *A Rhetoric of Motives* (Berkeley: University of California Press, 1969), 21.

he succeeded in showing the people of Memphis that he identified with them, at the semantic as well as the performative level, which is clear from the audience's enthusiastic, oral response.[17]

If the speaker has an extrovert personality and a vivid body language, the speechwriter may suggest obvious performative actions in square brackets to amplify her character: [Now leave the rostrum and approach the audience. Look at them and pause to increase suspense when having asked the rhetorical question. The story about your parents is then delivered by heart.] If the speaker, on the contrary, is introvert and uses few gestures, it is important to match her delivery as well. For instance, one should avoid a long, humoristic passages relying on a vocal dialogue with the audience. However, an introvert speaker may feel comfortable with arch and subtle humor making the audience smile or laugh silently. A way to oblige introversion and modest body language is to enrich the manuscript with figures of style, such as alliterations and anaphors, memorable metaphors, and *evidentia*; creating inner pictures though vivid appeals to the senses. In that way, a reserved speaker can still be perceived as charismatic and colorful.

INTERVIEW QUESTIONS FOR SPEECHES AND FOR SPEAKER PROFILES

Getting a sense of the character of the speaker and gathering material for a speech can be acquired by interviewing the speaker. Such interviewing can be aimed at both a specific speech and the development of a more general profile of the speaker's character and rhetorical profile.

When interviewing the speaker at the beginning of a specific speechwriting process, directed questions may help the speechwriter profile the speaker[18]:

- What is the speech about? What is your position on the issue?
- Why is it important? Can you be more specific?
- What do you enjoy doing in your spare time?
- What books have you read lately?
- What books (or movies) have made the greatest impression on you?

---

[17] The speech can be heard at youtube: https://youtu.be/bpnAJdztWOo.
[18] Thanks to journalist Anne Eisenberg for tips on interview techniques.

- What are your top three values?
- How did your childhood community influence the person you are today?

Avoid asking speakers explicitly how they argue and use language. Many speakers will have difficulties answering these questions in a way that would be useful to the speechwriting process. Instead, ask the speaker's permission to record the interview in addition to studying the speaker's earlier speeches and recordings of oral performances. If anything else fails, you must observe while doing the interview.

- Observe *how* the speaker talks.
- Observe the speaker's way of arguing and reasoning.

Most of these questions are also relevant when developing a speechwriter's guide to the speaker. Such a guide, also called a *speaker profile*,[19] can be developed as an internal document, a booklet, or an online resource that provides any writer with access to an understanding of the speaker's character, life experience, and rhetorical style. Instead of going through the process of interviewing before every speech, the *speaker profile* can be consulted. Such a profile is especially valuable if a speechwriter will be writing several speeches for the same speaker, or if several or different people are engaged in writing speeches for the same person. Any organization, company, party, or ministerial department where a leader gives many speeches will benefit from a speaker profile. Interviewing is a central task when developing the profile. Such interviewing will ask questions like the ones mentioned above (see other similar questions in Chapter 11, "Determining the Proper Style and Delivery"). Other questions could be about the speaker's attitude toward speechmaking and about speakers that she or he admires or dislikes. The interests, leisure activities, and cultural preferences of the speaker should be explored and noted. Does she enjoy opera or country music? Or both? What does she read? Or is she not fond of reading and prefer tennis instead? Knowledge of such interests and inclinations—cultural or otherwise—can be written

---

[19] The Danish rhetoric and speechwriting agency, *Rhetor*, for instance, develops such guides for their clients. See Simone Brendstrup, *Taleskrivning i Danmark: State of the Art 2017* (Speechwriting in Denmark: State of the Art 2017) (Fredriksberg: Rhetor - rådgivende retorikere, 2017), 23.

into the speaker profile and form a wide range of different sources that speechwriters can draw upon in their work. Besides interviewing a speaker, the profile can be developed through rhetorical analysis of audio and video recordings or of texts and manuscripts written by the speaker.

A good speaker profile will be constantly developed and kept up to date. New material, sources, and insights will be added, some might be removed. If a childhood story has already been used, it should be noted in the profile, so that the same material will not be reused in an inexpedient way.

To sum up: In order to characterize a speaker plausibly, a speechwriter has to know the speaker's private as well as the speaker's public persona. Characterization is based on the speechwriter's rhetorical research including interview, observation, and the study of former speeches, but it is also a dynamic act allowing the speechwriter to balance considerations of expedience with the speaker's own input, political advice, and expectations of the audience. Characterization is successful when it is easy for the speaker to make the speech her own during the rhetorical delivery. When her general oral communication—such as her improvisation and her dialogue with the audience after the speech—is similar to the prepared speech, then the speechwriter has grasped the speaker's character and strengthen her credibility.

CHAPTER 9

Writing for the Ear

Modern communication technologies have given rise to a new oral era.[1] The increased interest in public speaking and speechwriting as well as the more accepting and pragmatic attitude toward the field of communication can be observed in scholarly as well as in public discourse.[2] When characterizing modern speechwriting one realizes that orality and literacy are intertwined from the very beginning of the communicative process. Sometimes oral and written aspects are present simultaneously.

ORALITY AND LITERACY IN CONTEMPORARY SPEECHWRITING

Like the ancient ghostwriters (logographers), modern speechwriters still have to be able to *write* in a way that anticipates oral encounters between speakers and audiences in concrete situations, just as composers and playwrights do. They have to formulate speeches so that they will persuasively display themselves as a series of sounds in the present moment of the delivery in front of audiences who primarily perceive aurally. Listeners are constrained by the elusiveness of sound and will need a

---

[1] Walter J. Ong, *The Presence of the Word: Some Prolegomena for Cultural and Religious History* (New Haven: Yale University Press, 2002), 88; and Joshua Gunn, "Speech Is Dead; Long Live Speech," *Quarterly Journal of Speech* 94, no. 3 (2008), 344.

[2] In the preface of his book *Speechwright* (Michigan State University Press, 2011), William F. Gavin argues that the argument that hiring speechwriters is wrong, perhaps even immoral, is not made so much anymore (xii).

speechwriter's help to *stay attentive* and *remember* the speech thanks to clear structure, relatively short sentences with variation in length, and a simple syntax. Different types of repetitions, memorable stylistic features, and concrete examples will also ease the process of perception.

When sound waves reach the listener's ears, these listeners are directly confronted with the speaker both in a physiological and in a psychological sense. They meet, for instance, the *grain* of the speaker's voice, a concept introduced by Roland Barthes and defined as "the materiality of the body."[3] The listeners aurally sense the vibrations of the speaker's vocal cords, cartilages, bones, cavities, velum, tongue, and lips. According to Barthes, who introduced the concept *grain* in the context of classical singing, note that some voices have more grain than others, with Barthes preferring aesthetic performances with much grain.[4]

The listener's perception of the speaker's voice also unveils that speaker's mood and affections.[5] A voice can exceed the meaning of speech[6]: a voice is an expression of the speaker's whole life, experience, and current psychological state, often unveiled through *paralingual features*—aspects of the sounding voice that tend *not* to be transcribed when orality is transformed into literacy.[7] They include, for instance, respiration capacity, resonance, hoarseness, breathiness, vocal fry, and tension. These factors are highly important for the speechwriter to identify when seeking to accommodate the individual voice and its psychology in order to write for it in an adequate manner. Thus, to help a speaker make a speech her own, a speechwriter must aim at grasping the physiology as well as the psychology of the voice.

Basically, vocal sounds are air blasts made up by vibrations of the speaker's vocal cords. They hit the listener's tympanic membranes,

---

[3] In the article "The Grain of the Voice" [1972, 1977], which deals with the sensuous perception of classical singing, Roland Barthes introduces the concept *grain*: "The 'grain' is the body in the voice as it sings, the hand as it writes, the limb as it performs." See, *The Twentieth-Century Performance Reader*. Edited by Michael Huxley and Noel Witts. Routledge and New York. 1996, 54.

[4] Barthes, 50.

[5] Walter Ong, "Word as Sound," *Landmark Essays on Voice and Writing* (Hermagoras Press, 1994), 22.

[6] Joshua Gunn, "Speech Is Dead; Long Live Speech," *Quarterly Journal of Speech* 94, no. 3 (August 2008), 353.

[7] Richard Bauman, *Verbal Art as Performance* (Long Grove: Waveland Press, Inc., 1977), 19.

which start to vibrate, creating an energy that is first transformed into fluid energy in the inner ear, then into electric impulses in the ear cells of the inner ear, and then into nerve impulses of the acoustic nerve. These impulses are interpreted as vowels, semivowels, and consonants in the auditory and speech center in the brain's temporal fossa, constituting phonemes, syllables, and finally words and sentences.

During delivery, a speech is immediately reinforced by the acoustics of the concrete space. Moreover, the speaker's voice is simultaneously mixed with spatial sounds from the room and the present listeners, such as noise from the ventilation system, whispering, and coughing, actions that are taking place at the same time in the middle of the actual situation.[8] High sound level affects the speaker, who automatically raises his voice as an instinctive response. The speechwriter may have to simplify the speech and add performative advice in the manuscript if the situation is very noisy. This way, the speaker is prepared and able to respond deliberately to the situational constraints by using a slow tempo, precise enunciation, powerful dynamics, and pauses.

One should not forget, however, that delivery both aims at oral as well as *visual* perception. The audience watches the speaker and the body language accompanying the speech. Moreover, the speech may include *visual* material such as: (1) PowerPoint slides including text, graphical illustrations, and pictures and (2) handouts, often prepared by the speechwriter in connection with the manuscript.

Contemporary public speaking is, moreover, often recorded and broadcast on radio, television, or uploaded on the Internet, thereby attracting, sometimes simultaneously, a new, more distant, audience, who, like readers, are able to leaf through the discourse and rewind, review, and re-listen. In contrast to a present audience, a mediated audience might be able to observe the speaker in a close-up recording that unveils details of the performance, such as facial expressions, which the present audience is not able to see. However, an "authentic" transmission might also be chosen with cameras focusing on the situation as a whole as well as on the speaker's interaction with her audience—a parallel to live music recordings, where one also experiences the musician's dialogue with the audience.

---

[8]Walter Ong, "Word as Sound," 20–29.

"Video orality," then, has achieved *permanence*—originally a literary characteristic. On YouTube sound does not only exist when "going out of existence."[9] Watching and listening to a video-recorded speech therefore also promotes an observer's approach, thorough study, and analysis. Of course, evanescence and connection to the "real time" still mark the original rhetorical delivery in front of the present listeners, but the video recording may still influence the rhetorical choices of the speechwriter: When an Internet audience can watch a speech repeatedly, she might, for instance, choose not to use quite as many repetitions. However, repetitions help the listeners in the concrete situation, who experience the speech in the present moment of the delivery. The speechwriter and the speaker will therefore have to weigh pros and cons when deciding on a rhetorical strategy to accommodate the different audiences.

When the speech has been delivered, it may be uploaded on a home page or printed, e.g., in a newspaper as a *written speech*. The printed text might be based either on the speechwriter's manuscript or on a transcript of the rhetorical delivery. This way, the speech can be read, analyzed meticulously for topoi, argumentation, structure, and stylistic choices, unlike the listeners, who could discern some but not all of the intricate features of the speech. Consequently, a speechwriter sometimes prepares two manuscripts based on his knowledge on orality and literacy: the first aiming at the real-time rhetorical delivery and the latter aimed at the newspaper or the home page. Finally, the speech, or parts of it, may be shared as a text, sound file, or video. Passages of it may also be shown on television and quotations might be printed or brought in written media such as newspapers.

Modern speechwriting responds to complex situations, both oral and written, or a hybrid of the two. However, we argue that it still makes sense to maintain a separating line between orality and literacy when approaching speechwriting, both as a theoretical and as a practical topic; a position that is not to be interpreted as a nostalgic apology for oral speech. Our instances are pragmatic; profound knowledge of the ontology of orality as well as literacy helps speechwriters analyze individual rhetorical situations and may be used as a guideline especially when a situation is marked by *both* oral and written aspects. A speechwriter has to decide, for instance, how to target and prioritize specific

---

[9]Walter Ong, *Orality and Literacy. The Technologizing of the Word* [1982] (Routledge, London and New York, 1996), 71.

points when addressing different audiences of a speech. Is the rhetorical delivery aimed at the present listeners? Or is it to be considered a radio speech without appeal to sight? Or is it a video speech, primarily aiming at Internet audiences more distant in both time and space?

Archetypical differences between orality and literacy are:

Orality	Literacy
Speech is perceived by the ear	Text is perceived by the eye
When you listen to a speech, you are restrained by the limitations of *time*. Sound occurs in a present moment and disappears at once	Texts are material and have *permanence*. They can be read and re-read
As a listener, you primarily focus on understanding an utterance and interpreting it	As a reader, you can *re-read*, which promotes critical analysis
There are certain limits on both the performer and the audience's *memory span* in an oral situation	The written text promotes memorability because texts can be *preserved*
Oral artifacts, for instance political speeches and storytelling, are closely connected to a *concrete* situation where the speaker normally is directly confronted with an audience	Texts are not in the same way connected to a concrete situation. It is therefore often *uncertain* who is going to read a text and when it will be read
It is difficult to avoid sound artifacts. Sound waves often reach a receiver even though his attention is kept by something else	Visual artifacts call for a direct contemplation of the receiver
Speech is closely tied to the speaker and his *voice* and *body*	Texts *exist in themselves*
A speech is an act that *happens*	A text *is* because it is written down

Oral Perception and Memorability

If abstract theory stands alone without being concretized through examples, it will probably not be remembered, nor will highly concentrated presentation of a problem and sentences with complicated grammatical structures. A manuscript with the density of a stock cube not only has a negative impact on the listener's perception and memory span but also affects the rhetorical delivery of the speaker, who will have to use much energy reading and interpreting the prose and not have energy left for eye contact with the audience. Moreover, an overly compact manuscript might cause a monotonous delivery without gestures, and a restrained respiration.

If a listener's aural understanding is facilitated, on the other hand, it is possible to understand and remember speeches with many layers and nuances. Thus, a full manuscript should use relatively short sentences with marked rhythms, promoting the vocal delivery, and preferably use sentence constructions with active verbs. The speech should have a logical structure and not include too many parts and examples and narratives should be included to promote the listener's understanding of theoretical passages. An oral manuscript that is easy to overview and deliver also helps the speaker stay in contact with his listeners and support his argumentation with gestures and pauses. Maybe she might even dare to improvise parts of the speech since the clear structure makes it easier to return to the manuscript after the improvised bits.

Writing to Remember

Below are two illustrative examples of manuscripts facilitating memorability as well as persuasive rhetorical delivery. The first example is from the introduction to "A Whisper of AIDS. Address to the Republican Convention" delivered by Mary Fisher in Houston, 1992:

> I bear a message of challenge, not self-congratulation. I want your attention, not your applause. I would never have asked to be HIV-positive. But I believe that in all things there is a good purpose, and so I stand before you and before the nation, gladly.[10]

The sentences are relatively short and marked by active verbs in first person, present tense: "I bear," "I want," "I believe," and "I stand." The first two sentences are also characterized by antithetical nouns: "challenge"/"self-congratulation" and "attention"/"applause," adding a marked rhythm to the delivery. It seems obvious to read them aloud with pauses before "not" before the second noun and then emphasize "not" with a stress, to underline the contrast[11]:

> I bear a message of challenge, [pause] not self-congratulation. I want your attention, [pause] not your applause.

---

[10] http://www.americanrhetoric.com/speeches/maryfisher1992rnc.html.
[11] The delivery of the speech is uploaded on youtube.com: https://youtu.be/zB5K9k__SOo.

The second example is taken from the opening speech, 2012, delivered in the Danish Parliament by Prime Minister Helle Thorning-Schmidt. This part of the manuscript promotes both memorability and a persuasive rhetorical delivery:

> My vision – and the vision of the Government – is a public school where all children are learning more. All children. A school where order is maintained throughout classes. Where the kids are doing fine and are eager to study. Where they develop their personality and are becoming engaged participants in a living democracy. A public school where the teachers use their great knowledge about their subject and use the best teaching methods, and where they are treated with respect and trust.[12]

The periods are relatively short without deep hypotaxis, which promotes a good rhythm and a suitable respiration. Like in Fisher's speech, most verbs are active and in the present tense: "learn" (lærer), "develop" (udvikler), "use" (bruger), etc. The sentence which stands alone: "All children" (Alle børn) promotes a performative framing with pauses before and after the utterance and with a stress on "All" (Alle): [pause] Alle børn [pause]. The anaphor "where" (hvor) binds the passage together and advances the temporal and dynamic energy of the rhetorical delivery forming a crescendo. The anaphorical part might be interpreted as *immanent orality*, a concept introduced by the Danish rhetorician Jørgen Fafner in order to characterize material aspects of a discourse promoting a specific tone, rhythm, melody, tempo, and articulation.[13] When performed in that way, the anaphors seem to embody the vision of the prime minister, creating a connection between the *inventio*, *elocutio*, and *actio* of the speech. The vision is followed up by a concrete example, a narrative about the boy Emil, who attends a municipal school, adding

---

[12] Thorning-Schmidt (http://www.stm.dk/_p_13744.html, 2012): "Min vision – og regeringens vision – er en folkeskole, hvor alle børn lærer mere. Alle børn. En skole, hvor der er ro i timerne. Hvor ungerne trives og har lyst til at lære. Hvor de udvikler deres personlighed og bliver engagerede deltagere i et levende demokrati. En folkeskole, hvor lærerne bruger deres store viden om deres fag og anvender de bedste undervisningsmetoder, og hvor de nyder respekt og tillid," 7. Our translation into English.

[13] Jørgen Fafner, *Retorik. Klassisk og modern*, Chapter II and V (Akademisk forlag, København 1977) and "Lyrikkens væsen. Introduktion til fremførelseslæren" (*Retorik Studier*, 2/1978).

memorability and *evidentia* to the speech by appealing to several senses (smell, sound, vision):

> Let us take a boy who is 13 years old and is attending the 7th grade. His name can, for instance, be Emil. And the school day may, for instance, begin with math. The class learns about angles, equations, and percent. Math has moved from the classroom to the woodwork room of the school. Here is Emil building a birdhouse together with three classmates. The smell of wood, the sound of the saw, the correct angle of the roof of the nesting box – all that helps the doctrine of Pythagoras to stick in a better way.[14]

TIMELY WORDS—*KAIRÓS* IN SPEECHWRITING

The Greek concept *kairós* roughly means "timing" and is often used to describe important potentials of oral speech, though written discourse may also be interpreted as the right words to the right audience at the right time and occasion.[15] But unlike a writer, a speaker is present *in front of* listeners. This means that when improvising, the speaker is able to grasp the actual moment of the performative situation. Thus, the classical scholar Øivind Andersen emphasizes the sophist Alcidamas (died 375 BC), who was influenced by the procedures of the ancient court and popular assembly based on improvisation. Alcidamas argued that a speech never suited the situation better than when improvised, that is, when it was both created and delivered at the critical moment, in the actual *now* in front of the audience.[16]

The concept of *kairós* implies that rhetoric is deeply rooted in a situation, and that the situation should be considered one of the greatest

---

[14]Thorning-Schmidt (http://www.stm.dk/_p_13744.html, 2012): "Lad os tage en dreng på 13 år, der går i 7. klasse. Han kan for eksempel hedde Emil. Og skoledagen kan for eksempel starte med matematik. Klassen lærer om vinkler, grader og procenter. Matematikken er flyttet fra klasselokalet til skolens værksted. Her er Emil i gang med at bygge et fuglehus sammen med tre andre fra klassen. Lugten af træ, lyden af saven, den rette vinkel på fuglehusets tag – det får Pythagoras sætning til at hænge bedre fast" (Our translation into English).

[15]In the writings of Isocrates (436–ca. 338 BC) *kairós* is used in different ways: It means e.g. 'time', 'circumstances', or 'occation.' Øivind Andersen: "Rette ord i rette tid", *Rhetorica Scandinavica*, no. 23, 2002.

[16]Andersen, 23.

resources when selecting and choosing topics for the speech. But how can a ghostwritten speech embody *kairós*? Even though few contemporary speakers improvise whole speeches, they might find it suitable to improvise, e.g., parts of the introduction. Thus *kairós* can be achieved if the speaker responds to urgent situational aspects or acts happening simultaneously or just before the rhetorical delivery. In that way a speaker is able to anchor the speech in the present moment, even though most of it has been written by the speechwriter before delivery.

An illustrative example of an improvised introduction grasping the very moment can be observed in the incendiary political speech of M.C. Lyngsie, leader of the Danish labor movement. The speech was delivered in Nykøbing Falster the first of May, 1925, in front of a huge audience of frightened workers experiencing lockout. Given the situation, Lyngsie aimed primarily at inspiring courage and hope in the workers. Unfortunately, it was raining heavily when he ascended the rostrum outdoors and being an experienced improviser, he succeeded in using the bad weather strategically in his introduction and stirring up his audience:

> *People Tidings*! [Noise and applause!] *Diocese Tidings*! [New noise], and *Liberal Paper*! [Applause again] – tomorrow these newspapers will gleefully write that God is not on the side of the socialists: the rain was pouring down, their banners were limp, and the mood was poor. For the moment I fight with these folks, and I shall say to them: You are not right! [Here, Lyngsie spoke directly reporters]. Today heaven is crying because of the lock-outers' foolishness. Not because of us [Hear!]. The sky's moisture is falling in order to gain growth on earth, so that the plants can grow up and pay for the stupidity and loss, which the lock-outers cause the country.[17]

---

[17] "Folketidende! (Larmen og Bifald) Stiftstidende! (Ny Larm) og Venstrebladet! (atter Bifald) – disse Blade vil i Morgen skadefro skrive, at Vorherre er ikke med Socialisterne, for Regnen strømmede ned, deres Faner var slatne, og Humøret var sløjt. Jeg slaas for Tiden med de Godtfolk, og jeg vil sige til dem: De har slet ikke Ret! (Hr. Lyngsie talte her som ofte senere ned mod Referenterne). Naar himlen græder i Dag, saa er det ikke over os, men over Lockoutherrernes Taabelighed. (Hør). Naar Himlens væde falder, saa er det for at skaffe Grøde paa Jorden, for at Væksterne kan vokse op og bøde paa Dumheden og Tabene, som Lockoutherrerne forvolder Landet." Quoted from Jørgensen: *Danske taler*, 206–207 (Our translation).

Lyngsie creates *kairós* by referencing the bad weather and transforming its negative constraint and subsequently turning a despondent audience into an optimistic lot, taking the rain as a sign of heavenly sympathy. It seems clear from the transcription of the speech that he at once manages to get the attention of the audience. The introduction can also be interpreted as an inoculation strategy: The newspapers supporting the lockout will not be able to use the rain to ridicule the workers with great effect since Lyngsie has already preempted this option.

Many speeches have been praised for expanding and reflecting on the actual moment and its significance, which may also be imitated by contemporary speechwriters to achieve *kairós* on a more abstract level.[18] In Martin Luther King's "I Have a Dream" speech, delivered on August 28, 1963, at the Lincoln Memorial, King built up *kairós* by using the phrase "the urgency of now" and the anaphora "now is the time," which was repeated three times, reinforcing King's insistent call to America:

> We have also come to this hallowed spot to remind America of the fierce *urgency of Now*. This is no time to engage in luxury of cooling off or to take the tranquilizing drug of gradualism. *Now is the time* to make real the promises of democracy. *Now is the time* to rise from the dark and desolate valley of segregation to the sunlit path of racial justice. *Now is the time* to lift our nation from the quicksands of racial injustice to the solid rock of brotherhood. *Now is the time* to make justice a reality for all of God's children.[19]

In Barack Obama's speech "A World that Stands as One," delivered in Berlin on July 24, 2008, while Obama was still a candidate for president, *kairós* is primarily constituted through two anaphora: "Now is the time" and "This is the moment." "Now is the time," a quotation from King's "I have a Dream," leads to a long anaphoric passage where "This is the Moment" is repeated nine times:

> *Now is the time* to build new bridges across the globe as strong as the one that bound us across the Atlantic. *Now is the time* to join together, through constant cooperation, strong institutions, shared sacrifice, and a global commitment to progress, to meet the challenges of the 21st century. It was

---

[18] Andersen, 22.
[19] www.americanrhetoric.com (my italics).

this spirit that led airlift planes to appear in the sky above our heads, and people to assemble where we stand today. And *this is the moment* when our nations – and all nations – must summon that spirit anew.[20]

The intertextual references to the "I have a Dream" speech can be interpreted as *kairós* in a new sense, constituting a connection between the two speeches: if Obama were elected President of the USA in 2008, he would thereby also fulfill, at least parts of, King's dream.

What Does a Good Manuscript Look Like?

A manuscript prepared thoroughly for oral delivery should be considered a draft aiming at the rhetorical performance and often looks quite plain:

- The sentences are rather short with a variation in length and a memorable rhythm.
- The grammar is simple, using mostly parataxis and active verbs.
- Abstract passages are preceded or followed by concrete passages: examples or narration, etc.
- The disposition is logical and does not include too many parts.
- Figures of style and metaphors are used to increase memorability.
- The language is individually toned, fitting the speaker's voice and gestures.
- Some passages can be left open, allowing the speaker to improvise.

Contemporary speechwriting is embedded in complex situations with both oral and written characteristics: Speechwriters should therefore write for the ear as well as for the eye. The speechwriter must decide on a communicative strategy together with the speaker as a response to the constraints of the individual situation. If the original performance is to be considered the most important (and if a potential recording has an "authentic" character, focusing on the speaker's interaction with the present audience), the manuscript, as well as added advice on performance, should primarily aim at the oral situation and at aural reception. If the speechwriter is preparing a video presentation for Internet users, one must write a manuscript that considers orality and literacy at the same time. Thus, even though a video audience receives the speech

---

[20]www.cnn.com (our italics).

aurally, they are not constrained by the limitations of time since they are both able to review and re-listen. If the speech is both watched and read, the speechwriter may choose to prepare *two* manuscripts: one aimed at the listeners and another aimed at the readers of the home page or newspaper.

CHAPTER 10

Writing for the Eye: Pictures, Visions, and PowerPoint

In the twenty-first century, appeals to the eye are more present and important than ever before. We are surrounded by imagery and visual media, and most presentations use PowerPoint, Keynote, Prezi, or similar presentation technologies. Speeches are distributed via YouTube, Vimeo, and TED. Speakers and speechwriters need to take into account the visual aspects of public presentations, if they want their speeches to succeed. Relying on visual presentation technologies, however, also leads to the risk of removing the attention and effort from the powerful rhetoric of speaking to the eye with verbal imagery. So, while presenters may use presentation technologies to display images, a good speechwriter will be able to appeal to the inner eye of the audience, by drawing with words.

DRAWING WITH WORDS

Rhetoricians have known for centuries the power of talking to the eye. "Words," Aristotle writes in *On Rhetoric* "ought to set the scene before our eyes; for events ought to be seen in progress rather than in prospect." Cicero calls sight the keenest sense,[1] and the world's first appointed professor in eloquence, the Roman rhetorician Quintilian, writes that oratory fails its full effect:

---

[1] Cicero, *De oratore*, 2.87.357.

© The Author(s) 2019
J. E. Kjeldsen et al., *Speechwriting in Theory and Practice*,
Rhetoric, Politics and Society,
https://doi.org/10.1007/978-3-030-03685-0_10

[i]f its appeal is merely to the hearing, and the judge merely feels that the facts on which he has to give his decision are being narrated to him, and not displayed in their living truth to the eyes of the mind.[2]

A speechwriter, then, should not narrate, but display the facts in their living truth to the eyes of the mind. Time and again, the ancient rhetoricians encourage us to put events vividly in front of the audience so that they experience them as if they see them with their own eyes. The advice is equally valid today. Contemporary research in rhetoric, media studies, and cognitive psychology confirms what rhetoricians have been saying for 2000 years. Cognitive psychology, for instance, argues that memory is inherently visual: Humans experience, understand, and remember through two cognitive channels: an auditive, verbal channel that processes sound and verbal impressions, and a visual channel that processes images and visual impressions. This means that if speaker wishes to influence an audience, touch their emotions, and make them remember the message, they cannot just narrate and explain, they also have to show and display the message. Speakers, then, must combine the general with the specific and unite argument and image. This postulation is based on the simple dictum that if you want people to remember something, you have to make them see it.

Speechwriters and orators have been painting with words for at least 2000 years.[3] One of the most common rhetorical figures is the *descriptio* (gr. *ekphrasis*): the vivid verbal descriptions making something come alive before the eyes of the audience. In antiquity, the most common forms of *descriptio* were the detailed description of a place (*descriptio loci*), a person (*descriptio personae*), a situation or course of events (*description rei*), or the moment, season, or time of year for an act (*description temporis*). The same types of verbal descriptions are used by speechwriters today. A notable example of the use of visual appeals is the speech delivered by Ronald Reagan on June 6, 1984, commemorating the 40th anniversary of D-Day. The speech was delivered at the very spot on the coast of France where the soldiers went ashore 40 years earlier. The beginning paints pictures like a literary novel or a movie. It is a

---

[2] Quintilian, *Oratoria*, 8.3.61-2.

[3] Jens E. Kjeldsen, *Tale med billeder - tegne med ord. Det visuelle i antik retorik og retorikken i det visuelle* [Speaking with Images—Drawing with Words. The Visual in Antique Rhetoric and the Rhetoric of the Visual] (Oslo: Spartacus, 2011).

well crafted, memorable, and significant piece of oratory, so an extensive quote is in place:

> We stand on a lonely, windswept point on the northern shore of France. The air is soft, but 40 years ago at this moment, the air was dense with smoke and the cries of men, and the air was filled with the crack of rifle fire and the roar of cannon. At dawn, on the morning of the 6th of June, 1944, 225 Rangers jumped off the British landing craft and ran to the bottom of these cliffs. Their mission was one of the most difficult and daring of the invasion: to climb these sheer and desolate cliffs and take out the enemy guns. The Allies had been told that some of the mightiest of these guns were here and they would be trained on the beaches to stop the Allied advance.
>
> The Rangers looked up and saw the enemy soldiers – the edge of the cliffs shooting down at them with machine guns and throwing grenades. And the American Rangers began to climb. They shot rope ladders over the face of these cliffs and began to pull themselves up. When one Ranger fell, another would take his place. When one rope was cut, a Ranger would grab another and begin his climb again. They climbed, shot back, and held their footing. Soon, one by one, the Rangers pulled themselves over the top, and in seizing the firm land at the top of these cliffs, they began to seize back the continent of Europe. Two hundred and twenty-five came here. After 2 days of fighting, only 90 could still bear arms.

The speech was written by Peggy Noonan, who has explained that she was thinking cinematically. The cinematic character lies not only in the verbal pictures, but also in the planned use of television pictures. At the moment Reagan honored the soldiers with the words "these are the boys of Pointe du Hoc," the cameras would turn to the elderly veterans, who once were the young soldiers climbing the cliffs below.[4]

The power of the verbal description (ekphrasis) is threefold: It elicits emotions, it seems to document by presenting reality, and it is readily understood and remembered. In contemporary speechwriting, however, the vivid description is generally part of a story describing the actions of persons or the outcome of their actions. Rarer are descriptions that are

---

[4]Cf. Kathleen Hall Jamieson, *Eloquence in an Electronic Age: The Transformation of Political Speechmaking* (Oxford and New York: Oxford University Press, 1988), 162. Cf. Peggy Noonan, *What I Saw at the Revolution: A Political Life in the Reagan Era* (New York: Random House, 1990/2010). The inaugural speech by Reagan can be read and seen here: https://www.americanrhetoric.com/speeches/ronaldreagandfirstinaugural.html. The Reagan-quote is taken from this page.

not directly part of a story being told. However, detailed descriptions of things and sights are powerful devices, even when they are not part of a specific story. When the American actress Viola Davis in 2015, as the first African-American actress in history, received an Emmy for a leading role, she began her speech with a quote from the African-American abolitionist Harriet Tubman:

> In my mind, I see a line.
> And over that line, I see green fields and lovely flowers
> and beautiful white women
> with their arms stretched out to me over that line.
> But I can't seem to get there no how.
> I can't seem to get over that line.

The quote does not so much tell a story as it paints a picture of the struggles of African-American women slaves in the USA. Seeing the picture and seeing Mrs. Davis with the Emmy in her hand make the audience understand this struggle and the significance of the fact that the people who came after Tubman, people like Davis, are now climbing over the line that used to divide.

One of the main advantages of painting with words when writing speeches is that it activates a visually based rhetorical model of eliciting emotions.[5] If an orator wishes to elicit the emotions of the audience, the ancient rhetorician Quintilian writes, he must first elicit the same emotions in himself.[6] How does he do that? Or more relevant: How can a speechwriter help elicit the right emotions in the speaker? The orator, Quintilian says, can evoke the proper and appropriate emotions in himself through certain experiences known as *visions*: "whereby things absent are presented to our imagination with such extreme vividness that they seem actually to be before our very eyes. It is the man who is really sensitive to such impressions who will have the greatest power over emotions."[7]

---

[5] See Kjeldsen, "Talking to the Eye: Visuality in Ancient Rhetoric," *Word & Image* 19, no. 3 (2003).

[6] Marcus Fabius Quintilianus, *The Institutio Oratoria of Quintilian: In Four Volumes: 2*, The Loeb Classical Library (London: William Heinemann, 1921), Book 6, 2, 29.

[7] Ibid.

Rhetoricians of all times have emphasized the extraordinarily powerful effect of delivery: Without an efficient delivery the words, arguments, and emotions created by the speechwriter will inevitably fall flat, unless they are given "the fire that voice, look, and the whole carriage of the body can give them."[8] In order to transform his own delivery, his *actio*, into vivid evidence of the emotional importance of the case or argument, the orator must evoke these *visions* in his own mind:

> Shall I not bring before my eyes all the circumstances which it is reasonable to imagine must have occurred in such a connection? Shall I not see the assassin burst suddenly from his hiding-place, the victim tremble, cry for help, beg for mercy, or turn to run? Shall I not see the fatal blow delivered and the stricken body fall? Will not the blood, the deathly pallor, the groan of agony, the death-rattle, be indelibly impressed on my mind?[9]

The rhetorical use of visions has a three-step, visually based model of persuasion[10]: In the first step, the orator visualizes certain events in order to create the necessary visions. In the second step, these visions will move the orator and make him feel the proper emotions for the case or argument. The emotional movement will then affect the orator's whole figure and appearance into a visual presentation of these emotions. In the third step, the sight of the moved orator as a physical manifestation of the proper emotions will then evoke the same emotions in the audience.[11]

The rhetorical value of this method is that the orator's obvious emotion presents itself as visual evidence of the proper emotional character of the case. For the audience, the sight of the moved orator appears as a credible sign of the emotional truth of the case. This applies for the contemporary speechwriter as well. If you want to move the audience, you must first move the speaker, you do this through what the ancient Romans called *visiones* (lat.). Through such *visions*, you create images in the speech that first elicits the emotions of the speaker, which will then elicit the emotions of the audience.

---

[8] Quintilian, *Institutio*, 11, 3, 23.
[9] Ibid., 6, 2, 31.
[10] Kjeldsen, "Talking to the Eye."
[11] Cf. Cicero, *De Oratore*, 2, 45, 189.

The Visual Rhetoric of Place and Things

On May 1, 2003, President George W. Bush flew in a jet aircraft that landed on the aircraft carrier USS Abraham Lincoln. The carrier had just returned from the Persian Gulf, and the president was set to announce in a live television address that major combat in Iraq had ended. The photographs from the event generally showed two things: The first was the president, a former pilot himself, leaving the aircraft dressed in the flight suit, holding the pilot helmet under his arm. The second was the president addressing the crowd on the USS Abraham Lincoln, with a large banner in the background saying, "Mission accomplished." The president told the audience, "Major combat operations in Iraq have ended. In the battle of Iraq, the United States and our allies have prevailed." The president never actually said, "Mission accomplished"; nevertheless, this is what most people seem to remember from the speech. It is hard to recollect the words of a speech, but easy to re-visualize the president in front of the massive banner. The image of the claim that the mission accomplished turned out to be a problem for the president, since combat continued for several more years.

As with the verbally evoked images, pictures and photographs are efficient in grabbing the attention, moving the emotions, and impressing the memory. Speechwriters should be aware of this force and enhance the power of their speeches by taking advantage of the place the speech is given. Exploiting the ambience can be done by referencing the surroundings and by creating the right circumstances for photo opportunities. Ronald Reagan was efficient in such rhetorical use of the surroundings for his speeches in order to persuade and leave a memorable impression. In his first inaugural address of 1981, he had the ceremony moved to the west portico the Capitol in order to use the television pictures to underscore his claim that heroism is "both part of America's past and future."[12] While talking about the heroes of America—George Washington, Thomas Jefferson, Abraham Lincoln, the soldiers fallen in the wars for the nation—the camera offered the audience pictures of the national monuments to each of the three former presidents and Arlington National Cemetery. In the televised broadcast, words and images intertwined to form memorable pictures.

---

[12] Kathleen H. Jamieson, *Eloquence in an Electronic Age: The Transformation of Political Speechmaking* (New York and Oxford: Oxford University Press, 1988), 119–120.

This way of intersecting ambience and surroundings into the speech did not begin with television, but has been employed since antiquity. Cicero deliberately chose to deliver his first *Catilinarian oration*, the speech attacking the Roman Senator Lucius Sergius Catilina for conspiracy against the state, in the temple of Jupiter Stator. This temple was raised by the city's founder Romulus in gratitude to the gods for putting the Sabines, enemies of Rome, on the flight. Cicero allegedly chose this place because it was safe from an attack by the conspirators; however, he was chiefly concerned with the *perception* of safety and the rhetorical possibility it provided the audience for seeing Cicero as Romulus, and Catiline and his followers as the Sabines.[13]

Besides utilizing the place a speech is given, a speaker can use attributes and props as effective rhetorical tools, because the displaying of a physical object offers a visual appeal that affects the emotions and is readily remembered. During a TED-talk in 2009 on "Mosquitos, malaria and education," Microsoft founder Bill Gates presented a jar with mosquitoes on stage. "Malaria, of course is transmitted by mosquitoes," he told the audience and lifted the lid of the jar, letting the mosquitos out. "We'll let those roam around the auditorium a little bit. There is no reason only poor people should have the experience." The audience laughed and applauded, some of them slightly hesitant and uneasy, but everyone turned their full attention to the stage. Gates then assured that these mosquitoes were not infected; however, using them as a prop, he efficiently made his point. It even got him on the evening news in the USA, and the talk was mentioned in many media outlets across the world.

Not all use of attributes, however, is rhetorically effective. At a speech at the party conference of the Dutch party "Christian Democratic Appeal" in 1995, the newly elected chairman of the party, Hans Helgers, wanted the audience to understand that he would listen to members and voters. To illustrate his message, he put two large ears on his head. It was a memorable, but unfortunately also a laughable sight.[14] A similar visual appeal intended to express approachability was presented by Ton de Lange, a student board member in Leiden University in the Netherlands speaking to junior students. de Lange had ripped the threshold from

---

[13] Ann Vasaly, *Representations: Images of the World in Ciceronian Oratory* (Berkeley, Los Angeles and London: University of California Press, 1993), 40–87.

[14] Jaap de Jong, "Stekkers, geweren en stropdassen Theatrale effecten in toespraken," *Onze Taal* 9 (2014), 245–247.

door of his office and threw it on the floor before students as a symbol of his open door policy.[15]

Because props and attributes draw attention to them and will stick in the memory of the audience after the speech, it is important that the prop clearly signifies the central idea or argument of the speech. Furthermore, props are not only remembered because their simplicity and visuality stick in the mind of the audience, but also because they appeal to photographers. When a speech uses a prop persuasively, new audiences will see pictures of the prop in the paper or online. When US general Colin Powell advocated before the UN Council for an invasion of Iraq (on February 3, 2003), one of the most widespread pictures from the presentation was a photograph of Mr. Powell holding a replica vial of "anthrax." Powell used this prop to illustrate how little anthrax it would have taken to shutdown the US Senate during the attack in 2001.

One of the most salient uses of a prop at a TED talk was made when Dutch chief of Defense Peter van Uhm presented a machine gun on stage in order to make the audience understand why he chose the gun as his instrument to contribute to a better world.[16] The audience gasped when the machine gun was carried in, but van Uhm used the uneasiness to make his point:

> For you, and you heard already, being so close to this gun may make you feel uneasy. It may even feel scary. A real gun at a few feet's distance. Let us stop for a moment and feel this uneasiness. You could even hear it. Let us cherish the fact that probably most of you have never been close to a gun. It means The Netherlands is a peaceful country.

As it is the case with using the visual surroundings rhetorically, the use of props has been employed since antiquity: Orators in court would tear the cloak of their clients to show the honorable wounds received in battle, they would carry in orphaned children to evoke compassion, and they would reveal swords dripping with blood.[17]

The use of props doesn't have to be complicated. On the contrary, simple use of props is usually the best. This is evident from one of the

---

[15] Jong, "Stekkers, geweren en stropdassen."

[16] TED talk by Peter van Uhm, November 2011. http://www.ted.com/talks/peter_van_uhm_why_i_chose_a_gun/transcript?language=en.

[17] Quintilian, *Institutio Oratoria*, 6, 1, 30–34.

world's successful public speakers, the Swedish professor of international health Hans Rosling. He has successfully and entertainingly explained complex issues with the use of everything from boxes and apples to Lego bricks and toilet rolls. Besides his efficient use of simple props, Rosling is praised for his world-renowned presentations using Digital Presentation Tools (DPT) to illustrate global trends in health, development, poverty, and economics.[18]

THE RHETORIC OF DIGITAL PRESENTATION TOOLS

While Rosling manages to use DPT in a persuasive and entertaining manner, this kind of efficient use is unfortunately not very common. A rhetorical problem with DTP such as PowerPoint or Keynote is that these technologies are mainly speaker-oriented and neither content-oriented nor audience-oriented.[19] The standard setup and fixed formats that make the task of communication comfortable for the presenter often come at the expense of content and listeners. The price paid is presentations empty of information, lacking in content and endlessly tedious. We've all experienced an instructor or speaker standing in half-shadow with his back to the audience, reading in a staccato voice:

- each
- word
- on
- every
- single
- slide.

Very often speakers using DPT serve the audience with rapid, short sequences of thin information. DPT is therefore not just an alternative method of giving presentations, as cultural critic Neil Postman states; any

---

[18] https://www.ted.com/talks/hans_rosling_shows_the_best_stats_you_ve_ever_seen?language=en.

[19] Edward R. Tufte, *The Cognitive Style of PowerPoint* (Cheshire, CT: Graphics Press, 2003); Jens E. Kjeldsen, "The Rhetoric of PowerPoint," Seminar.net. *International Journal of Media, Technology and Lifelong Learning* 2, no. 1 (2006). See: http://seminar.net/files/Kjeldsen_powerpoint.pdf.

technology is also an ideology.[20] Indeed, most presentation programs, such as Microsoft's PowerPoint, are technologies, which not only change our way of communicating, but also our thinking.

In general, such software makes us think and speak in isolated blocks, instead of in coherent context, totalities, narratives, or linear reasoning. Each block invites us to think and speak in separate, hierarchizing sections and points. Presentation programs encourage us to use particular forms of visual material and defined formats and to use ready-made visual material and animations, even if they have no clear relevance to what is being said. Finally, such software invites ritual conformity of visual style.

The most obvious rhetorical problem with the standardization in programs such as PowerPoint is the bullet points. The program's basic structure, and thereby the speeches and talks using it, are but listing of everything in bullet points. These bullet lists can help unorganized speakers to be a little more organized, and for many audiences, they may "create the appearance of hard-headed organized thought. But in the reality of day-to-day practice, the PP cognitive style is faux-analytical."[21]

The bullet point approach, so common in business life, often leads to superficial and simplified ways of thinking. In the first place, bullet points are too general and say things that are applicable to any kind of business activity: Cut costs! Boost earnings! Get a bigger share of the market! Add to this the fact that lists state critical relations without specifying their connection in detail. For lists can only describe three kinds of relation: sequences, priorities, and association. But they can neither explain relations between elements nor clarify narrative or causal relations. In the third place, bullet points omit and suppress important lines of reasoning as to how something works and is interconnected.

When using PowerPoint, the templates, prescripts, and bullets will encourage the speechwriter to construct speeches that invite the audience to passive, rather than active listening. Because the software is constructed to make choices for the user, we are encouraged by the templates to concern ourselves less with rhetorical considerations of what we want to achieve, what we have to do, why we should do it, or how. Instead, the program invites the users to fill the format with whatever content we happen to have. We are invited not to make arguments, to

---

[20] Neil Postman, *Amusing Ourselves to Death: Public Discourse in the Age of Show Business* (New York: Penguin, 1986).

[21] Tufte, "The Cognitive Style," 5.

tell stories, or to examine our subject in detail, but merely to present an outline of the speech, which often means the speaker is reduced to reading up points in the dark with her back half-turned to the audience.

This kind of speechmaking is not likely to arouse the attention of an audience and persuade them. Exposed to point after point, through long series of slides, the audience is reduced to mental stenographers without contact or deeper understanding of what they are told.

We recognize this from our own experience. Most of us have tried to take notes and believed thereby that we understood what we were writing while what really happened was that the mere act of note taking prevented us from reflecting over the actual meaning of the words. In this way, technology risks posing a barrier to the speaker and the audience, instead of building a rhetorical bridge between them. Writing speeches with DPT invites the speechwriter to present statements, not to reflect, make arguments, and tell stories.

Even though DPT as a technology tends to invite the user to focus on form instead of content and message, many speakers have used such technology with rhetorical success. The co-founder and CEO of Apple, Steve Jobs, was admired for his presentations using the program Keynote. One key to his presentation success, besides his thorough and meticulous preparation, was the insistence on avoiding bullet points and keeping every slide simple and aesthetically pleasing. The slides generally had only a picture, sometimes a few words, or a simple and easy-to-read graph or chart. Jobs also combined the use of DPT with simple props onstage and always wrapped his company and products into a larger story.

While the use of DPT is omnipresent in business presentations, it has been an uncommon tool in political speechmaking. However, in Scandinavian and European political speechmaking, it is now more common to provide the speaker not with a traditional written manuscript, but instead with a slide presentation that is sometimes accompanied by a list of talking points, helping the speaker as she is talking through the slides.

While most speeches using slides too often end up making the speaker reiterate facts instead for communicating vividly, telling stories, and presenting arguments, slides can be very efficient in presenting a case. One example of this is the famous slideshow presentation by former US Vice President Al Gore, called "An inconvenient truth," who also became the core of the Oscar-winning movie of the same name. In this and several other presentations, Al Gore efficiently used graphics, illustrations, and photographic images to make and support rhetorical argumentation.

One of his strategies of visual argumentation has been titled *visual chronology*. This term signifies the use of images or graphics to show the chronological development of a process such as the shrinking of the North Polar ice cap, for example. The second strategy, titled *visual analogy*, allowed for comparing entities, such as when Gore visually displayed how much ice has actually disappeared and then analogically illustrated how much of the USA would vanish if a corresponding amount of territory disappeared.[22]

A special instance of the use of slides in politics is Obama's State of the Union addresses. Since 2011, the Obama administration has made available a so-called *Enhanced version* of the speech online at the White House homepage. When giving the SOTU addresses to Congress, Obama, as presidents before him, did not use any kind of DPT for the audience present in Congress. However, the online video versions used a split screen, allowing viewers to see both the president and slides underscoring his message. The slides presented graphs and charts supporting the claims of the speech, including pictures of children, workers, soldiers, and the president interacting with ordinary Americans. The enhanced online versions allowed citizens to "follow along with the speech as [they] watch in real time, view charts and infographics on key areas, tweet favorite lines, and leave notes."[23]

The Obama administration's enhanced version of the SOTU and its pre- and post-activities for the speech are the most recent changes in a trend that has moved the speech from exclusively addressing Congress to increasingly addressing the American population. While Obama is addressing Congress, the enhanced online version directly addresses the citizens.[24]

Furthermore, before 2015, the White House used to only send out an embargoed copy of the speech to the press, meaning that the press could see the speech, but could not report on it until a designated time. The public, on the other hand, was not provided with a copy until after the speech. In 2015, however, the White House made an online version

[22] Jens E. Kjeldsen, "Strategies of Visual Argumentation in Slideshow Presentations: The Role of the Visuals in an Al Gore Presentation on Climate Change," *Argumentation* 27, no. 4 (2013).

[23] https://www.whitehouse.gov/the-press-office/2015/01/20/remarks-president-barack-obama-prepared-delivery-state-union-address.

[24] Jens E. Kjeldsen, "The Rhetoric of Digital Presentation Tools in Politics. The Case of President Obama's Enhanced State of the Union," *Design Issues*, 2019 (forthcoming).

of the full manuscript publicly available on its site before the speech was delivered; this version was also accompanied by selected slides.

The changes in the presentation of the State of the Union speeches exemplify how the White House increasingly began making efforts to reach a wide online audience and give people a range of ways to consume the speech. It illustrates that contemporary speeches work in new and different ways from traditional speechmaking. In short, while a speechwriter used to just write words, viewers now have to understand the message and utilize the possible benefits of online distribution, multimodal communication, and the use of DPT.

HOW TO HANDLE DIGITAL PRESENTATION TOOLS
AS A SPEECHWRITER

Since DPT isn't going away, speechwriters should try to adopt an active approach to this communication tool. The first is to evaluate the speaking situation and determine if the speech would be better off with the use of DPT. If not, then it should not be used. Most times, political speeches are better off without presentation tools.

As speakers and speechwriters, we should not be thinking of how to fill in the templates of computer programs such as PowerPoint. We should be thinking of purpose, goals, and means. What do we want to achieve? How can we best achieve it? What tools will help us best? And what are the technological limitations and possibilities? We should emulate Cicero, performing a rhetorical analysis of the situation, the audience, and communicative tools in relation to intention.

It has become common to talk these days of Media Literacy, i.e., people's ability to decode, understand, and relate to media and media statements.[25] The time has now come for us also to think about Media Rhetoricity or rhetorical competency.[26] If Media Literacy represents the ability to read and interpret media statements, Media Rhetoricity represents the ability to create and communicate such statements: to write instead of reading, to code instead of decoding, and to influence instead of being influenced. Among these skills is the selection of appropriate and persuasive communication tools such as PowerPoint.

---

[25] James W. Potter, *Media Literacy* (Thousand Oaks, CA: Sage, 2005).
[26] Kjeldsen, "Rhetoric of PowerPoint."

Practical skills require theoretical and rhetorical understanding. It is therefore important for speechwriters to understand the significance of Multimedia Learning. The supplementing of a speech with texts, pictures, and sound involves at the same time the software's pedagogical possibilities and limitations. It has to do with the way we humans perceive and decode information.

As we noted at the beginning of this chapter, cognition research has given us three hypotheses or theories that describe how the human brain works.[27] The first hypothesis is that we process information through two separate channels: an auditive and verbal channel which processes sound and verbal impressions, and a visual channel which processes images and visual impressions.[28] In a presentation using DPT, the speaker's words and any sounds or sound effects used will be picked up by the ears, while words and pictures on the screen are picked up by the eye. Our working memory will then connect, select, and organize the auditive and visual impressions through the respective channels, before the verbal and visual modalities are finally united in the long-term memory.

The second cognitive hypothesis teaches us that both these human information channels have limited processing capacity. This is particularly relevant in the processing of multimedia impressions when exposed to DPT. Third, real learning requires considerable cognitive activity in both channels. When in a learning situation, we are exposed simultaneously to words, images, and sound, we therefore run the risk of cognitive overload. In the progression from sensory impression to sensory memory and thence to working memory and finally to long-term memory, all teaching and learning entail the risk of cognitive overload.[29] If we are too busy seeing, we are not listening properly. If we are too busy listening, we might not process the information on the slides.

Using DPT constantly comes with the risk of cognitive overload. Because we are continuously processing different representations such as written texts, design, pictures, graphics, animation, and sound effects,

---

[27] Richard E. Meyer, *Multimedia Learning* (Cambridge: Cambridge University Press, 2003); Richard E. Meyer and Roxana Moreno, "Nine Ways to Reduce Cognitive Load in Multimedia Learning," *Educational Psychologist* 38, no. 1 (2003), 43–52.

[28] Allan Paivio, *Imagery and Verbal Processes* (Hillsdale and New York: Lawrence Erlbaum, 1979). Mayer and Moreno, "Nine Ways."

[29] Meyer and Moreno, "Nine Ways."

our brain does not have enough capacity to process the speaker's words. Retention and processing of the many different representational forms absorb our thinking capacity and lead to cognitive overload. Because both verbal and visual information come so rapidly and fragmentally, listeners can neither process and retain the information in their working memory nor transfer it to their long-term memory.

The solution is rhetorical and a simple one. In the first place, the speechwriter must remove everything not directly pertinent to the main focus and desired aim of the speech—away with irrelevant pictures, disturbing animations and sounds without function. Variety is positive but only if relevant and functional.

Second, speechwriters must create redundancy. This can be done in two ways: (1) repeating ideas over a period of time or (2) repeat them simultaneously, that is, communicate the same content in different ways and at the same time. By repetition over time, speechwriters can create diachronic redundancy, as when repeating verbally or visually a point presented earlier. Speakers can say or show the same thing in different ways, for example, by reformulating the same points, giving different examples, or first presenting something orally then in writing, or first with an illustration and then in words.

Speechwriters can also create synchronic redundancy, which is a simultaneous repetition, by communicating something both verbally and visually at the same time. We can describe the relevant elements in a picture, emphasize what the audience should note on the screen, or simply read the text out loud. Manuals on the use of PowerPoint often advise presenters not to read out what's on the slides. This is hammered home with exclamation marks: Don't read out what's on your slides! But pedagogically it's in fact quite a good idea. For in this way the message is communicated through both the recipients' verbal and visual information channels. Occasionally reading quotes or short texts from the slides will make the presentation more engaging. However, speakers who repeatedly read from bullet points, from text on every slide, or who are too reliant on the slides as their real manuscript, will surely bore the audience.

As noted, we should be aware that PowerPoint (and similar presentation software) is a multimedia tool. But we should also remember, as pointed out in Chapter 1, that presentations are done orally. The use of text, sound, and pictures should support the person speaking, not replace the speaker. We would therefore do well to remind ourselves of the traditional rhetorical aims of persuasion, teaching, and entertaining.

We should also remember rhetoric's doctrine of *inventio*, which teaches us how to find the best content and the most convincing arguments. It teaches us to prefer exploring one central argument in depth rather than superficially reeling off a number of different arguments. In the same way, rhetorical doctrine tells us about the appropriate development of our theme, *dispositio*, that the different sections of our disposition have different functions: The introduction should arouse interest and win goodwill and credibility. The presentation of the matter should be brief, clear, and concise. Our argumentation should provide proof of our theses and refute our opponents' objections. Stories and vivid descriptions should be used to evoke the imagination and emotions of the audience. Our conclusion should summarize and appeal to feelings and action.

The waffling chat that often accompanies presentations with DPTs would also benefit from greater attention to the rhetorical requirement that the language we use should not only be clear, correct, and appropriate, but also vivid. The use of tropes and figurative language sharpens our ears and structures our thinking, including anecdotes and descriptions, alliterations and assonances, metaphors and metonyms. These verbal devices are not given free play when we use lists in DPT to present our thematic content.

To prevent these general rules about arguments, disposition, and the use of language from petrifying into stiff genres, such as templates and prescripts in presentation software, they are always subordinate to rhetorical requirements for attention to functionality and regard to the concrete situation. The speaker must choose the right moment (*kairos*) to say what is pertinent and appropriate (*aptum*). Functionality before form.

The Power of the Visual

Ever since Gorgias in his *Encomium for Helen* argued that rhetoric and visual impressions are irresistible, humans seem to have believed that imagery and pictures are especially powerful. Used in the right way, imagery, whether material or verbally evoked, does seem especially well suited for eliciting emotions. For instance, material pictures, used in DPT, are also efficient in documenting facts or supporting verbal utterances. As we have argued in this chapter, in a traditional speech, appealing through storytelling and argumentation strengthens its rhetorical power when exploiting the visual. We argued in the first chapter that one of the most powerful ways to create community is to tell the story of the group. The stories should be told in ways that appeal to the inner eye. This is what Barack Obama did well in his keynote address to the Democratic Convention in 2004, weaving his own life story into the fabrics of the US' history. Most importantly, the story and the argument were infused with vividness: There he was, the black man with the odd name, on the enormous stage in Boston, transmitted to millions of television screens. "Tonight is a particular honor for me," he said:

> because, let's face it, my presence on this stage is pretty unlikely. My father was a foreign student, born and raised in a small village in Kenya. He grew up herding goats, went to school in a tin-roof shack. His father, my grandfather, was a cook, a domestic servant.

The story of generations of hard work and perseverance that helped bring Obama in front of this huge audience is not just the story about Obama, it is also the story about the USA and the American dream.

We use vivid stories because they turn our messages into something present and compelling. The specific and vivid, that which has presence, engages the audience. It makes them involved, and the stories stick in our memory. We remember stories that appeal to the eye, not bullet points for the ear.

But we should be aware that stories sometimes run the risk of being just stories. The audience may enjoy a vivid story, but they are not necessarily moving audiences in the direction a speechwriter wants them to move. A research study that focused on television news in the USA can illustrate this. Researchers made two versions of a news segment about unemployment: One group of viewers was shown a vivid story about the difficulty and distress of an unemployed individual, living in the suburbs of Chicago. Another group was presented with national facts and statistics about the increasing unemployment.

The question posed was this: Which group was more likely to be persuaded that unemployment was a problem, the group that got a story of individual hardship, or the group that was presented with numbers and facts? The researcher's conclusion was surprising:

> Contrary to much conventional wisdom, news stories that direct viewers' attention to the flesh and blood victims of national problems prove no

more persuasive than news stories that cover national problems impersonally – indeed, they tend to be less persuasive.[30]

The reason that flesh and blood stories and vivid representations can be less persuasive, the authors write, is perhaps because:

> they are so successful as melodrama. Viewers may get so caught up in one family's trouble that they fail to make the connection back to the national condition. Overwhelmed by concrete details, they miss the general point.

Vivid stories and detailed descriptions may arrest the attention and entertain the audience, but they do not necessarily persuade them. So, a speech that aims not only to entertain, but also to persuade should make sure that story told functions as an argument. Obama's story was not just a story. It was also an argument: an argument about him and about the USA. If this young man has come so far, then he can go even further. And if a person with his background can make it, then we can all make it, and thus the ostensible conclusion that the American dream is alive, and that this man—Obama—is a promising leader.

Keeping in mind that the visual is powerful, will help speechwriters write better speeches. Painting with words and drawing pictures with sentences will captivate the mind of the audience and make them remember. Beginning a speech with a vivid image will help put the speaker in the right mood, and when experiencing the emotions of the speaker, the audience will be influenced by this mood. As speechwriters, we can use verbal imagery at critical points in our speeches. We can apply them in places that should be remembered, as well as at places we wish to elicit the emotions of the audience. In places where we see the need to change the mood of the audience, verbal imagery can be introduced to change the emotions of the speaker and thus of the audience. When painting with words, it is important to be aware that salient imagery in speeches and stories will stick out and be remembered. It is therefore important that the visual parts are closely connected to the central message and argument of the speech. As speechwriters, we should wrap our argument in a story and tie our story to an image. The image will make the audience remember the story, and the story will make them remember the argument.

---

[30] S. Iyengar and D.R. Kinder, *News That Matter: Television and American Opinion* (Chicago: University of Chicago Press, 1987), 42.

A speech can appeal to both the inner and the outer eye. By this, we mean that besides evoking mental images through words, speechwriters should consciously think about how to use props and attributes rhetorically. The clever use of one or a few selected props can be very rhetorically salient. Like the use of verbal imagery, it is important not just to use any kind of prop, but to only use props that clearly connect to the message of the speech. Also the surroundings for the speech can be rhetorically exploited.

The use of DPT can be a tricky matter. Speeches should not be written in slides. Most presentations using DPT tend to put the speaker, literally, in the dark, and to expose the audience to enumeration of facts and fragmented lines, while forgetting about traditional values of speechwriting such as storytelling and argumentation. At the same time, DPT can be used persuasively if the speechwriter consciously and sparingly uses the ability of slides to appeal to the eye, and simultaneously remember to make the use of DPT a tool for a credible speaker, a good argument and vivid storytelling.

CHAPTER 11

The Ethics of Speechwriting

A Speechwriter's Code of Ethics

At the 2015 World Conference of the *Professional Speechwriters Association*,[1] a passionate debate erupted when a proposal for a *Speechwriter's Code of Ethics* was put forward to the members. Some members eagerly encouraged the creation of a document that could make the rules of conduct for speechwriters explicit, and guide them in their daily work. Equally important, a code of ethics was considered a necessary step toward the professionalization of the profession. Others found that such rules unnecessarily constraining and impossible to create, since the ethical issues of speechwriting are multifaceted and situational. A speechwriter must be loyal not only to the truth, but also to the client, to the audience, and to herself. Rules would either be empty banalities or too specific to apply. Thus, prudence, not general rules, was put forward as the proper solution when encountering moral and ethical dilemmas and challenges.

The association did create a code of ethics and published it online.[2] It was introduced by a preamble stating that because speechwriting is an ethically fraught and complicated job, speechwriters have yearned for "some

---

[1] Organized by The Professional Speechwriters Association (see https://www.vsotd.com/speech-writers-association) at the *Georgetown University (McDonough School of Business)* on October 7–8, 2015.

[2] The code can be found online at https://www.vsotd.com/PSA/CodeOfEthics. Accessed January 6, 2019.

© The Author(s) 2019
J. E. Kjeldsen et al., *Speechwriting in Theory and Practice*,
Rhetoric, Politics and Society,
https://doi.org/10.1007/978-3-030-03685-0_11

generally agreed-upon ethical guidelines to show their leaders, their clients, their colleagues and their listeners what speechwriters should and should not do with their peculiar powers of persuasion." Acknowledging the difficulties in creating ethical rules the association noted that:

> This is the imperfect document that our association's leaders, helped by advice from working speechwriters around the world, have produced. It is a living document, subject to periodic elaboration, updating, reconsideration and revision.[3]

The code itself consists of seven points:

1. Plagiarism: Speechwriters never plagiarize.
2. Confidentiality: Speechwriters keep matters involving clients as confidential as the clients demand and expect.
3. Conflict of interest: Speechwriters take assignments only after sharing with clients potential conflict of interest.
4. Fees: Freelance speechwriters are open about their basic fee structure, including the factors that call for variation.
5. Candor: Speechwriters are willing to speak "truth to power." That means confronting the client when asked to include deceptive, misleading, or false material.
6. Audience: On all assignments, the speechwriter serves listeners as well as the speaker—respecting their time, and considering their intellectual interests and their individual and collective needs.
7. Mission: Speechwriters use all their abilities to make clients better communicators.

We assume that all agree that the ethics of communication is understood as necessitating honesty in the exchange of ideas and message, and that specific measures such as facts, or distinguishing right from wrong, can secure such standards. We also assume that communicators know that ethical messages enhance credibility and believability and that ideas projected for persuasive objective are well supported and that they abide by moral precepts. Yet, we all recognize that the opposite is equally plausible and history is replete with dire examples and consequences whereby the manipulator and the deceiver can appear authentic and credible while

[3] Ibid.

the message is anything but. In the name of unethical and false speech, horrendous atrocities have been committed, making the understanding and implementation of ethical standards critical for good and proper communication. We must also realize the difficulties listeners have in discerning ethical from unethical speech, or that they are able to identify the manipulative communicator. As Richard Johannesen, a scholar of the study of ethics in communication, noted, "We should formulate meaningful ethical guidelines, not inflexible rules."[4]

Our ethical challenges are confounded by the very theories of rhetoric and the genres they espouse to fit a speech type to a given situation seeking to divert audiences into a specific mood and receptiveness. It is for this very reason that Plato and the philosophers opposed the study of rhetoric altogether and referring to it as akin to cookery—or an art molded in the hands of the cook/rhetor who is able to produce that most tasteful and appealing results. Calling on rhetors/speakers to realize the strength and weaknesses of a given speech type and the advantages of given emotional appeals are but examples of such calculations; strategies to maximize the effect of a rhetorical act. There is nothing unethical about such strategizing unless one takes a purist approach. Yet, the very process of adopting speech to people can be taken as somewhat manipulative.

When narrowing the focus from communication in general to the practice of speechwriting, we must address additional ethical constraints that pertain to the message construction by those that speak and practice wordsmithing. The very act of writing speeches for others and putting words in the mouth of others is often taken as unethical. This is so, we assume, because people expect that one's speech is or ought to be pure and original. Individuals need help in multiple ways and often resort to professionals whose expertise can make one's life easier, more productive, and efficient. Yet, when it comes to one's speech, our words are taken as a direct extension of our being and hence the expectation that they are original; that they are "ours" and no one else's. But this is wishful thinking as the sense of pure speech assumes that individual never learns to speak better, or that they never imitate others who speak well, or that they never adopt words and phrases that enhance one's presentation or learn from others how to organize better one's speech. In truth, we all

---

[4] Richard L. Johannesen, *Ethics in Human Communication*, 3rd ed. (Prospect Heights, IL: Waveland Press, 1990), 17.

imitate, learn to do things better, and seek to adopt improved practices. Except for the few gifted orators, most individuals learn to speak well in multiple ways and given the Greeks' emphasis on teaching speech by imitating, even requiring declamation of the great speeches of known orators, the notion of pure speech is simply a wishful thinking.

AUTHENTICITY AND THE MYTH OF LEADERSHIP

As mentioned earlier, the most challenging ethical question that speechwriting faces is a question of authenticity. Put in a question form; should the person speaking be the person constructing the words of the speech? And relatedly, what is ethical or unethical about the practice of speechwriting? Here, we must turn to the practicality of speechwriting and, as we have already discussed, a long-standing practice that dates back to the ancient world. The Old Testament tells us that Moses as the leader of the Israelites in Egypt had a speech impediment and that he relied on his brother Aaron to speak for him. Pharaoh did not seem to mind who was speaking to him and understood perfectly well the pleas presented. The sophists became prominent in the fifth century BCE precisely because those who went to court to argue their case needed experts in public advocacy to teach them the art of speaking in public. Aristotle's contribution to the art of rhetoric by codifying it and presenting a thoughtful treatise titled *On Rhetoric* streamlined the teaching of the art of public speaking. He considered rhetoric a *techne*, or an art that is based on a "set of productive principles or practices," while facts and testimonies were considered extrinsic, or those that exist prior to having "to invent them to an audience."[5] The distinction between intrinsic and extrinsic components of the rhetorical process further illustrates the degree to which the speechwriter brings to a given speech draft a theoretical understanding of the variables involved. Invention, the key variable to rhetorical development, is not based solely on a speaker or speechwriter's innate skills but critically, also on known theories and practices that stood the test of time. In short, even the development of a rhetorical act is based on past experiences and hence are not purely original or individually related to one person at a given time and place.

[5] Sharon Crowley and Debra Hawhee, *Ancient Rhetorics for Contemporary Students*, 2nd ed. (Boston: Allyn and Bacon, 1999), 7.

In the modern era, explicating some of the ethical concerns from the American presidency, for example, brings us to note that to one degree or another, all presidents beginning with George Washington had speechwriters work on their speeches, and that the practice of speechwriters employed by the executive predates the official title of speechwriter by some one hundred and fifty years. Speechwriters, as Ritter and Medhurst remind us, appear in different shapes and form and they are not always called "speechwriters."[6] Presidential aides of different sort and profession have been employed as speechwriters. Perhaps the most important point to make about speechwriters is that their function has never been that of stylists, in charge of the ornamentation of speeches and not of their invention. To the contrary, many presidential speechwriters worked closely with the president and covering much more than just the stylistic aspects of speeches.[7] For a long time, presidential speechwriters remained anonymous, leaving the mystery of quality speeches (or lack thereof) solely in the hands of the president. This tradition was broken when one of President Dwight Eisenhower revealed the inner-working of speechwriters and the president, and with the rise of presidential libraries, the public had access to the speechwriting process, its various drafts, inputs and such, further chipping away at the mystery of the speechwriting process.[8] For better or worse, speechwriters of presidents are known by name and even by prominent speeches they have drafted.

Given the growing awareness of speechwriters by name as well as their particular role in a given setting and circumstances, the question of ethics in speechwriting is front and center. Following the stipulations of Ritter and Medhurst, they confront the question of ethics by pointing to the need to go beyond wordsmithing when considering the work of speechwriters. The words constructed, they argue, cannot be separated from the larger context or exigency of the moment that necessitates a given speech and that "[i]t always exists in a dynamic relationship with people, policies, practices, and circumstances that give shape and substance to the discourse."[9] Put differently, examining a presidential speech

---

[6] Ritter and Medhurst, 6–7.
[7] Ibid., 8–9.
[8] Ibid., 9–10.
[9] Ibid., 12.

requires much more than a narrow appreciation of the text in question but a comprehensive assessment of the complex situation.

The question of authenticity, or who wrote the speech, is not just a matter of speechwriting but an involved process that puts text and context as interdependent. Ernest Bormann, writing in the context of rhetorical criticism, laments the rise of speechwriters as a class of professionals and attributes this phenomenon to the rise of the mass media.[10] He also considers the work of ghostwriter most destructive because their primary influence is on a speaker's style and given the fact (and quoting Marie Hochmuth) that "style is the man himself, then a close scrutiny of the details of style should tell us what manner of man is doing the speaking, and in what relationship he conceives himself to be with his audience."[11] We agree that ghostwriting poses a challenge to the critics of rhetoric, but our concern is with the practice of speechwriting and not in its artistic quality. The yardstick of the rhetorical critic is not identical to the measure of success or failure audiences assign to speakers and their speeches, which is our main focus. Bormann's critique of speechwriting goes beyond style. He also argues that "deception is inherent in the practice of ghostwriting": The speaker acts as if the words he says are his and the character the words display are really him.[12] This, Bormann considers, is deceitful because audiences falsely believe that speeches are written by the speaker, and the effectiveness of a ghostwritten speech is based on this deception.

A speaker finishing his speech with acknowledgements to the ghostwriter would destroy the effectiveness of the speech as well as his own credibility. Justifying speechwriting with the argument that a president, a prime minister, a university president, or a business leader, necessarily needs to delegate is unfortunate, according to Bormann, because it "inherently trivializes the study, teaching, and practice of speechmaking."[13] There is a substantial difference between booking flights and carrying bags for a leader, and crafting his thoughts and words. The reason for the deceit,

---

[10] Ernest G. Bormann, "Ghostwriting and the Rhetorical Critic," *Quarterly Journal of Speech* 46 (1960), 284–288.

[11] Ibid., 285

[12] Ernest G. Bormann, "Ethics of Ghostwritten Speeches," *Quarterly Journal of Speech* 47 (1961), 262–267.

[13] Ernest G. Bormann, "Response (to Franklyn S. Haiman's "Ghostwriting and the Cult of Leadership")," *Communication Education* 33 (1984), 304.

writes Franklyn S. Haiman, is more fundamental than the pragmatic issue of limited time. If lack of time was the sole concern for speakers using ghostwriters, then they would not only delegate the writing, but also the delivery. That, of course, doesn't happen. The real reason for the use of ghostwriting, he argues, is that those in position of authority and their audiences wish to create and perpetuate "a myth that authority figures are all-seeing, all-knowing, and all doing, a cult of leadership which endows the father or mother figures with superhuman capacities and turns away from the reality that in any group, organization or society the functions of leadership are, to one degree or another, inevitably shared."[14] In organizational rhetoric, Matthew W. Seeger points out there is both a theory and a practice of "symbolic leadership," which is consistent with Haiman's myth of the cult of leadership: The leader is expected to "behave in ways consistent with the illusion of personal causation, control, and direction of the larger social entity symbolically represented."[15] In essence, then, if the myth of leadership exists, if it compels leaders to employ ghostwriters, and if ghostwriting results in an organizational product that does not primarily represent an individual, then "criteria other than how the speech was produced must be used to judge ethics."[16]

THE SEPARATION OF WORDS AND POLICY

In truth, the separation of speechwriting from policy making is part of the ethical understanding. Those who see the two as completely separate tend to view speechwriters as wordsmithing professionals who write independently of context and constraints of time and place while the more sophisticated view brings policy-makers and speechwriters together, seeing the value of words emerging out of given situation as responding to situational constraints. Articulation, then, is a limited view of speechwriters, while considering them advisors to an executive, among other advisors, is a more productive way of understanding the speechwriting process.

---

[14] Franklyn S. Haiman, "Ghostwriting and the Cult of Leadership," *Communication Education* 33 (1984), 301–304.

[15] Matthew W. Seeger, "Ghostbusting: Exorcising the Great Man Spirit from the Speechwriting Debate," *Communication Education* 36, no. 4 (1985), 353–358, 357.

[16] Ibid., 357. Cf. Matthew W. Seeger, "Ethical Issues in Corporate Speechwriting," *Journal of Business Ethics* 11, no. 7 (1992), 501–504.

This view also addresses the ethical question of authenticity in speechmaking as it puts the process as advisory and equates it with other forms of advice and counsel that an executive seeks. Put more succinctly, it cannot be that the work of the speechwriter is suspect because of the charge of "putting words" in the mouth of a speaker while other advisors' input is taken as "legitimate."

The need for advisors, aides, including experts in policy, technology, and communication ought to be taken as part of any organization with speechwriters and editors included. This point can be further strengthened with the corollary of the court system from antiquity onward, those appearing in the court of law are represented by lawyers who are well versed in the intricacies of the legal system and critically, they speak on behalf of their clients. There is nothing unethical about professionals taking over the representation and advice of individuals confronting a legal challenge. The same, then, can be said of speechwriters who are experts in the particular area of speechmaking and whose advice and input include the actual drafting of speeches.

The question of authenticity, then, needs to be expanded to include different sorts of advice a speaker/leader receives and that cumulatively generate the rhetorical product. In this sense, the contribution of the speechwriter is but one of several kinds of input that help construct a rhetorical act, such for example, a speaker seeks a speaking venue, an adviser offers several options, and a speechwriter drafts a speech based on the topic requested and the venue selected. It cannot be that the speechwriter alone is marked for ghostwriting.

Ethical considerations of speechmaking and speechwriting are warranted for the primary realization that language is power and as such it burdens its users and consumers to discern the honorable intent from the dishonorable. And because facts and truths are only as convincing as the language used to advance them, the best that rhetorical acts can produce is approximation or probabilities of what is true or factual. Rhetoric, then, can be dangerous when used by extremists and unscrupulous individuals and for this very reason, "by studying rhetoric we can become alert to its potential for misuse and learn to recognize when a speaker is seeking to manipulate us."[17] There is, then, a corrective in rhetorical

---

[17] George Kennedy, "Prooemion," in *Aristotle on Rhetoric: A Theory of Civic Discourse* (New York: Oxford University Press, 1991), viii.

acts; though it is often misused and abused, as a method of "inventing" speeches, it can also provide the tools of discerning the manipulative and the unethical by opening the door to questioning arguments, assessing the strength of evidence, questioning intent, discovering ploys, and identifying fallacies in reasoning.

We also recognize the limitations that ethical standards offer. For example, the rational criterion assumes that rational assumptions and truth overlap and that a "rhetorical act that violates the truth criterion may be judged unethical." Yet, as Scott and Smith remind us, civility and decorum and other semblance of a rational discourse are instruments of power and can mask injustice and the "have nots."[18] The psychological criterion assumes that effective rhetorical acts are favored over ineffective, yet effectiveness cannot be equated with ethical. A more important way to assess effectiveness in rhetorical acts is to consider the social implications and effects of a given rhetorical act.[19] Finally, speechwriters need to be reminded that imitating great speeches or portions thereof has to be guided by ethical standards whereby borrowing text from another source without attribution is considered plagiarism while citing lines from past great orators can enhance a speech without compromising its authenticity.

Since he announced his presidential candidacy in June 2015, Donald Trump, who during the presidential campaign has appeared regularly on television networks and addressed multiple audiences throughout the nation and quite frequently, gave only few teleprompter-based speeches. Two such speeches stand out: one to AIPAC (American-Israel Public Action Committee, March 20, 2016) and one titled a "foreign policy" speech of April 26, 2016. Trump even prided himself on not being a scripted speaker and has thus offered himself as an authentic politician and not a puppet in the hands of speechwriters and political advisors. That Donald Trump has changed presidential politics in the USA is now better appreciated than earlier when his initial forays into the campaign were just underway and often accompanied by much skepticism. And though the implications of his successful candidacy are larger than the scope of this book, the implications for speechwriting

---

[18] Cited in Karlyn K. Campbell and Thomas R. Burkholder, *Critiques of Contemporary Rhetoric*, 2nd ed. (Wadsworth Publishing, 1997), 118.

[19] Ibid., 119.

are significant nonetheless. At the heart of the critical view of speechwriter, scripted speeches and fully developed speech texts are equated with the authenticity of the speaker vis-à-vis the audience. The case of the American presidency, the practice of speechwriting commenced with George Washington and followed by the vast majority of presidents with some exemplifying more involvement than others but almost all in need for others to draft, edit, and provide feedback to early drafts of speeches.

The growing understanding that speakers are dependent on their speechwriters has promoted the notion that they are not able to think and speak for themselves and are too careful and cautious in their public utterances that they need these professionals to save them from making errors or from stating the wrong thing or unintentionally offending audiences. This growing public perception is not always without merit though it also replete with faulty assumptions about the role of speechwriters.

Yet, Trump has touched a nerve. Dismissing the "handling" of speeches by speechwriters, he was able to offer a larger critique of American politics practiced by an elite and insiders who carefully frame issues and provide rhetorical lines that advantage an inner group of political operatives and not necessarily the interests of the larger community. That a considerable segment of the nation looked for a non-politician to govern the nation and with it the call for changing traditional practices such as carefully designated speeches is very much the makeup of the Trump candidacy and presidency. This tension could be more acute in the conflict between Republican Party leaders and Trump and the call for tempered and measured speech opposite Trump's preference for the crude, the direct and at times, even the offensive. There is no doubt that many would like to have Trump use speechwriters to moderate his statements in speeches and debates and follow more traditional rhetorical venues. The fact that on two occasions, Trump focusing on foreign affairs required a prepared speech text attests to the enduring quality of well thought through rhetorical acts. Yet, the overall dismissal of speechwriters as cosmetic handlers has caught speechwriters in the middle of a major quandary that can be taken by many as aiding politicians to offer careful presentations instead of raw messages. This, we believe, is a false dichotomy and our intent here to refute such a notion. At the center of our view is the role of the speechwriter as an adviser in the construction of messages for greater receptiveness but not at the expense of truths.

Speechwriters can and often are essential to many individuals not well versed in the rhetorical process.

The issue of authenticity must be unpacked in order to fully understand the role and function of speechwriters. Authenticity in the rhetorical process lies in the words uttered by the speaker and the conviction that accompany them. It does not mean, however, that earlier phases in the preparations of a given speech or statement are also solely the work of the speaker. Most individuals consult others in the construction of messages and the range of such helpful measures can include asking for feedback over initial points, outlines, or drafts, reading a speech aloud for feedback before finalizing it or even asking for suggestions for different versions of the same message. Yet, a growing problem over authenticity does exist. In the late twentieth century, rhetoric scholars have problematized the separation of *inventio* and *actio*. "The Divorce Between Speech and Thought" from *Eloquence in an Electronic Age* (1988) by Kathleen Hall Jamieson, for instance, discusses the implications of splitting up the rhetorical *partes*. She sees this development, which is partly caused by an increased number of speeches, contrary to ancient Greece and Rome when the first three *partes, inventio, dispositio*, and *elocutio* were more centrally resided with the speaker.[20] A recurrent objection of her work is that speechwriters help shape our perceptions of politicians who are, on the other hand, all too ready to take credit for someone else's word. In that way, ghostwriting clouds our opportunity to know politicians as they really are. The contemporary politician has been turned into an actor. Jamieson emphasizes, however, that it remained an ideal to deliver your own words. Nixon, for instance, accused his rival John F. Kennedy for being a "puppet who echoed his speechmaker" even though Nixon had a huge speechwriting staff himself.

Trump's critique notwithstanding, the ideal of speakers crafting their own words from initial outline to a final speech and delivery is simply not practical in an age of continuous and daily speech acts by political operatives. What is practical, then, are the principles of ethics that must guide the speechwriting process, whether solely in the hands of the speaker or when aided by advisors and speechwriters. First and foremost, the idea, thesis, or objective of speakers must be theirs, at least in spirit and intention. Speechwriters should not put in the speech ideas not espoused by speakers.

---

[20] Jamieson, *Eloquence*, the following quotes are from pages 204, 217, 218.

Though speechwriters have known to be involved in policy making, and often to advantage the speech, speaker and speechwriters must share and agree on the ideational message of the speech. Second, speeches must adhere to the principle of the public good, of pursuing worthwhile objectives and policies. A code of ethics for speechwriters may be necessary to ensure that they do not support or encourage the faulty or the manipulative. Their commitment to the pursuit of the truthful and the factual must be emphasized. Third, we recognize that the *inventio* and *elocutio* can allow speakers to phrase messages differently and that the range of such statements can run from the crude to the eloquent. Finally, if we take for granted the principle that speakers speak to people in order to change attitudes or modify positions, speeches must exclude offending statements. Outrageous statements may find some adherents but they do not endear the speaker to the larger community that likely also includes those not yet convinced or still hesitant to accept the speaker's objectives. If speakers can assess the full impact of their speeches, then speechwriters have the added responsibility of pointing such eventualities to the speaker. However, they must be brought to the table in the first place.

CHAPTER 12

The Functions of Speechwriting in Contemporary Society

Ghostwriting and speechwriting are a controversial issue. As we have made clear so far, the challenges and problems of using speechwriters have been debated since the ancient Greeks. So why do we use speechwriters? Why should we? Are the challenges so many, and the advantages so few that speechwriters shouldn't be used? In short: What are the functions of speechwriting in contemporary society?

ON THE PAGE OR OFF-THE-CUFF

Perhaps the transition from the Obama to the Trump administration in the USA has not only yielded insights into numerous aspects of politics including presidential speechwriting but also crystallized several issues of importance. From the careful and measured Obama's rhetoric to the off-the cuff and repetitive line of Trump's speechmaking, the functions of speechwriting have become easily identified. The mere commentary on Trump's *First State of the Union Address* of February 28, 2017, considered unusually strong and effective, was made in the context of the many non-teleprompter based-speeches. We cannot assess this comparison lightly and simplify it to following or not following a well-prepared speech text that was put on the teleprompter. There are ample examples of US politicians who did well with the off-the-cuff speeches, such as Harry Truman, and whose rhetoric was more limited when following a speech text. Donald Trump got elected with mostly off-the-cuff rhetoric

© The Author(s) 2019
J. E. Kjeldsen et al., *Speechwriting in Theory and Practice*,
Rhetoric, Politics and Society,
https://doi.org/10.1007/978-3-030-03685-0_12

while Obama was more heavily reliant on the teleprompter. Yet, the very commentary on Trump's State of the Union address is indicative of the overall function of the value of speechwriters. In the midst of a highly controversial entry into the White House and multiple crises, the address was well received and comments abound spoke of the President's ability to use the speech to pivot back his agenda and counter initial setbacks (or so many thought). We expect our leaders to present well-crafted speeches and that means that professionals who understand the role of good oratory advance the work that goes into them. Issues of status and credibility are often on the line when the public assess the value of speeches of leaders or prominent individuals. Rhetorical tradition is expected and any diversion from it is sure to be commented and sometimes even criticized. Rhetorical tradition offers stability and continuity in the midst of the unknown and for the individual speaker, a well-prepared speech can stand for the essence of one's leadership qualities.

Much can be risky in public speeches, and hence, speechwriters who work closely with their "clients" can assess early on the merit of a specific line or paragraph and even how an idea will or will not resonate with a given audience. They can point to potential advantages or pitfalls as well as generate expectations of audience reaction. The professionalization and function of speechwriters are crucial then for the success or failure of given public figure. The Trump presidency may prove, in the more unflattering way, how crucial oratory is and how critical its function can be when put in the context of both routine and crisis situations. The future of speechwriting is as promising as its past. Public speeches will always necessitate the help, advice, and input of those expert in public oratory. Those who need speeches—leaders in the political, social, and business arenas—are not always proficient public speakers, though some are. Hence, the work of speechwriters is needed though their work is often obscured and hidden.

With the comparison above, we suggest that the functions of the speechwriters include being a primary advisor to a leader in the communication arena. Here, we mean a person who can help a speaker frame an issue and write a fitting speech, an individual who is familiar with the speaker and hence able to direct a speech such that it avoids pitfalls and setbacks. These key functions of the speechwriter assume expertise in the art of rhetoric and its key variables such as strategizing a given speech to a particular audience and setting to accommodate a warranted informative or persuasive appeals. Significantly, the functions of speechwriters depend on an organizational setting that allow them to function to the fullest degree. This means being taken seriously, that others appreciate their work and allow them the necessary access to the leadership entrusted with the public speeches. Considering speechwriters as less valuable or as second-tier advisors will not secure the effective speech. And as discussed earlier, speechwriters that are also involved or are considered part of the policy-making team can help secure strong speeches as well as let other advisors appreciate how words selected to explain policy are central to the policy itself. Speechwriters that are relegated to the backroom will likely see their speechwriting assignments finalized by non-expert and in the end will likely reduce the quality of the speeches.

THE VALUE OF CRAFTING MANUSCRIPTS FOR OTHERS

One of the obvious, but often overlooked functions of speechwriting is the creation of a written text. First, and most importantly, the writing can function as a form of collaborative thinking. The many people that are often involved in speechwriting work in unison, developing what the organization thinks and believes, while gathering the best arguments and examples for the position or idea. The final manuscript and the delivered speech are the manifestation of the position an organization takes, and it reflects the rhetorical working through of the issue that has been carried out.[1] This also provides perspective to the common demand of authenticity of a speaker. The employment of speechwriting, as already mentioned, has been criticized for creating speeches that are not a truthful representations of the speakers, since it is not the speakers themselves who craft the speeches. This may be correct in some cases, but the critique misses an important distinction, because it is based on the assumption that the speaker is a private individual. This assumption, however, is only partly true. A prime minister, for instance, is a specific person, but this person speaks in the *role* of prime minister, not as an individual. The prime minister does not primarily represent him- or herself, but the government as an institution.

A related function and benefit of speechwriters and aides contributing to manuscripts is that the text can be carefully prepared; positions

[1] Cf. Jens E. Kjeldsen, *Rhetoric as Working Through*. Paper Presented at the Norwegian Media Researchers Conference in Bergen, Norway (Medieforskerkonferansen, October 20–21, 2016).

and arguments therein thought through, and language formulated in the most precise, nuanced way. In this way, speechwriting allows for an institutional working through of the issues and arguments, a collective thinking about policy and values.[2]

There is also an aspect of necessity to the speechwriting collaboration. The world of today, especially in politics, is so fragmented and complex (e.g., in relation to legislation or to the multitude of stakeholders in every case), that the speaker is often unable to know all that is necessary to know in order address the issues pertinent to the speech.

The written text also has pragmatic functions, such as the ability to be used as manuscripts and text for teleprompters. In Scandinavian countries, for instance, the written text is sometimes provided as a paper handout for reporters and others. This is most common in politics, and especially at the party conventions. Here, handouts of important speeches are available to reporters during the speech, making it convenient for them to follow the reasoning and to quote correctly in their reporting.

Among the two most frequently mentioned functions speechwriting have for a speaker is first, that the speaker's natural or lacking credibility and ability to persuade can be improved through the carefully prepared manuscript, and the effectiveness of the speaker's message can be enhanced. Second, that the speaker will be able to deliver more speeches than she is able to write herself.

While the question of authorship and authenticity continues to be a rhetorical and ethical challenge for speechwriting as a practice and profession, it also clear that the practice of speechwriting and advising during the writing performs important functions for speakers, organizations, and society. One benefit for all, is that speechwriting, when performed properly, will provide better speeches. "Better speeches" are those that are rhetorically worked through by several minds, in order to put forward the best available means of persuasion, so that every speech provides the best arguments for the case. As we have suggested, "better speeches" are speeches that are both consolidated in the organization and are engaging and convincing.

Of course, speechwriting is not without problems for speakers, organizations, and society. Kathleen Hall Jamieson has pointed out how the

---

[2] Cf. Kjeldsen (2016).

use of speechwriting risks separating knowledge from communication, creating a *divorce between speech and thought*. When a speaker does not carry out the research and thinking necessary to write a good speech, the speaker has not really thought the case through, but just read the message out aloud. The phases of gathering the material, working through the case, thinking about and adapting it to the audience, organizing and formulating it, are all parts of rhetorical thinking that not only educate the speaker, but often will change the arguments, reasoning, and positions of the speaker during the work.

In the USA, presidential speechwriting in "The rhetorical presidency," (the presidency since Theodore Roosevelt and Woodrow Wilson) has bypassed Congress and instead addressed the people directly and in support of legislation and other initiatives.[3] Both Presidents Barack Obama and Donald J. Trump have done so, espousing direct communication between a political leader and the electorates. Likewise, prime ministers, cabinet ministers, and state secretaries are considered to have a *duty* to "constantly defend themselves publicly, to promote policy initiatives nationwide, and to inspirit the population."[4] For better or worse, political speechwriting is an integral part of this form of *rhetorical leadership* that dominates governments and parliaments across the world. Political rhetoric and speechwriting attempting to influence parliaments and politics by using the populace as a rhetorical means create a specific dynamic in the interaction between political actors and institutions. This trend of rhetorical leadership is largely independent of the phenomenon of speechwriting; yet, it is still closely connected due to the necessity of a given politician to address the general population, both as a whole and in its segmented forms, creating a special demand for professional rhetorical help.

An Old Profession in a Digital World

Even though speechwriting is a more than a 2000-year-old practice, it has continuously evolved, and appears to take new directions in our time. An increased awareness of the subject of speechwriting has emerged among politicians, bureaucracy, communication professionals, and the public. Most people now know that leaders do not always

---

[3] Jeffrey K. Tulis, *The Rhetorical Presidency*, 4.
[4] Tulis, 4.

write their own speeches. Part of this trend in politics and organizations is an increased professionalization of communication efforts such as speechmaking and speechwriting. In Europe ministries and departments, leaders and employees are deliberating on how they may improve the departmental speechwriting processes, which for many have ended up as rather rigid and bureaucratic approval processes. In Norway, for instance, the Department of Trade and industry made changes to the traditional line format and established a speechwriting group of three people. In a similar fashion Ministry of Education and Research, carried out a reorganization of workflow in order to facilitate the speechwriting process.[5]

We also find innovations in the private sector of speechwriting. When writing corporate speeches for an executive of a US company such as UPS (United Parcel Service), for example, the speechwriter should consult the warehouse operative to tell the company's story.

Perhaps the most significant changes for the practice of speechwriting are the increasing interaction, even fusion, with technology. An obvious example is the use of presentation tools by speakers. Speechwriters used to write words, now they also have to create slides with pictures, figures, and bullet points. As we have suggested in Chapter 9, this use of presentation tools has already changed what a speechwriter does and is. Social media also affects the role and function of speechwriting. Perhaps the most significant development in this regard is the use of tweets in politics. President Trump has radically altered presidential communication by the use of tweets in the employ of politics. Initially during the campaign and continued into the presidency, Trump has changed political communication with short statements that reach millions. While the president generated many of the tweets, some of his tweets were written with the assistance of an advisor. This collaborative work has opened the door to a new feature of speechwriting. Despite extensive commentary regarding Trump's factual errors and misspelled words, his tweets have accompanied every controversial issue, often used for strategic objectives as in his infamous tweet about firing the Director of the Federal Bureau of Investigation (FBI), hoping that there are no tapes of their private conversation. We assume that if tweets are going to become a staple of

---

[5] Simon Stjern, "Jeg prøver å skrive det jeg tror de ville skrevet selv" En kvalitativ undersøkelse av tre taleskriveres arbeid med å konstruere karakter i politiske taler. Master thesis, Oslo University (2017).

political communication, they, too, will required a more systematic help of assistants/writers to ensure an effective messaging.

Another trend in speechmaking, and thus in speechwriting, is parallel to the movement from traditional oratory toward technology-assisted talks. This is the move away from the use of manuscripts in general. Talking without text is probably most common in business speeches. Many business and organization leaders even claim that they do not do speeches at all: They just have meetings and conversations with employees, partners, and stakeholders. Even though CEOs and business leaders give many oral presentations, they generally do not consider these as speeches, since they are not prepared as manuscripts. Still, we argue, these presentations perform the same rhetorical functions as traditional speeches and are best conceived as speeches. Some of these them have been called *micro speeches*: instances of short verbal addressed and structured remarks that leaders make to audiences in situations that are not considered by the parties involved as formal instances of oratory or speechmaking.[6] This could be short remarks in connection with a gathering, a meeting, or minor celebrations of employees and anniversaries. Microspeeches can be used at such events to exemplify or make explicit the expectations of a meeting, the values that the organization shares, its goals, and other similar rhetorical functions. In the daily life of any organization, there are countless instances allowing for valuable micro speeches. Nadja Pass points to three important rhetorical functions for such speeches[7]: (1) Creating community, unity, and a sense of each other's competencies. Any gathering in the organization can be utilized in this way, because any gathering provides an opportunity to mention the shared values and the people embodying these values. (2) Gaining understanding and accepting of values, strategies, or organizational changes. This as well can be done in many ways and situations; for instance, when welcoming a new employee or sharing the reasons for a promotion. (3) Establishing the leader as host and chief executive. This, for instance, can be done when introducing participants at a meeting, speakers at a

---

[6] Nadja Pass, "Hverdagens mikrotaler skaber fælles fodslag" (*"*The Everyday Micro Speeches Create Common Ground"), in Jonas Gabrielsen and Mette Møller, *Ledere, der taler - taler der leder* ("Leaders That Speak—Speeches That Lead") (Frederiksberg: Frydenlund, 2014), 99–114.

[7] Pass, "Hverdagens mikrotaler."

conference, or through introductions or conclusions to meetings, workshops, or other kinds of gatherings.

These kind of speeches, microspeeches and otherwise, do not require a manuscript. In some cases, the use of a manuscript will even be counterproductive, because it will be seen as to formal or even inauthentic and feigned. Does this mean that speechwriters should not be concerned with such speeches? No. We believe that this kind of rhetorical communication naturally belongs the sphere of speechwriting, even though it does not necessarily involve writing. The job of a speechwriter in the future will not only be crafting written speeches alone; it will include assisting speakers with oral presentations without manuscripts. This may involve coaching speakers in general or help developing specific speeches or presentations orally, without the aid of a manuscript.

Researchers at Roskilde University and Copenhagen Business School[8] have even argued that speakers should refrain as much as possible from using written manuscripts, because this tends to make speakers stiff, formal, and buttoned-up. Furthermore, as we have described in our chapter on character, the tone and style of a speaker is very difficult to establish in a written text. Finally, many speakers find it challenging to use a manuscript convincingly, so they end up with an artificial, unengaging reading aloud of a text. In such situations, manuscripts restrain more than they enable. In a sense, this view is in line with research on oral societies, such as ancient speechmaking, where speeches were written down *after* they had been delivered: "Learning to read and write disables the oral poet," Walter J. Ong writes in his book *Orality and Literacy*.[9]

Researchers critical of the use of manuscripts, therefore, advocate that rather than writing words down, *speeches should be talked into being*. The role of the speechwriter, then, becomes less of a writer, and more that of an aide or a coach that continuously teaches speakers mnemonics and delivery, and informs the speaker on how to develop structure, parts, and content that are easy to remember and deliver. In many ways, such rhetorical thinking and delivery are similar to the delivery of poems, songs,

---

[8] A central advocate for this approach is Jonas Gabrielsen from Roskilde University, who previously worked at Copenhagen Business School. Gabrielsen is co-author of *The Power of Speech* (with Tanja Juul Christiansen, Hans Reitzels Forlag: Copenhagen, 2010). He is also co-editor (with Mette Møller) of *Ledere, der taler - taler der leder* ("Leaders That Speak—Speeches That Lead") (Frederiksberg: Frydenlund, 2014).

[9] Ong, *Orality & Literacy*, p. 59.

and the telling of stories in oral societies. Researchers have argued that oral performances such as Homeric poetry from ancient Greece and the narrative storytelling and poems of modern former Yugoslavia were talked into being.[10] Stories were first told and then written down. Their metric and formulaic character was created orally, and this character made it possible for the narrator, the rhapsodic, to remember long stories and poems. The poems and stories were created as prefabricated parts that were then stitched together during the telling. This kind of rhapsodic rhetoric not only enables a narrator to remember each part, and thus the whole story, but also to make the telling longer or shorter by adding and removing parts, and even changing the storytelling creatively by moving parts around.

In contemporary speechwriting and speech coaching, this kind of oral Lego-brick rhetoric is considered beneficial because it makes speeches easier to remember and to deliver, and because it is thought to lead to much more natural, dynamic, vivid, and engaging speeches. The words are the speaker's own, and she is not tied to the constraints of a manuscript. Instead of writing manuscripts and working hard to remember the script, speechwriter, and speaker can spend more time on determining the goal of the speech, analyzing situation and audience, and then adding examples and important facts that the speaker knows by heart or can easily learn and recall.

Surely, as we have pointed out, the art of speechwriting is changing both culturally and technologically, and talking speeches into being has many advantages. Still, it would often require what speakers do not have: time. The constraints of limited time are still the most important reason for using speechwriters in the first place.

So, even though speechmaking and speechwriting may be changing, the central place of speechwriting continues. Even though speakers and speechwriters more than ever before have to contemplate the goals, ethics, constraints, procedures, and the problems and values of speechwriting. The art of writing speeches for others is more prevalent and important than it has ever been. In the future, this prevalence and importance is likely to become even more significant.

[10] Ibid.

CHAPTER 13

The General Steps in the Speechwriting Process

The speechwriting process discussed here has been implemented and activated rather inconsistently, often conditioned by the individuals involved and the circumstances surrounding specific speaker and speech assignment. There are also different traditions that determine the speechwriting process as evidenced in the discussion here about the differences between the more structured European and the more flexible and even inconsistent American approaches to this process. In general, we note that some speakers would have a heavy hand in the speech preparation while others would get involved only in the final stages of editing and rehearsing the presentation. Some speakers would forward an outline as a guide to speechwriters while others would leave this task to speechwriters. Yet, regardless of the level of speaker-speechwriter interaction, key steps are always included in the process even if their implementation is more or less structured. Following the classical perspective of the rhetorical process, we develop in this chapter the key phases in the speechwriting process, assuming that once the comprehensive picture of the process is understood, any shortcut would still fall within the full framework of the process. The general steps are:

1. Selection of topic.
2. Assessing and understanding the speakers and their voice as well as their natural way of speaking. Here, style and delivery would mitigate message construction.

3. A complete understanding of the speaker's relationship to the topic. Is the speaker following a known track, building a message on previous speeches, or is this a new message altogether?
4. Understanding the background, context, and precedents that can potentially affect but also constrain the speech.
5. Identification and understanding of the audience(s).
6. Determining the appropriate style and delivery for the audience and setting.
7. Determining the key points and outlining the speech.
8. Drafting the speech and generating feedback.
9. Completing and, if operative, submitting speech text to the speaker.
10. Feedback, editing, and approval of the speech.

A note of caution is necessary here. The above list is suggestive of a comprehensive consideration of the variables involved yet the sequential outline is flexible and not necessarily rigid. For example, it is possible that a topic selection would be followed by an outline of major points or arguments deemed essential, or that an initial outline of general objectives would dictate the framing of the topic. It is equally possible that an audience concern or views would pivot the entire speech topic and dictate its parameters. The speaker's review of the speech can take place at any phase and not just toward the completion of the drafting. We also recognize the different types of speechwriters including the professional, the adviser, and the specialist, and that each would function in a different setting and organization.

The Selection of Topic

The selection of topic is variably a matter of situation, speaker, and audience. Speech topics can arise from the speaker who feels the need to address a situation or be generated by the audience (flexibly defined) calling on an individual to address an issue that it, too, arises out of a specific situation. Some topics are known in advance and allow for detailed preparations while others can arise suddenly, putting pressure on all involved to finalize a speech and rather quickly. We note, for example, that President Barack Obama had a team of speechwriters and that they were divided by speech genre. One of the authors here, during a visit to the White House in May 2016, met one of the President's speechwriter whose responsibility was to write ceremonial speeches. Some of these speeches were known in advance and prepared accordingly, while others had to be written in rather condensed fashion.

In general, the clearer the topic or the more specific its focus, the tighter is the speech, its outline, and overall organization. And relatedly, the clearer and the more specific the topic, the easier it is for audiences to follow and recall specifics therein.

SPEAKER AND SPEECHWRITER

Given the uniqueness of writing speeches for clients, the speechwriter has to understand the person for whom the speech is written. The speaker, in a rhetorical sense, is the authority behind the speech. When a speech is written for a client, the speechwriter is much more than a wordsmith. The speechwriter is an individual who knows and understands the speaker and to a degree assumes a persona that is outside oneself. The speechwriter writes for the speaker's conviction, for the speaker's concerns, and with the speaker's sense of timing, style, decorum, and rhetorical proclivities. Importantly, the speechwriter is not without potential influence over the speaker and the topic. Familiarity with the speaker can also yield mutual respect that can translate into a fusion of ideas and rhetorical direction. In short, an effective working relationship between speaker and speechwriter can yield an effective speech.

Specific questions that can guide the speechwriter in discerning the quality, character, and relationship of speaker to the topic at hand can include the following:

1. Who is the speaker?
2. What is the speaker's background, both personal and professional?
3. What is the speaker's record of accomplishment as a public speaker?
4. What are the speaker's rhetorical habits?
5. What is the speaker's relationship to the topic selected and the audience at hand?
6. What assessment can the speechwriter draw from the above variables and what impact do they have on the speechwriting process?

Background, Situation, and Context

The speech topic is always situated in a given context but is also affected by a larger context and history and is informed by related issues, concerns, and constraints. The speechwriter needs to understand the background of a given speech topic, previous statements made regarding the selected topic as well as constraints that need to be realized in order to produce a workable thesis and a solid rhetorical plan. As noted in the previous point, a solid understanding of the speaker's persona as well as all related constraints is essential for assessing the merit and direction of a given speech and its rhetorical construction.

Specific questions that can guide the speechwriter in discerning the relationship between background, context, and situation, the speaker and the topic:

1. What is the immediate background for the specific topic?
2. How did the speech topic come about?
3. What previous stands, positions, and counterpoints have or can potentially constrain this particular topic?
4. What is the larger situation and background that may affect the speech?

Identifying the Audience

A speaker has always an audience and sometimes more than one audience to consider. The speech exists because the speaker has an audience and its concerns, aspiration or questions are the reason for considering the speech in the first place. The speechwriter needs to comprehend the audience the speaker has targeted because the writing of the speech must relate to the audience selected. Specifically, the speech is addressed to an audience whom the speaker assumes has the ability to act accordingly, whether by agreeing with the speaker's proposal, taking the speech as advice for further action, or in opposing the message. Knowledge and understanding of the audience, its beliefs, values, as well as demographic information would dictate matters of substance, style, and delivery as well as minimize friction and disagreements. This task is further complicated when more than one audience is addressed or when the audience is large enough to include a wide range of views and opinions, such that no one proposal or idea can satisfy the majority. The appeals of the given speech must then be strategized such that the speaker can still maximize the appeal to the widest audience possible. This is undoubtedly the challenge of most political speeches addressed to large multitudes.

Specific questions that can guide the speechwriter in assessing the audience for a given speech:

1. What are the characteristics of the immediate audience (in terms of demographic and psychographic variables)? Here, assessment of age, education, locality as well as psychological variables such as known attitudes, beliefs, or state of mind can be helpful if not altogether crucial to the speech.
2. Is there a larger audience that must be rationalized (a secondary media-based audience)?
3. Can audience variables inhibit the speech or parts of it thereof?
4. What persuasive strategy is to be selected for the speech given the audience assessment?

Determining the Proper Style and Delivery

Style, or the choice of words, is detrimental to the success of the speaker in effecting the desired change. In contemplating the style, the speechwriter will resort to word choices, metaphors, and other linguistic devices that can enhance the effectiveness of the speech. The speaker's stylistic habits will dictate the most suitable style for a particular speech but so would the topic at hand suggest the proper style. In some cases, the speechwriter will suggest a stylistic direction while in other cases the speechwriter will let the speaker follow the style best suited to the topic and audience. It is equally plausible that a given speaker will maintain a consistent style over different speaking occasions while other speakers will adopt the style to the speaking occasion.

Emphases on style, character, and authenticity are crucial and key to successful speech making. Speechwriters need to figure out if in a given setting they are to create the voice of the speaker or that of the organization. These two options require serious considerations that must consult unique organizational setting, cultural differences, and alternative bureaucratic structure. For example, while some US presidents considered their speechwriters as limited to stylistic word smithers, others saw no difference between policy issues and their speeches thereof. In principle, emphasis on the oral style would guarantee the success of a speech.

Style, however, should not be taken as the dressing of a speech but the essence of the speaker's performative quality.

Delivery, or the way we say things, is equally an important variable in the success of a public speech. Here, we recognize that different occasions and different audience may necessitate alternative modes of delivery. A very formal speech may call for a forceful but also an eloquent delivery while some presidential speeches occasioned informal speeches and milder delivery mode that proved to be more successful than formal ones. Specific questions that can guide the speechwriter in determining the suitable style and delivery mode:

1. What are the speaker's common stylistic devices?
2. What stylistic consistencies the speech must employ, if any?
3. What stylistic decisions are proper relative to the topic at hand?
4. What stylistic decisions are proper relative to the audience at hand?
5. What is the speaker's most comfortable delivery mode?
6. What is the most fitting delivery mode for the particular speech and audience?
7. Can the speaker adapt to a changing delivery mode or does the speech need any modification to suit the speaker's known delivery mode?

Drafting the Speech

The speechwriter is a researcher first and whose insights into a given topic begins with a complete understanding of the topic, its context, and history. Though not always practiced, an effective drafting of a speech ought to begin with an outline that functions as a rhetorical skeleton on which the speech is build. The outline of the speech, in general, ought to follow the selection of the speech topic, even if only tentatively planned as well as some key points that the speaker and others' associates have drafted as an initial guide.

Who submits the outline depends on the unique features of a given organization. The practice of outlining must be mastered for producing an effective speech as it allows an early preview of the overall parameters of the speech and its main points.

Drafting a speech can be the speechwriter's best take on the speech assignment. The most creative phase of the speechwriting process is now underway. With the situational constraints fully realized and the outline in place, the speechwriter is well informed and ready to commence the writing of the speech as well as assessing the kind of evidence needed therein. All things being equal, this phase is the most exciting one. However, recent experiences have informed us of numerous occasions when time was compressed enough for the writing process to be short and for the creative process to be challenged by severe time constraints. Another complicating factor lies in the potential of several speechwriters assigned to draft the same speech or portions thereof.

Specific points that ought to guide the speechwriter in drafting the speech:

1. Determining the thesis and the objective of the speech.
2. Identifying the primary points to be raised.
3. Developing sub-points that explain, rationalize, and support the main points.
4. Supplying the evidence and reasoning for each point.
5. Deciding on the sequence of the main points.
6. Developing an introduction and conclusion.
7. Researching needed information (dates, facts, statistics, etc.).
8. Assessing the strength of the evidence.
9. Writing for the ear and creating vivid language.
10. Working with other speechwriters and staff members, and if necessary, stitching together parts of the speech.
11. Finalizing a clean draft for further review.

Feedback and Editing

Given the principle notion that a speechwriter works for a client, the importance of feedback and further editing is critical and essential to the process. The speechwriter can assess the creative product when feedback is forwarded and additional input is requested. Some speakers will return the speech draft for additional work, including minor or majors revisions. Other speakers will leave the editing process to self and/or to close aides and exclude the speechwriter who drafted the speech. Even if the speechwriter is not involved in additional editing, the final speech is an important document that the speechwriter should attend to in order to fine-tune future speechwriting assignments, discerning from the editorial habits and changes made the speaker's persona and rhetorical preferences.

A Master Rhetorical Plan

The speechwriting process can be further understood by considering all the essential variables of the rhetorical process. By this we mean that the speechwriter considers the variables of the speaker, the speech, the situation, the audience, the mode of communication, and possible constraints that may affect each of these variables. The principle idea we forward here is that all these variables are organic and dynamic and that they can overlap each other to produce a unique collective often referred to as a rhetorical plan. Briefly, the speechwriter ought to ask whether a specific speech topic should be delivered to a particular audience at a particular time. This essential question the speechwriter has to ask of the speaker, even if only theoretically, assuming that reflecting on the topic vis-à-vis the audience, circumstances, and constraints would provide the necessary justification for the speech. The speechwriter, when the speaker-speechwriter relationship is effective and productive, ought to be a rhetorical advisor first and that ought to include giving an honest assessment of advantages and disadvantages of a particular speech plan as well as suggesting a direction, a pivot, and any unique perspective to be taken. What we have in mind is the development of a brief that summarizes key points of an upcoming speaking engagement.

The speaker: Here the speechwriter develops a biographical sketch as well as a good account of the speaker's public speaking experience that is helpful to the speechwriter; what we have referred to as a *speaker profile*. Understanding the speaker's preferred style and delivery as mentioned before is crucial for writing speeches but so are the constraints that can influence a given speech by the particular speaker. Some constraints are personal to the speaker such as specific weaknesses related to speaking in public and others could be some unique tendencies that can affect the speech. For example, some known speakers preferred short sentences. Other constraints can be "political" in the sense that there are limits to what can be said over a particular issue. Not all thoughts or ideas that a speaker has in mind should be stated publicly since some items could send the wrong message or be interpreted in such a way that they can diminish the objectives of the speech.

Some points to consider:

1. Is the speaker the best person to deliver this particular speech?
2. How much rhetorical maneuverability does the speaker has in developing the speech topic and expressing the desired message?

3. Has the speaker addressed the topic or audience, or both in the past? What past reactions can tell the speechwriter as preparations for the future speech are underway?

The speech: The speech topic is often an answer to a prevailing question or issue raised. Ostensibly, the issue at hand directs the development of the topic and as such it limits its range and scope but also adds focus and complexity.

Some points to consider:

1. What is the nature of the topic? Is it very specific or general?
2. Are there essential points that must be included? How detailed should the speech be?
3. Is the issue conditioning the speech a problem to be solved? And can the speech advance the issue at hand?

The situation: By definition, every situation is a set of constraints that directs the speech in a specific way. The physical location may dictate unique speech requirements (inartistic proof) as well as influence the overall speech (artistic proof). A cemetery will likely dictate a somber speech while a political rally may be too raucous for a long and formal address. A speech at a business gathering may be best pursued as a semi-formal speech with minimal attempts at humor that often backfire. Some speeches ought to be direct and to the point while others may benefit from the inclusion of a narrative portion. Some speeches will be very formal and long as befitting a well-planned address while others, such as those addressed to the media and the invisible audience of millions, short and strategic.

Some points to consider:

1. What is known about the immediate context?
2. What is unique about the physical situation of the speech?
3. What is known about the larger situation including cultural and social setting? Can they affect the speech?
4. How formal should the speech be, if at all?

The audience: Speeches are addressed to audience and not to self. The speechwriter needs to drive this point that whatever is said, is for the benefits of others who attend to the speech as well as the media in attendance. Audiences are empowered to accept a viewpoint, agree to a proposal, and even act according to set recommendations the speaker has made. Audiences, then, should be treated carefully.

Some points to consider:

1. What is the makeup of the audience?
2. What is unique about the particular audience? It is unified in its view or not? How large is it and are there multiple audiences?
3. Does the audience possess the potential to ameliorate the situation that called the speech in the first place?
4. And relatedly, can the audience advance the cause the speaker assigned to the speech? How?

The mode of communication: The medium of addressing audiences can vary from a small and informal group that can hear the speaker without the use of loudspeakers to a larger audiences that can be reached only by the use of a public address system. Televised speeches can reach millions and so can skyped speeches. The size of the audience often dictates the mode of communication and in turn, they affect the speech and the speaker in determining range of topic, structure and level of formality, and the amount of information therein. Since speeches are addressed to audiences, the range of sentiments and attitudes must be calibrated such that the speaker can maximize the sought effects of the speech. Audiences such as the "American people" will dictate a rhetorical range different from a local speech to a heavily partisan audience, and even in this eventuality, a segment of a "local speech" can be transmitted via the web and re-positions the speech for a mass audience that might react quite differently than the local audience.

Index

A
Abbott, Tony, 9
Acropolis, 34, 35
actio, 55, 67, 139, 149, 175
Adenauer, Konrad, 103
ad populum, 18
Aeschines, 32, 35
Against Eratosthenes speech, 123
Agora, 34, 35
Alcidamas, 33, 34, 140
alliteration, 21, 73, 129, 160
American presidency, 43, 44, 49, 78, 169, 174
American Promise speech, 80
American republic, 47
amplificatio, 35
anaphora, 73
Ancient Greece, 3, 27, 30, 33, 41, 66, 123, 175, 185
anecdote, 20, 56, 61, 63, 66, 126
antimetabole, 21, 71, 72
Antiphon, 32, 33, 41
antithesis, 35, 67, 71–73
appropriateness, 68
aptum, 68, 160

Arab spring, 9
Areopagus rock, 34
arête, 64
arguments, 1, 15–18, 31, 34, 36, 55–61, 63, 64, 66, 67, 69, 72, 74, 82, 83, 85, 88, 91, 98, 108, 119, 120, 123, 124, 126, 133, 146, 149, 152, 154, 155, 160–163, 170, 173, 179–181, 188
Aristotle, 27–29, 41, 60, 62, 64, 76, 122, 145, 168, 172
Athenians, 31, 32, 35
Athens, 30, 31, 33–37
Attic orators, 32
authenticity, 41, 46, 47, 50, 51, 119, 120, 124, 168, 170, 172–175, 179, 180, 191

B
Ballantine, Arthur A., 108
Barthes, Roland, 134
Bergerac, Cyrano de, 82
Bible, the, 23, 121

Biblical times, 3
body language, 14, 19, 120, 124, 128, 129, 135
Bormann, Ernest, 107, 170
Boston Bombing, 112
Bouleterion, 34
Bournemouth Conference, 17
Brandt, Willy, 79
Branham, Robert, 20
Bruges speech, 17
Bundeskanzler, der, 44
Burke, Kenneth, 10, 15, 128
Bush, George W., 7, 39, 42, 44, 70, 150
business rhetoric, 90

C
Cairo, 9
Call of the Wild, 21
Campbell, Karlyn K., 75, 76, 85, 173
canons of Rhetoric, 81
captatio benevolentiae, 62, 63
Carter, Jimmy, 80, 94
Catilina, Lucius Sergius, 151
CEO, 8, 66, 68, 91, 155, 183
ceremonial speeches, 29, 31, 35, 77, 92, 189
Challenger disaster, 10
Chappaquiddick address, 73
characterization, 50, 51, 65, 119–121, 124, 125, 131
chiasmus, 22, 23, 72
Churchill, Winston, 71, 72, 127
Cicero, 24, 28, 36, 37, 145, 149, 151, 157
Civil Rights Act, 94
clarity, 68, 105, 122
Claudius, 37
Clinton, William Jefferson (Bill), 128
Cold War, 23

Conservative Party, 87
Constitution Day, 87
consubstantiality, 15, 128
contio, 36, 37
Coolidge, Calvin, 80
corporate speechwriting, 46, 48, 51, 57, 88, 91, 119, 171
credibility, 3, 11, 17, 28, 29, 64, 122, 131, 160, 166, 170, 178, 180

D
Danish Prime Minister, 19, 71, 127
Davis, Vioila, 148
D-Day, 146
decorum, 68, 173, 189
deliberative speeches, 29, 31, 76, 79
delivery, 1, 3, 4, 11–13, 22, 28, 37, 49, 55, 81, 99, 100, 103, 107, 120, 122, 123, 128–131, 133, 135–139, 141, 143, 149, 171, 175, 184, 187, 188, 190–192, 194
Demosthenes, 31, 32, 35, 41
descriptio, 146
Dictionary of Affect in Language, 53
digital presentation tools, 153, 156, 157, 163
Dionysius of Halicarnassus, 41, 123
Dionysos, theater of, 35
dispositio, 55, 67, 98, 160, 175
Dromos, 35
Dutch, government, 45, 53
Dutch minister of Foreign Affairs, 22, 62

E
Eisenhower, Dwight, 80, 169
ekphrasis, 146, 147
Ellemann-Jensen, Uffe, 71

elocutio, 55, 67, 98, 139, 175, 176
enthymemic reasoning, 65
epideictic speeches, 29, 49
ethics, 4, 28, 40, 41, 46, 47, 50, 52, 59, 81, 165–167, 169–171, 175, 176, 185
Ethnographic research, 50
Ethopoeia, 33, 41, 50, 51, 65, 119–123
Ethos, 29, 51, 63–65, 92, 119, 120
eunoia, 64
European Parliament, 8, 85
European politics, 41, 44, 95
European Union, 72
evidentia, 129, 140

F
Fafner, Jørgen, 139
Fallows, James, 113
farewell address, 77, 78, 82, 88
Favreau, Jon, 40, 111
figures of sound, 73
Fireside chat, 10, 19, 107, 108
Fisher, Mary, 138
Ford, Gerald, 82
Forum Romanum, 36, 37
Frederik, Crown Prince, 71
Freeman, Martin, 72

G
Gates, Bill, 151
Gavin, William F., 109, 133
Germany, 44, 48, 101, 127
Gettysburg Address, 12
Gifford, Gabrielle, 23
Gillard, Julia, 9
Gorgias, 32, 160
grand style, 24, 69, 84
Greece, 32, 120
Greek period, 1

H
Haiman, Franklyn, 170, 171
Hamilton, Alexander, 79
Hannan, Daniel, 8
Harald, King, 86, 87
Harding, Warren G., 42
Harvard, Graduation Speech, 62
Harvard University, 63
Hawthorne, Nathaniel, 79
Helgers, Hans, 151
Hermogenes, 122
Hitler, Adolf, 4, 19
Holy Roman Empire, 3
Hoover, Herbert, 108
humor, 45, 61, 62, 69, 71, 120, 126, 129, 195

I
I have a dream speech (Martin Luther King), 73
Inaugural address, 21, 43, 72, 77–81, 94, 100, 102, 114, 150
intellectual horizon (the speaker's), 125, 127
Internet, 3, 7–10, 24, 127, 135–137, 143
interview questions (for speaker), 59, 129
inventio, 37, 55, 67, 139, 160, 175, 176
inventional, 40, 59, 83
iron curtain, 71, 72
irony, 71, 72
isocolon, 73
Isocrates, 32, 33, 35, 140

J
Jackson, Andrew, 79, 81, 94
Jamieson, Kathleen H., 19, 75, 76, 85, 122, 125, 147, 150, 175, 180

Johannesen, Richard, 167
Johnson, Lyndon B., 80
Judicial speeches, 30, 123

K
kairós, 140–143
Kennedy, Edward, 73
Kennedy, John F., 17, 21, 70, 77, 80, 114, 122, 175
Keramikos, 35
King, Martin Luther, 11, 17, 73, 142

L
Labor Day speech, 87
Labour Party, 17, 72
Lange, Ton de, 151
Latimer, Matt, 7, 39, 48
Lehrman, Robert, 55
Lincoln, Abraham, 4, 150
Lincoln Memorial, 142
literacy, 16, 133, 134, 136, 137, 143, 157, 184
logography, 30, 32, 33, 36, 37, 41, 119
logos, 29, 64, 65
Lyngsie, M.C., 141
Lysias, 31–33, 41, 51, 123, 124

M
MacArthur, Douglas, 80
manuscript, 22, 32, 49–51, 69, 100, 102, 103, 105–107, 120, 121, 126, 129, 135–139, 143, 155, 157, 179, 180, 184, 185
Medhurst, Martin J., 40, 42, 79, 81
megaphone, 3
memorability, 73, 137–140, 143
memoria, 55, 67
Merkel, Angela, 127

metaphor, 61, 65, 67, 71, 72, 96, 111, 124
metic, 33
micro speeches, 183, 184
Middle Ages, 3
middle style, 24, 69
Moley, Ray, 80, 114
multimedia, 158, 159

N
narrative, 16, 17, 23, 33, 60, 63, 64, 85, 86, 110, 121, 138, 139, 154, 185, 195
National eulogies, 22, 77, 84
neo-aristotelian criticism, 47
Nero, 37
Netherlands, the, 44, 45, 84, 95, 151, 152
New Year's speech, 19, 86, 87
Nineteenth century, 2, 81
Nixon, Richard, 109
Noonan, Peggy, 20, 21, 39, 93, 95, 110, 111, 147
Northern Europe, 44, 45, 95

O
Obama, Barack, 7, 10, 17, 23, 40, 115, 142, 161, 181, 188
Occupy Wall Street, 9
Old Testament, 168
Olympic games, 31
Ong, Walter J., 133, 184
on Rhetoric, 2, 27, 28, 41, 91, 145, 168, 172
onomatopoeia, 73
Opening Address, 85, 86, 127
orality, 13, 16, 73, 120, 133, 134, 136, 137, 139, 143, 184
Oslo Cathedral, 23

P

paralingual, 134
paralipsis, 72
paranomasia, 68
partitio, 61, 63
pathos, 23, 29, 64, 65
Paul, apostle, 34
Pearce, Barnett, 20
Peloponnesian War, 33, 35
Pericles, 32, 35
Perlman, Alan, 50, 124, 125
persona, 3, 30, 52, 120, 121, 128, 131, 189, 190, 193
personal experience, 126
philosophers, 27, 28, 33, 37, 62, 167
phronesis, 64
Pierce, Franklin, 79
pistis, 60, 64
Plato, 27, 35, 41, 167
Pnyx, 34, 35
policy, 2, 29, 30, 40, 42–44, 48, 49, 52, 76–79, 81, 83–85, 87, 95, 96, 99, 100, 109, 111, 113, 114, 152, 171–173, 176, 179–181, 191
Political action committees (PACS), 18
polyptoton, 68
polysyndeton, 124
Postman, Neil, 153, 154
Potter, Harry, 62, 63, 66
Powell, Colin, 152
PowerPoint, 92, 135, 145, 153, 154, 157, 159
praeteritio, 72
prepon, to, 68
President, 7, 9, 19, 23, 36, 42–44, 47, 51–53, 55, 59, 60, 62, 71, 77–83, 85, 94, 108–114, 127, 142, 143, 150, 155, 156, 169, 170, 178, 181, 182, 188, 189
presidential election, 2016, 18
Prime Minister, 9, 20, 23, 44, 45, 66, 85–87, 100–103, 139, 170, 179
professional speechwriter's association, 32, 165
public address, 3, 20–22, 60, 82, 94, 122, 196
public speaking, 2–4, 15, 20, 21, 24, 27, 28, 66, 82, 92, 119, 121, 133, 135, 168, 194
Pythagoras, 127, 140

Q

Quintilian, 28, 37, 41, 56, 145, 146, 148, 149, 152

R

radio, 3, 10, 18, 24, 88, 107, 135, 137
Rasmussen, Lars Løkke, 71
Reagan, Ronald, 10, 20, 42, 44, 51, 53, 80, 93, 110, 125, 146, 150
Renaissance, 9, 27, 37
Rhetorica ad Herennium, 24
rhetorical figures, 21, 22, 35, 67–74, 106, 146
rhetorical theories, ancient, 24
Roman Empire, 3
Roman period, 2
Roosevelt, Franklin D., 10, 12, 42, 73, 79, 94, 107, 114
Roosevelt, Theodore, 181
Rosling, Hans, 153
Rowling, J.K., 62, 63, 66

S

Scandinavia, 44, 46, 49
Second World War, 18
Seeger, Matthew W., 171
Seneca, 37, 66

Seward, William, 79
simple style, 24, 69
Sophists, 1, 27, 31–33, 41, 168
Sorensen, Theodore, 80
speaker profile, 130, 131, 194
Speech from the Throne, 84
Spencer Diana, Lady, 21
Spencer, Earl, 21, 22, 73
State of the Union Address, 70, 77, 83–85, 115, 156, 177, 178
statistics, 17, 126, 161, 193
Stoltenberg, Jens, 23
storytelling, 16, 23, 137, 160, 163, 185
style, 3, 9, 18–22, 24, 25, 28, 37, 40, 41, 44, 46, 47, 50, 51, 55, 64, 67– 69, 72, 74, 78, 79, 81, 85, 88, 90, 99, 100, 103, 108, 111, 114, 115, 120–125, 128–130, 143, 153, 154, 170, 184, 187–192, 194
Switzerland, 45, 48, 52
Syracuse, 1

T
Tahrir Square, 9
TED-talk, 151
teleprompter, 3, 9, 28, 173, 177, 178, 180
television, 3, 10, 11, 13, 18, 19, 24, 82, 88, 110, 135, 136, 147, 150, 151, 161, 162, 173
Thatcher, Margaret, 17, 87, 88, 127
Thorning-Schmidt, Helle, 19, 20, 127, 139, 140
Thucydides, 32
Timmermans, Frans, 22, 62

topoi, 29, 56, 57, 59, 136
topos, 56
Trachalus, 37
Trump, Donald, 7, 9, 173, 174, 177, 178, 181
Tubman, Harriet, 148
Tulis, Jeffrey, 43, 113
Twenty first century, 7

U
Uhm. Peter van, 152
Ukraine, 22
United Nations Security Council, 22
Utøya, Island, 23

V
Veto Message, 77, 78, 82
video, 8–10, 14, 72, 131, 136, 143, 156
Vietnamization speech, 60
vividness, 56, 68, 148, 161

W
Warnock, Mary Baroness, 62, 63
Washington, George, 42, 79, 150, 169, 174
White House, 39, 41–43, 51, 52, 55, 57, 82, 93, 94, 108, 111, 113, 114, 156, 157, 178, 189
Wilson, Woodrow, 181

Y
YouTube, 9, 129, 136, 138, 145

The manufacturer's authorised representative in the EU is Springer Nature Customer Service Centre GmbH, Europaplatz 3, 69115 Heidelberg, Germany. If you have any concerns regarding our products, please contact ProductSafety@springernature.com

Printed and bound by CPI Group (UK) Ltd, Croydon, CR0 4YY
23/03/2026
02076672-0002